D1434014

THE LAND OF
LOST CONTENT

The Land of Lost Content

The Biography of Anthony Chenevix-Trench

by

MARK PEEL

The Pentland Press
Edinburgh – Cambridge – Durham – USA

First published in 1996 by
The Pentland Press Ltd
1 Hutton Close,
South Church
Bishop Auckland
Durham

ISBN 1–85821–400–9

Typeset by Carnegie Publishing, 18 Maynard St, Preston
Printed and bound by Bookcraft Ltd, Bath

Contents

Acknowledgements

ANTHONY CHENEVIX-TRENCH, like so many brilliant men, was a complex and controversial personality whose life and work elicited sharply contrasting opinions. There were those who felt that the more contentious issues which dogged the latter part of his life might make a biography of him painful reading for his family. That I felt able to proceed with my efforts to present a full and balanced portrait of this fascinating schoolmaster says much for the unblinkered co-operation and support I received from Anthony Chenevix-Trench's family, most notably his daughter, Jo Homfray, and his sons Richard and Jonathan Chenevix-Trench. Others within the family to whom I am grateful include John Chenevix-Trench (nephew), John Homfray (son-in-law) and John Chenevix-Trench and Delle Fletcher (cousins).

I would also like to place on record my thanks to the following who, either in conversation or in print, shared their recollections of Anthony Chenevix-Trench with me.

Margaret Addison, Richard Allison, The Lord Annan, John Arkell, Hew Balfour, Nicholas Barber, Oliver Barnes, James Baxter, Mary Bevan, Roger Bevan, Hugh Bruce-Watt, Bobby Bourne, Humphrey Bourne, Anthony Bowen, Prebendary Patrick Brock, David Brydon, Roddy Buchanan, The Rev. Dr Bob Burn, Michael Burton QC, Colin Campbell, Fred Carr, Chris Carruthers, Margaret Charlie, Charles Clark, Jonathan Clark, Nigel Clark, Cameron Cochrane, Dick Cole-Hamilton, Stacy Colman, James Cosby-Ross, Peter Coshan, Beryl Courtney-Embley, Colonel Tom Craig, Patrick Croker, The Lord Dacre,

Professor John Dancy, Rupert Daniels, Peter Dixon, Sir Kenneth Dover, John Elwick, Kate Eveling, Sir Eric Faulkner, John Foot, Aidan Foster-Carter, Jumbo Fuller, Will Garfit, Charles George QC, Peter Gladstone, Noel Gibbs, The Rt. Hon. Lord Glendevon PC, Tom Goldie-Scot, Nigel Goodman, David Goude, Christopher Gowan, The Hon. Lord Grieve, Simon Groves, David Guilford, William Gurney, Raymond Hawthorn, Richard Henriques QC, Joe Hills, Michael Hoban, Tom Holden, Peter Holt, The Viscount and Viscountess Hood, Richard Ingrams, Sir William Jaffray Bt., Nigel Jaques, Jerry Jarrett, Richard Jenkyns, Basil Johnson, Jane Jones, Stephen Kemp, Bill Kennedy, David Kennedy, Sir Ludovic Kennedy QC, Francis King, Rawle Knox, Peter Lawrence, Colin Leach, Ross Leckie, Laurence Le Quesne, Michael Leslie, Cyril Little, Professor Sir Hugh Lloyd-Jones, The Hon. Jamie MacKay, Alastair McCracken, Mike McIntosh-Reid, David McMurray, Robin Macnaghten, The Rev. Canon David Main, Freddy Mann, Martin Marix-Evans, Cim Mellor, Cameron Miller, Howard Moseley, Gracie Murdoch, Fergus Murray, David Natzler, Dick Newell, David Orchard, The Lord Palmer, Christopher Pemberton, Bob Philp, George Preston, Anthony Quick, Geoffrey Rae-Smith, Richard Raven, Michael Ricketts, Nick Ridley, Gavin Roynon, Alastair Reid, Bill Sadleir, Lt. Col. Edward Sawyer, Simon Scott, The Very Rev. Dr Ronald Selby Wright, Michael Seymour, Charles Shelton-Agar, David Smout, Colin Smythe, Robert Sopwith, Paul Sowerby, John Stevenson, Joy and Philip Stibbe, Nigel Stoughton, Peter Stuart, John Symes, Colin Tipple, Philippa and Walthy Tooth, Professor Jim Urmson, Alan Waddell, Humphrey Ward, Robert Watkins, The Rev. David Weekes, Jean Weekes, Tom Wheare, Doris Wight, Richard Wilcock, Bill Williams, Nico Williams, Jo Wilson, Pam Wilson, Tim Wilson-Smith, Ian Winstanley, Patrick Wormald, Sir Brian Young, Sir Roger Young, Tim Young.

It is invidious to single out individuals but in this context I would like to mention Tim Card, the Vice-Provost of Eton College, as a quite invaluable source.

Others whose help and kindness I readily acknowledge are Tim Clark, Clerk to the Council at Bradfield College, Antony Collieu, the Librarian, Bradfield College, Mark Curthoys, Archivist, Christ Church, Oxford, Alasdair Fox, Clerk to the Governors of the Fettes Trust, James Lawson, The Librarian, Shrewsbury School, Alexia Lindsay, Archivist, Fettes College and Paul Quarrie, sometime College Librarian, Eton College.

In particular I'm most indebted to Commander Godfrey Chenevix-Trench for reading over the chapter on his brother's childhood, to Robin Lorimer for reading the one on Shrewsbury and Oxford, to Professor Dick Hare for the one covering the war years, to Michael Charlesworth for the Oxford and Shrewsbury chapter after the war and to Murray Argyle for the Bradfield one. John Anderson, Michael Meredith and Canon Peter Pilkington kindly read through the Eton chapter and Margaret Buchanan-Smith and David Rhodes the Fettes one. All of them were a tower of strength with their corrections, suggestions and illuminating observations.

Above all I would like to convey my appreciation to Sandra Edwards for her meticulous typing of the script, to Sir William Gladstone for consenting to write the Foreword, to Neil Henderson and Tony Pocock for acting as wise and trusted confidants throughout the writing of this book and, finally, to Mary Denton for her supportive work in the production of the book. Needless to say, I accept full responsibility for any errors which remain.

Edinburgh,   *Mark Peel*
March 1996

Foreword

By Sir William Gladstone, Bart

I FELL UNDER THE SPELL of Tony Chenevix-Trench's captivating personality and brilliant but lightly worn intellect at Christ Church in 1946. A large number of us freshmen who had been in the armed services for a longer or shorter part of the war joined a few veterans, including Tony, who had come up to the college in 1938 and had now returned to complete their degrees. Some of them had been majors or lieutenant-colonels and some had suffered appallingly in mind or body or both. Tony seemed to have been able to throw off his dreadful experiences as a prisoner-of-war of the Japanese, and was the life and soul of the college. He was splendid company, President of the Junior Common Room and a leading light in the revival of the Boat Club, the Twenty Club and several other entertaining institutions. He regaled us with delightful anecdotes and penetrating but generous observations on human nature.

Tony decided on a schoolmaster's career and returned to Shrewsbury where as a pupil he had been a bright star in a luminous classical firmament. I was fortunate to join the staff there a year later, so our friendship ripened, as did our exchange of views about schoolmastering. His interest was in drawing out the best from boys as individuals, and it was in this that his genius was always employed. That is what he meant when he said that he was an empiricist and not (for which I thank heaven) an educationist. Naturally, for one of his academic prowess, Oxford exerted a strong pull, but after a short return there he soon realised that he was a schoolmaster and not a don. He returned to Shrewsbury as soon as a good opportunity presented itself.

In spite of his personal doubts and reservations, and his actual refusal of Charterhouse, inevitably it was not long before he became a headmaster. He was no administrator and, as he himself said, no politician. He showed wonderful powers of improvisation and ingenuity in getting out of scrapes as an individual, but in an idealistic and indeed an innocent way he was, in his chosen profession, a man without guile. He had none of the cunning or calculating qualities required in politics as 'the art of the possible'. He had none of the politician's ability to gather and calculate support, nor to wait for the right moment to pounce.

The recording angel knows that Tony achieved a great deal at Eton, both for Eton as a school and for so many of its pupils who liked and admired him. Yet he left with an understandable sense of failure. Perhaps there was something deeper than his weakness in administration or politics, or his recognised personal shortcomings: was his reluctance to delegate or to ask for advice due to a deep-seated lack of self-confidence? I believe that it was, and that an appreciation of his personal humility is a key to understanding the man. In a character of many contradictions it was this quality which led to his erecting barriers against seeking advice and help.

Year after year a group of us used to foregather during the Christmas holidays for what was ostensibly a shooting holiday in Scotland. Most of us were schoolmasters (including my brother Peter, then at Shrewsbury, and Michael Ricketts, then at Bradfield) but never did a word of 'shop' pass between us. Huddled round a log fire playing Battleships or clad in enough layers to make Tony appear almost spherical, we enjoyed a long series of uproarious holidays, enlightened by his exquisite turn of phrase

and his fund of lightly (or sometimes heavily) embroidered anecdotes. He was a real countryman and, incidentally, a very
effective shot at wild pheasants, duck, pigeons and anything else
we could by subterfuge induce him to aim at, including at least
once, I am ashamed to say, a blackbird.

It was the misfortune of Tony, and of Elizabeth and their
children, that the devils of the Japanese captivity came to revisit
him when he was still in middle age. But he bounced back
astonishingly at Fettes and he died, as perhaps he would have
wished to die, at the helm.

Mark Peel deserves the gratitude of all who knew Tony for
writing this absorbing account of a man whose life and character
were full of paradox. The author grinds no axes, and strives only
to describe Tony as he was; and in this he triumphantly succeeds.

Hawarden,   *William Gladstone*
March 1996

Introduction

As britain awoke from the long, hard winter of 1962–63 the news that Anthony Chenevix-Trench had been appointed Head Master of Eton brought a spring to the step of all those who bemoaned the growing sense of drift and complacency in the country. For over a decade a Conservative government had been in power and now, in its sinking dotage, its reactionary class-bound image looked increasingly out of touch with a post-war generation eager to reform the major institutions and make them more accessible to those outside their exclusive walls. In such circumstances, the appointment of an outsider, with youthful looks and fresh ideals, to this most prestigious of educational establishments offered hope and succour for the future.

To insiders, the appointment was no surprise. Since his scholarship to Christ Church, Oxford, at the tender age of sixteen, Tony Chenevix-Trench was a name to be reckoned with. Born into an eminent family, Tony, the youngest of four boys, strutted effortlessly through Shrewsbury and Oxford, winning prizes and plaudits in equal measure. For all his brilliance, however, he was no mere academic intent on winning fame in his chosen field. When an opportunity to return to Shrewsbury came his way, the temptation proved irresistible and there, apart from one brief return to Oxford, he saw out the next eight years, becoming an outstanding schoolmaster. Before he had even been appointed a housemaster, the Archbishop of Canterbury was attempting unavailingly to woo him to Charterhouse as headmaster.

Tony eventually succumbed to overtures from Bradfield and there began eight years of arcadian bliss as he, in conjunction with his wife Elizabeth, invested it with a Camelot-style aura. An honest rural establishment was transformed into something greater and Tony became a national figure. He was appointed to the influential Robbins Committee into higher education, the only headmaster to be so honoured, and when Eton came looking for his services the interest seemed inevitable rather than surprising. Moreover, they were prepared to up their terms to get him. Not many outsiders dictate to Eton, but these were special times and he was the coming man. In such a heady atmosphere, he, like Churchill, could be forgiven for thinking that his life up to then had been but a preparation for this hour. Alas, how often do the Gods elevate their favourites to undreamed of pedestals only to see their rivals send them crashing. Once installed, his sureness of touch rapidly deserted him as he confronted a stubborn establishment in liege to 500 years of history.

In July 1970, less than seven years after his auspicious appointment, Head Master and College parted company on unhappy terms, leaving a once proud thoroughbred in search of his former pedigree. It took nearly a quarter of a century for history to have her say on these troubled times but, when eventually it did, the repercussions could hardly have been more devastating.

In a book, *Eton Renewed*, charting the school's history from 1860 to the present day, the college's Vice-Provost, Tim Card, when reviewing the Chenevix-Trench era, made some passing references to the late Head Master's propensity for alcohol and corporal punishment. He also gave lie to the previously unchallenged contention that Tony had resigned prematurely on grounds of physical strain and stress by outlining categorically the reasons behind his dismissal. These comments by Tim Card hit a raw nerve in the British establishment, sparking a heated debate in the press over the man and his supposed offences. For several days the controversy dominated the letter columns of *The Times* with a host of old boys, Etonian and non-Etonian alike, rushing to the defence of their former Head Master. Other columnists proved less charitable: their own painful reminiscences giving full credence to Tim Card's unflattering portrait.

As Tony's reputation lay pierced and bloodied like the toga of some murdered Caesar his faithful band of Mark Antonys was entitled to inquire whether all his glories, conquests, triumphs and spoils had shrunk to this petty measure. And yet for all the heat generated by supporters and opponents alike, the debate had barely deviated from Tony's role as a flogger, this most British of obsessions, omitting the many other facets of a talented school-master whose flair for exploration and discovery had originally prompted Eton to secure his services.

Whether it was in the palatial splendour of Imperial India or the well-groomed nursery of Shrewsbury, Tony's formative years were spent in perpetual sunshine. As he indulged his love of books depicting the noble feats of great men his vivid imagination conjured up a world where goodness finally triumphed over evil. For many, such dreams would have vanished amidst the Japanese barbarities of the Asian jungle but for Tony, a prisoner on the notorious Burma Road, his past acted as a trusted shield in his successful struggle for survival. He returned to more congenial surroundings, his faith unimpaired. Once he had committed him-self to teaching, this resolve to uncover the unfathomable depths of individual potential became his greatest motivation. Apart from his pocket-size appearance which had him repeatedly mistaken for one of his pupils, the witty self-parodies, the outlandish pranks and the flouting of pomp and circumstance gave him the common touch. Amidst the rigid conformity of the immediate post-war public school such unabashed familiarity was a revelation. He could pull it off as a teacher, as a housemaster possibly, but surely not as a headmaster. For as a breed they were austere figures of distant authority whose way of life, according to Anthony Sampson in *The Anatomy of Britain* combined monasticism with worldly ambition. Throwing convention to the winds, Tony on becoming a headmaster decided to go his own way, challenging others to follow his example. Conferences, committees, assemblies, rules and routine, the usual province of headmasters were of secondary importance to a man whose prime concern remained ministering to his flock, particularly those who veered from the straight and narrow.

To make his ideal a reality Tony ran an open-door policy which made him accessible to all and sundry. The long hours, the easy rapport, his belief in progress, all were reciprocated in kind. Many chose to be guided by his star and Bradfield became the talk of education in England. Had Tony come up with a style that offered a model for the future? The media clearly thought so as they pondered his elevation to Eton, 'I believe I have met a prophet,' wrote Vincent Mulchrone of the *Daily Mail* on 11th July 1963, 'a practical, pragmatic teacher, who has it in his heart to inspire and transform our society through our children.'

In truth the Trench style contained much that was open to chance, particularly in the strange world of Eton where administration not participation was the key to success. When Etonians, conditioned to a strictly formal relationship with their Head Master, were inundated with overtures of friendship, their response was less than forthcoming, particularly since his tendency to heap praise on everyone indiscriminately rather devalued the currency. Masters, too, beguiled with promises and panegyrics began to grow weary of the flattery when words weren't matched by deeds. A desire to please everyone had precisely the opposite effect as Tony gave contradictory undertakings which he couldn't possibly fulfil. To his critics his reliance upon charm as opposed to aloofness and method was fatal to the running of such a large institution and their merciless opposition exposed an Emperor devoid of robes. His enforced abdication brought about much agonised soul-searching severely undermining his confidence. A talk to the sixth form at Fettes several years later on the romance of his idyllic childhood invoked a wry comparison with the problems that beset him thereafter:

'Since those 'Paradise days', romanticism, classical reticence and harsh reality have torn me in three. I suppose that is why much later I became an unsatisfactory Head Master of Eton. Head and heart have always been at odds and heart has usually won at the expense of head.'

However, if this was a confession for past mistakes, it wasn't a blueprint for future change. Nothing would induce him to ditch his philosophy or even amend the more fragmented parts. Writing to his nephew John in 1976 he cheerfully acknowledged that 'Trenches are very quixotic animals . . . My dear friends regard me as a naive unworldly freak. No matter, I like it that way.' Such an admission, rare for any leader, passes for the musings of an incurable optimist who, whatever the fates, hasn't forsaken the untainted innocence of his youth. To the reader such gentle premises would appear a far cry from his craving for corporal punishment but Tony's complex approach to discipline was but the most striking paradox in a career grounded in educational unorthodoxy.

CHAPTER I

INDIA – STAR FROM THE EAST

Tony chenevix-trench was born into a family of distinction and service. His great, great paternal grandfather, Richard Trench (1774–1827) married the author Melesina Chenevix, daughter of Richard Chenevix, Bishop of Waterford. The Chenevixes and probably the Trenches, too, were of French Huguenot stock, refugees from persecution; the former from Picardy the latter from La Vendée. They settled in Ireland at the end of the seventeenth century from where they achieved considerable renown in military and ecclesiastical circles, none more so than Richard and Melesina's third son, Richard Chenevix-Trench (the Chenevix was added in 1873).

A man of abundant energies, Richard Trench numbered the poet Tennyson among his friends at Cambridge where their mutual love of poetry and literature brought them together in an aesthetic group known as the Apostles. A prolific author and poet himself, Trench nevertheless found his greatest vocation in the Church, becoming in turn Professor of Divinity at King's College, London in 1845, Dean of Westminster in 1856 and Archbishop of Dublin in 1864. It was in this last capacity that he waged an abortive campaign against Gladstone's disestablishment of the Anglican Church in Ireland. Had Trench's reputation not been sullied by a brief flirtation with the cause of radical insurgency against the throne of Spain in 1830 he, it is rumoured, might well have gone on to become Archbishop of Canterbury.

Like many clerics Trench came across as somewhat eccentric. As an old man he had long feared the onset of paralysis. At a grand dinner party he turned to his young neighbour and said, 'It has come at last, I knew it would.'

'What has come, Your Grace?' she asked.

'Paralysis. I have been pinching my leg for five minutes and have felt nothing.'

'Indeed you must not concern yourself about it, for it is my leg you have been pinching.'

This story had been told of others and the Archbishop's descendants doubted its veracity until his grandson Ralph as a young man was presented to a very old lady. 'Trench', she said. 'Trench. Is that your name? Any relation to the Archbishop?'

'He was my grandfather.'

'Oh, was he? Well, I'm the girl whose leg he pinched.'

In 1832 Richard Trench had married his first cousin, the then Frances Mary Trench (1809–1890). Their large family of eight sons and six daughters gives some idea as to why, by the turn of the century, it was rare to find a village from Belfast to Cork without at least one Chenevix-Trench in residence, well loved as a family for their acts of mercy during the great potato famine of the 1840s. Then, legend has it, one ancestor, casting his Huguenot origins to the winds, assembled all his tenants, flung open his doors and said, 'My house is yours. What I eat, you eat. If we starve, we'll do it together.'

Richard and Mary Chenevix-Trench's third son, Charles, opted for a career in the army and was just seventeen when posted to the Crimea. Once peace had descended he was employed by the governor of Gibraltar as an additional ADC where his duties allegedly included transmitting a request from the governor to the visiting Lord Cardigan, the *bête noir* of the Crimea, for him to take leave of the colony.

In the Franco-Prussian war of 1870–71, Charles Chenevix-Trench took service leave and offered his services to the recently formed International Society for the relief of the sick and wounded from which grew the Red Cross of today. His duty was to carry medical stores to the wounded of both sides. A respected British mediator, Charles was the soul of discretion as he constantly passed from one side to the other on his mission of mercy without disclosing state secrets. When he died in 1933, aged 95, one of the oldest Royal Artillery officers, *The Times* observed that, 'like so many of his generation his faith was simple and deep and he carried it out in his life.' This faith, coupled with an enduring attachment to Britain and her proud destiny in the world, instilled in him a noble concept of service which, intentionally or otherwise, found a ready echo in his large family.

When ADC to the governor of Bermuda, Lieutenant-General Sir Henry Lefroy, Charles had fallen for Sir Henry's daughter Emily. They married in 1874 and she bore him seven sons, two of whom fought in the Boer War, 1899–1902, five in the First World War and two in Hitler's War as well. Dick, the oldest, after seeing action with the Indian Army in the Far East, joined the Indian Political Department where years of distinguished service gained him a knighthood. Max, the third son, whose life of soldiering in South Africa and Egypt promised so much, met an untimely end on the Western Front in 1914. Christopher, the fourth son, died on active service in South Africa, aged twenty. Of the remaining three, all of whom were educated at Wellington, Ralph's work with the Royal Signals won him the MC in 1916 and Laurence's sterling exploits as a staff officer with the Royal Engineers, were rewarded with the DSO, CMG and Legion of Honour. The youngest, Alfred, was also seconded to the Royal Engineers during the First World War before transferring to civil engineering afterwards; his business ability a notable attribute in a family never renowned for its financial acumen.

The one exception to this military lineage was Charles and Emily's second son, Charles Godfrey, commonly known as Jack, who trod his own separate path to eminence. Educated at Loretto, a small Scottish public school outside Edinburgh on the windy Firth of Forth, Jack came under the benign influence of its famous headmaster, H.H. Almond, who mixed spartan rigour with an enlightened concern for the welfare of all his pupils. An outdoor fanatic himself, the informally clad Almond insisted that a Loretto education comprise a full exposure to the whims of the harsh Scottish climate. Aside from cold baths, bare knees and physical endurance, Loretto had much of merit to offer. The food was edible, the atmosphere excellent and the opportunities for self-fulfilment profuse. On many occasions, with the blessings of the headmaster, Jack would take to the hills to go birdwatching and shooting, dogs in attendance and beer in ready supply. Indeed so fired was he by his enthusiasm for nature that he even took a year out from school to live with the gypsies, learning Romany in the process.

Although Loretto's Classical education was reduced to little more than excessive learning of ancient texts by rote, Jack's fascination and aptitude for the Classics never deserted him. He won a scholarship to Lincoln College, Oxford, before his selection in 1900 for the Indian Civil Service. The Empire then offered many interesting opportunities for employment and we can safely surmise that India would have appealed to Jack's sense of romanticism as well as to his flair for languages. At any rate, in the following year, 1901, he was assigned to the Central Provinces, a vast area directly administered by the British, where for the next twenty-one years he worked in a number of different capacities, rising to the important position of Commissioner of Settlement. Official work aside, one of his more enduring feats was writing the first grammar of a remarkable Aboriginal tribe, the Gond, numbering two and a third million people living between the River Narbada and the Deccan. They had no written language and Jack's efforts persuaded the grateful natives to christen him a 'Gond with a white skin.' It was also during this period that Jack was to marry Margaret Blakesley, a union born of serendipity somehow in keeping with the mystique of the British Raj.

Margaret Blakeley's origins were half English and half French.Her paternal grandfather was Joseph William Blakesley, Dean of Lincoln, who by strange coincidence was a great friend and fellow Cambridge apostle of Richard Chenevix-Trench. His marriage to Margaret Wilson Holmes, daughter of the Rev. Thomas Holmes, brought him seven sons, the fourth of whom was John Blakesley, an engineer, who married Louisa Batallaird. The Batallairds were descended from the Chevalier, Vasse-St Owen, and lived dangerously during the French Revolution, and, as radicals, under Napoleon III. Louise herself, the daughter of political activist Paul Batallaird and his English wife Charlotte, had vivid memories as a small child of the Prussian Siege of Paris in 1870–71 and the horrific Commune riots which followed.

Later, in more peaceful times, she was to meet her husband, then studying in Paris, and they married on 12th November 1886. After their marriage Louise and John Blakesley set out for India where John took up an appointment as Engineer to the South Mahratta Railway and it was on 5th May 1888 that Margaret May was born. Louisa's ill-health forced the family almost immediately to return to Europe, first to Paris and then to London where they settled in the decorous suburb of Kew. There the domestically educated Margaret remained with her family until she travelled out to India in 1909 by boat to visit her uncle Edmund. who, ironically like Jack, worked in the Central Provinces for the Indian Civil Service. On board she happened to meet and befriend Jack's sister Maude. When they were met by their respective hosts in Bombay, Jack came face to face with Edmund for the first time.

According to Margaret, commonly known as Margot in later years, Jack had told Edmund he would like to marry her and Edmund told Margot that would be a splendid idea! They duly married in 1910 and during the course of the next decade Margot presented Jack with four sons, Christopher, Richard and Godfrey preceding the youngest, Tony, born at Kasauli in the Punjab on 10th May 1919. Within six months of his birth Tony was brought to Britain by his mother to begin a two-year nomadic spell during which they stayed with various sets of relations so that Margot could supervise the schooling of Christopher and Richard. By the time they returned to India in 1922, their father had moved to Udaipur to begin a new and important chapter in his Indian adventure.

The city of Udaipur, comprising 30,000 inhabitants, was the capital of the Rajput state of Mewar ruled over by the sunborn Sisodia family for over 1,100 years. Situated on cliffs of white marble overlooking the azure depths of Lake Pichola, the city's crowning jewels were its island palaces — cool, colonnaded retreats of marble — concealing secret gardens and curious frescoes. In the main palace, the Maharajah lived with his palace guard bedecked with chain mail armour and carrying great spears. They were the heirs of generations of Rajput resistance to the Mogul Emperors at Delhi and their commitment to a medieval life-style was more than matched by that of the chief nobles whose large estates were owned rent free in return for spells of feudal service. It was into this Oriental time-warp that the Chenevix-Trench family stepped when Jack answered an urgent request by the Mewar Dhakar to undertake the state's land settlement. There is no doubt that the tenants of Mewar had serious and justified grievances which in July 1923 became channelled into an extraordinary burst of lawlessness against the Udaipur state troops after the Dhakar had rejected recommendations from Jack's three-man commission that substantial concessions to the tenantry be granted. Viewed uneasily by his employers, sensing a troublemaker in their midst, Jack with his benign charm was a universally revered figure amongst the ordinary people; guide, philosopher and friend in one. Godfrey Chenevix-Trench recalls that twenty-nine years later in 1955, two full decades after Jack's retirement, his parents revisited Udaipur for the first time since Indian independence in 1947. Somehow the news leaked out and thousands of 'poors and rottens' flocked in from the country- side to greet them. Some had walked for two days.

Jack's wisdom and benevolence inevitably left its mark on his children. His love for the Classics found a ready response from all four boys: Tony was introduced to Herodotus at the age of 6. Similarly, his acute powers of observation were able to communicate the excitement of discovery in the world of creation, infusing Tony with that sense of wonder that never deserted him. Because Jack received only six months leave every three years, he remained severed from the rest of his family for long periods once his wife and children returned home. It was a source of constant sadness to all four boys that they didn't get to know their father better. How eagerly Tony used to await his father's letters from India, such was the sense of fun and interest they conveyed interspersed with gentle moral advice, so subtly expressed that it never came across as pontificating.

Home for the Chenevix-Trench family in Udaipur was an oblong, white two-storey house not far from the Residence and overlooking a dusty level stretch of ground, the Chaugan, on which from time to time the State cavalry used to exercise. Bougainvillaea covered the lower part of the house and a big tree shaded part of the upper verandah to which every sunset would fly a slow procession of large, fruit-eating bats. With a staff stretching to a dozen, the lives of Godfrey and Tony were well supervised and never dull. One of their greatest thrills was to ride behind the State cavalry on their ponies, Marmalade and Marmaduke, resplendent in their uniforms, courtesy of the Lancers. Another was to dress up in the remnants of their mother's old evening dresses. Otherwise they happily played with local Rajput boys on equal terms or learned the elements of Hindustani in discourse with the servants. Their Indian *ayah* was a sweet, gentle woman in whose eyes the boys could do no wrong except that of unkindness. She kept a whole litter of Siamese cats in Tony's chest of drawers which one day led to his discovering kittens. During the hottest summer months she would accompany Nanny and the boys to a small hotel in Simla amidst the foothills of the Himalayas. In 1923 when an attack of mumps forced a change of venue into a two-room log cabin, a large tailless ginger-coloured monkey slipped quietly into Godfrey's room only to be confronted by the *ayah* and an aluminium saucepan. Years later in Somerset, the saucepan with its enormous dent would be proudly displayed to visitors.

And then there was Nanny, alias Elsa Thorne, young, kind and devoted to the Chenevix-Trenches. She used to drive the boys in a horse and carriage late in the afternoon to Saheli Bagh (the Slave Girl Garden) or along the road skirting the Fateh Sagar Lake ringed by scrub-covered hills where they once saw a wolf. Nanny had never been abroad before, and was convinced that danger lurked behind every bush. Tony later recalled the time she confused a herd of goats coming down the hill with a herd of tigers. On another occasion when the six-year-old Godfrey stumbled into a hollow awaking a very large boar, distinctly inclined to retaliate, Nanny stamped angrily telling it, 'Shoo you nasty, dirty beast'. And shoo it did, eliciting scant surprise from her charges. For Nanny was Nanny and her word was law. Many years later her homilies would frequently grace headmagisterial texts on Founder's Day to illustrate some profound truth.

When Tony left India in 1925, not returning until 1940, he took away with him a host of happy memories, an imagination swelled by exotic surroundings and a confidence buoyed by his imperial grounding. Yet for all the riches emanating from his pampered lifestyle the paternalist ways of his father had inculcated in him, however tentatively, an understanding that those born into privilege must wear the robes of high office lightly. The 'have nots' who weren't invited to the palatial banquet and who supped on scraps outside still had their rights and their dignity.

On returning to Britain, the Chenevix-Trenches settled for a year at Petham in the depths of the Kent countryside before moving on to Westgate-on-Sea where Godfrey and Tony attended their first school. In 1927, the years of wandering ended when Jack paid out £1,955 for a home in the Somerset village of Aller, close to the edge of Sedgemoor, the scene of Monmouth's ill-fated rebellion against James II in 1685. Relics of his struggle and the bloody reprisals that followed, ruthlessly orchestrated by the notorious Judge Jeffreys, littered the sleepy towns and hamlets of the county.

Aller Manor was a rambling three-storey Georgian house, set amidst acres of woods with a sprawling garden leading up a hill at the back to lush meadows at the top where ponies gently grazed. Here in this enchanting pastoral setting the Chenevix-Trenches with a host of cousins in trail, turned their back on the outside world to find their own pleasures and entertainments in one another's company when they gathered for school holidays.

For Godfrey and Tony the novelty of getting to know their elder brothers proved doubly sweet such was their willingness to take them under their wing inspired, maybe, by the gentle advice tendered to Christopher by his absent father: 'How did you find the small brothers? Stick to them and you will never regret it. If four brothers hang together they can defy the world.'

Philippa Tooth, who was adopted by Tony's mother while her parents remained in India, remembers all the brothers being marvellous, particularly Tony, her elder by three weeks. He would always escort her to the top of the hill in the garden to console her during bouts of homesickness following separation from her parents. Tony's affection was reciprocated when Philippa was called upon by Nanny to come and hold Tony's hand to comfort him while she pricked the boils which constantly afflicted him. Such an ordeal would be stoically endured with only the odd tear betraying the pain that racked him. Traumatic scenes like this were happily rare departures from the atmosphere of fun and laughter that invariably filled the household.

Rarely was there a dull moment with a host of different activities on offer be it dressing up in Indian finery, tending the local wildlife, or playing hide and seek with the gardener Gullidge, commonly known as Gul-Gul. Devising an assortment of games was an essential part of the routine since they gave expression to the boundless torrents of vitality that flowed through the family's veins. Aside from keenly contested duels of soldiers in the nursery, Tony instigated a romp called the 'hog hunt' when he and Godfrey chased Philippa (the hog) around the house to see how many hog-hits they could get with soft boxing gloves. To the outsider these capers might appear rather malicious in design but Philippa, reared in the ways of a tomboy, clearly relished the challenge of evading her pursuers. These close family affinities survived the children's rare forays into the outside world. Philippa cherishes the memory of Tony rushing over to her at a children's dance after she had partnered Godfrey and shouting, 'My turn now, Hog,' forcing a hurried explanation from their chaperon that such a name was very much a term of endearment.

Presiding over the proceedings at Aller was Tony's mother. She was an intelligent, cultured woman, formidable and strict, but very kind and not averse to having her slight French accent gently mocked. The day would begin with her saying prayers before breakfast with all the maids present. Meals would be the occasion for lively, intelligent conversation, sometimes spoken in French at Margot's behest, a special drawl entering the Chenevix-Trench voices when something amusing was uttered. In the evening the entertainment would feature either a game of sardines or a get-together around the piano to sing their favourite hymns and folk songs. No day would be complete without Margot reading some stirring piece of literature to the children in bed. Particular favourites were Chesterton's *Ballad of the White Horse, Chevy Chase*, the old song of Percy and Douglas that moved Sir Philip Sydney's heart more than a trumpet, Kipling's stories, Kingsley's heroes, Greek myths and Horatio holding the bridge. In a radio broadcast shortly before he died Tony acknowledged the enormous debt he owed his mother in childhood, not least for providing him with this grounding in literature. 'The words still sing in my mind like music'. The little boy who had found that his early childhood 'passed in Paradise' further discovered that absorbing great literature helped him become 'passionately romantic and idealistic'.

These ideas were to survive the ordeal of being sent away to boarding school at the tender age of eight. In common with most prep schools of that vintage, Highfield, near Liphook in Hampshire, was a bleak, unforgiving institution presided over by its autocratic headmaster, Canon W.R. Mills, a portly cleric universally known as the Bug, much wedded to old-fashioned theories of crime and punishment. Rarely would a day go by when the Bug would not admonish his charges from the pulpit or in school assembly about their misdemeanours. Hovering over such chilling diatribes was the shadow of the cane, a sanction rigorously applied to classroom loafers or late night revellers in the dormitories, not expecting one of their headmaster's nocturnal prowls along the corridors. Such severity was denounced from the perspective of fifty years on by one of Tony's contemporaries, Ludovic Kennedy, the writer and broadcaster, who clearly loathed the headmaster and everything he stood for. His views were echoed by two other eminent contemporaries; Antony Storr, the psychiatrist and writer, and Robin Maugham the novelist.

Brutality aside, however, the school wasn't devoid of virtue. The facilities were good and the staff were highly proficient both in their classroom teaching and their encouragement of extra-curricular activities. With the faithful Godfrey to act as his prop, Tony survived his first term, Christmas 1927, smoothly enough, the only discordant note on an otherwise promising initial report being struck by his French master who complained that he was 'silly and troublesome in class'.

The following term, however, his progress was abruptly halted by a recurrence of ill-health that had first plagued him when he was only a year old. A combination of lung congestion and suspected rheumatic fever confined him to prolonged periods in the sanatorium, the prelude to a whole year away from school. When he returned in May 1929 he saw Sir Maurice Craig, a specialist, about sleepwalking after he had lost his front teeth in a nocturnal excursion. Another term's absence was the result. This appeared to do the trick. From then on the rest of his education was able to proceed unimpeded.

Led by the Bug himself, who was a hard taskmaster in Latin, the school demanded high standards from its pupils. Only some-one of Tony's exceptional intelligence could easily surmount the pressure. Ludovic Kennedy remembers sitting next to an ink-stained Tony in class and envying his ability to construct Greek sentences while the rest of them laboured wearily away, yet gratefully accepting his help when the opportunity presented itself. Although Tony's later reports sometimes drew attention to his general carelessness and inaccuracy, there was no doubting his love for the Classics or his aptitude for them.

In March 1932, three months before his thirteenth birthday, Tony followed in the footsteps of all three of his brothers by winning a scholarship to Shrewsbury. 'He is well advanced intellectually for his age,' wrote Canon Mills on his final report as Tony collected prizes for English and the New Testament in addition to a special prize for the best literary contributions to the school magazine. Thanks to his tutoring in literature at home, Tony never lost his intoxication with words. The result was some highly polished pieces of prose and poetry from one so young. the emphasis on rural imagery reflecting the love of the countryside his father had instilled in him.

One such, written during the Lent term when Tony was eleven, was this:

A Frosty Morning

It is a beautiful morning. It has frozen in the night, and nature has decked everything with silver dew and a white mantle of frost, which sparkles like diamonds in the early morning sun. The air is fresh and crisp, and filled with the twittering of the small morning birds. The old, familiar woodland path is transformed into some wonderful fairyland, where all the bracken and boughs of the great gnarled old oaks, blades of grass, twigs and all are covered with a shining mantle of silver and white. We wander aimlessly on in this wonderful place, hardly daring to breathe lest it should disturb the quiet and beauty of this paradise such as no artist could ever hope to paint. Soon we come to a beautiful stream, rippling gently along, the branches entwining over it forming a snowy white canopy, and the small flowers, all in white too, peep out on its banks. At last, with a great effort, we have to wrest our eyes from this wondrous sight and retrace our steps. But first we go

to the top of a hill nearby, and before us is a great carpet
of silver. Here and there a pine tree rears its head, hoary
with frost, from the wood. We then, much against our will,
have to go home.

A.C-T.

Two years later, during the Lent term of 1932, Tony contributed
this poem called *The Sirens*:

There is a land beyond the rising sun,
    Where voices chant for ever on the shore,
Of weary sorrow past, and sad toil done,
    Of calm, and wondrous peace for evermore.
Here, or here, do the Sirens lie
Singing sweet songs to the starlit sky,
    Where the foam gleams white in the hard moonlight
And the lonely sea-birds, wheeling, cry.

Here in the fragrant summer twilight
    A ship came sailing by
Breaking the stillness of the growing starlight,
    As swift their oars they ply
When, as the first great golden star was peeping,
    Across those solitary deeps came sweeping
The glory of the Sirens song nearby.

Ply, ply your oars, ye oarsmen, lest ye, heeding
    The magic beauty of its sweetly pleading,
Should tempted be to rest a little space,
And as ye hear the beauty of their singing
    Across the glassy rippling waters ringing
Ye turn your prows toward the fatal place.

Academic prowess aside, Tony clearly enjoyed his time at Highfield. He was too small and unco-ordinated to shine at any of the major team games but his speed and pluck won him laurels in the boxing ring. Such spirit typified his approach to school life making him gregarious and popular, even though there were occasions when this jauntiness was taken too far. One incident became so etched in his memory that Tony recounted it years later (with a touch of poetic licence surely) to a group of head-masters at Marlborough.

During his penultimate year there developed a particular High-field craze called Missionary Journeys (they were reading the Acts of the Apostles in scripture) which consisted of crawling about at 6am in pyjamas, exploring the cockloft between the tiles and the top storey ceilings. It was possible to go a long way and Tony re-called that it had all the ingredients of glamour — dark, mysterious, daring and illegitimate — so beloved by prep-school boys. One summer Sunday morning Tony and a friend penetrated into this mysterious land when the companion pushed Tony with a singular ill-timed playfulness. He slipped off the beam, went through the lath and plaster and fell with considerable force onto the Head-master's bed bringing with him pounds of dust and debris. The Bug's initial consternation rapidly turned to fury, his angry cry of 'You little beast' echoing around the room as he thrashed the startled boy there and then amongst the rubble of the bed.

Such a blot on Tony's copybook didn't distract from his generally sound disciplinary record and reconciliation was com-plete when the headmaster appointed him a school prefect for his last term. Tony left Highfield secure in the knowledge that, physi-cal size apart, he was well prepared to undergo the tempestuous journey into adolescence.

CHAPTER 2

SHREWSBURY AND OXFORD –
IN SEARCH OF THE HOLY GRAIL

For a family previously unaligned to any particular school, it might have seemed strange that Jack Chenevix-Trench should have placed all his eggs in one basket by his choice of Shrewsbury for all four of his sons. Historically, no member of the family had previously graced its portals and geographically Shropshire was some distance from Somerset. Highfield, however, had developed close contacts with Shrewsbury over the years and their generous endowment of scholarships was particularly alluring to a father on a modest salary of £1,000 with four intelligent boys to educate.

Founded in 1552 by Edward VI, Shrewsbury owed its eminence to a triumvirate of great headmasters whose combined tenure of office, spanning an incredible 110 years, took the school from the 18th to the 20th century. Samuel Butler, who assumed the headmastership in 1798, besides being a pioneer of the monitorial system long before Arnold established something similar at Rugby, ushered in at Shrewsbury that combination of Godliness and good learning which later became the touchstone of Victorian enlightenment in the public schools.

Butler was succeeded by one of his own pupils, Benjamin Hall Kennedy, the greatest Classical teacher of the 19th century and the author of the famous *Shorter Latin Primer* that remained essential reading for generations of prep-school Classicists. He in turn was followed in 1866 by another Salopian, Henry Whitehead

Moss, well remembered for instituting the school's move to Kingsland on the southern side of the city overlooking the River Severn. Here in this picturesque setting, which so enraptured the journalist and writer Sir Neville Cardus, when assistant cricket coach there, the modern school began to take shape. By the 1930s the Victorian legacy still abounded with its rich Classical tradition, its sporting fanaticism, fervent house loyalties, robust discipline and unseemly squalor all to the fore. To Brian Inglis, later editor of *Private Eye*, the school then was "as regimented as boys in a remand home" but, for all the restrictions, serious and petty alike, the general quality of the Common Room, enlivened by its share of eccentric characters helped sustain the school's premier ranking in select circles.

Tony's arrival coincided with that of H.H. Hardy, whose succession as headmaster to the absent-minded Canon H.A.P. Sawyer heralded a break in Salopian tradition. For, unlike the overwhelming majority of his predecessors, Hardy was a layman, whose brief but distinguished military past made him well suited to the increasing administrative demands that went with the job. As befitted a soldier, Hardy was a strict disciplinarian, his brusque demeanour commanding respect rather than affection but, underneath this forbidding exterior, lay a generous heart and a passion, like that of Almond of Loretto, for the great outdoors. This led to increased opportunities for pupils to explore the delights of the Shropshire countryside on their bicycles, or climb the Welsh hills on supervised expeditions. Such outings were manna for Tony who had inherited his father's love for the open spaces, and who revelled in energetic hikes up Cader Idris, Wales's second highest peak.

Diminutive of stature with thick black hair, a sallow complexion, dark eyebrows, protruding ears and sensual lips from which there passed a musically seductive voice, Tony cut quite a dash as a new boy in School House, his lack of inches both a source of amazement and amusement. One story has it that during his first term he could fasten his collar around his waist; another which he loved to relate was the occasion he was requested by one of his masters in class to take a note he had just composed to the headmaster. Tony duly obliged and Hardy, having read it, promptly tore it up before consigning it to the waste-paper basket. Itching to discover its content, Tony crept back into Hardy's classroom during the lunch break to piece the remnants back together. On completion, he absorbed the following unflattering observation, 'Have you ever met such a funny little boy before?'

Such an idiosyncratic appearance could have marked him out for excessive mocking by his peers but, fortunately, his wit and insidious charm came to his aid, shielding him from potential ridicule. Never one to lack confidence in repartee, Tony could wriggle his way out of most tight corners. Notorious for his disorganisation and tardiness, Tony one day confronted the head-master, a stickler for punctuality, as he struggled to make it into chapel on time:

'Dear me, late again, I see, Trench,' muttered Hardy.
'Oh are you, Sir?' replied Tony. 'So am I!'

His precocity didn't confine itself to the headmaster. Others in authority were subjected to the Trench humour, none more so than Harry Dawson, the pedestrian Latin master who had been badly wounded in the First World War. Boys used to sit through his lessons with their legs in the air, and taken in by the legend that Dawson's leg was wooden, Tony reputedly once stuck a hatpin in it as he walked around the class only to be convulsed by horror when he realised that the rumour lacked foundation. Like all boys Tony enjoyed the occasional bout of classroom baiting whenever an inviting target appeared. Essentially a conformist and an achiever, he could entertain his peers knowing there would be clear limits to his buffoonery.

Settling well into the Classical Fifth, Tony was soon at home in this academic cauldron and fulfilling the high expectations held out for him. To a man his masters found him keen, alert and ingenious in class with a scholar's desire for approbation. 'He evidently means business,' wrote the headmaster at the end of his first term, 'and will make a success of his time here.' Just over a year later, in March 1934, he won the coveted form prize, awarded each term to the person with the most marks in all subjects, for the first time, a prelude to the fistful of trophies he was to lay claim to over the course of the next three years. 'Doing very well, almost inconveniently young to be so high in the School,' Hardy was to remark at this stage. Into the sixth form at the age of fifteen, his diet became an increasing round of Latin and Greek with some English, French, history and divinity thrown in for good measure.

In line with the great public schools and the acclaimed standards set by the likes of Kennedy, the Classics department at Shrewsbury ranked with the very best. In addition to Dawson, whose disciplinary problems couldn't mask real scholarship and kindness, the leading lights were J.M. Street, an acerbic Unitarian from Liverpool, so hated by Richard Cobb, the historian, R.W. Moore, later Headmaster of Harrow, R.J. Pitts-Tucker, House Tutor in School House and later Headmaster of Pocklington, and Stacy Colman, a brilliant Old Salopian and sometime Fellow of Queen's College, Oxford. In their insistence upon the highest of linguistic standards combined with their encouragement, they all, particularly Street, were to have a profound effect on the young Trench whose own impish flair somewhat mesmerized them in turn. Colman remembered Tony as 'a lively little boy; a leader in the form who gave you answers with a half wink. If he was caught out in argument, he would bluff away'.

Although he was imbued with the interests and good taste of
the scholar there were flaws to iron out; grammatical blunders
in his Latin prose, and a lack of accuracy in his Greek iambics
not to mention, according to his English master, S.S. Sopwith,
the family failing of 'being a little too allusive and figurative in
his essays'. Even after winning his scholarship to Christ Church,
Tony was never allowed to rest complacent in the quest for true
perfection. But these were the reservations of hard taskmasters
intent on turning out the most erudite of scholars. Tony's excellence at composition, his catholic taste in reading, his elephan-
tine memory, his depth of ideas, his powers of insight, his clarity
of thought and his abilities in the subsidiary subjects made him
a real teenage prodigy.

So impressed was Hardy, a proficient Classicist himself, that
he was moved to write of the fifteen-year-old Tony, 'If he
doesn't presently get two Firsts at Oxford it will be disreputable
of him!' A year later the prediction began to assume a compelling
accuracy as Tony, in January 1936, still aged only sixteen, won
an open scholarship to Christ Church, Oxford, his English essay
and general paper, according to Hardy, 'getting astounding marks
for a boy of his age'. Hardy had hoped that Tony would go to
Balliol the following year but Christ Church, out to lure promising
scholars before they gravitated to Balliol, stepped in boldly with
a scholarship of £100 per annum.

Confronted with such an enticing *fait accompli*, Tony's father,
not surprisingly, grasped the nettle on the proviso that his son
could delay entry till October 1937. Christ Church willingly
assented and Tony returned to Shrewsbury for another five terms
to refine his skills at the feet of great men, and to lay claim to
the whole gamut of school prizes on offer to aspiring academics.
With a number of able scholars in residence, he didn't lack for
competition. One such contender was Robin Lorimer, Tony's
closest friend at Shrewsbury, who also happened to be in School

House. Lorimer recalls Tony's immense irritation when he, not Tony, was awarded the Kittermaster Greek Iambics prize for a piece of Greek poetry which Tony considered unduly pedantic.

There were other awards which also eluded Tony's grasp but the disappointments were few and far between amidst the general acclamation. His last year in particular was something of an *annus mirabilis* for on Speech Day, Tony made off with the pick of the silverware including the Form Prize with a record number of marks, the Moss Prize for the best Classical Scholar in the school and the John Millington Exhibition for leavers. Eclipsing all these triumphs was the gratification of emulating his brother Christopher in winning the beautiful Sidney gold medal — the school's most prestigious award — for distinction in composition. An excursion into the uncharted waters of the history department even saw him gain *Proxime Accessit* in the British History prize. Given that the Upper Classical Sixth in his last year, which included the head boy, Geoffrey Lane, a future Lord Chief Justice, was, according to Street, the best in his forty-four years at Shrewsbury, bar the vintage year of 1917–18, this was no mean achievement. But then, according to Lorimer, Street considered Tony to be the best pupil he ever taught. By the time he left Shrewsbury, Tony reckoned there was very little from a psalm to a nursery rhyme that he couldn't turn into Latin or Greek verse.

Although Tony's academic accomplishments did attract some latent resentment — the Duke's French prize became known as the Flukes Trench prize when a Classicist stole the modern linguists thunder — he suffered little from the gibes of the uncultured fringe. Character aside, Tony was helped by the undue tolerance residing at Shrewsbury during this period. Lorimer remembers School House, under the enlightened influence of J.R. Hope-Simpson, possessing an intellectual atmosphere where discussion on a broad range of cultural subjects was the norm.

The tone of these discussions alternated between the highbrow
and the glib, the latter a Salopian trait at which many, including
Tony, excelled. Accustomed to the limelight since earliest days
in India, Tony loved to recreate that sense of court life in which
he could dominate the stage and play to the gallery. Many a
personal experience involving something amusing or bizarre was
often turned into a cracking good story, its material shamelessly
embroidered to maximise its effect. Extensive quotations from
literature and one-to-one conversations, particularly of a cerebral
nature, were very much his speciality too. Lorimer recalls relaxing
for over an hour in a communal bath with Tony deep in Classical
talk oblivious to the thickening scum around them.

    With a mind so eager to be stimulated it wasn't surprising that
Tony should participate in so many of the school's cultural activities. In addition to his membership of the debating society
— 'His speeches sometimes lacked construction', commented the
Salopian – he was president of the Halifax Society, winning official
plaudits for his talk on 'The Post-War Novel'. He also took the
part of Aegisthus in *The Agamemnon* of Aeschylus and co-edited
the *Salopian* with Lorimer, circumventing the usual hazard of
unmet deadlines by making up much of the material himself. If
all this activity wasn't enough to keep Tony's nose to the grind-
stone, he and Lorimer learnt German in their spare time from a
new master, Frank MacEachran, whose arrival in 1935 quite took
the school by storm. A compelling teacher with a passion for
poetry he introduced a private reading group which met two
evenings every week in winter, chiefly to read Dante's *Inferno*.
In common with countless Salopians, who over the next forty
years fell captive to the magnetic powers of this remarkable man,
Tony's appetite for literature, already prodigious, was further
whetted.

    Although his lack of size ensured that Tony's career in cricket
or football never progressed beyond representing his House he

found ample compensation in other sports. Apart from captaining the school fencing team and the House running team he was a gifted Fives player and rowed at Bow for the Doctors First IV⋆ To all of them he brought his usual brand of steely determination, particularly on the precipitous steeplechase course where, undaunted by potential hazards, he would plough through muddied streams, reinforced hedges and icy water-jumps. Such tenacity was on view in the House steeplechase championships in his final year, when in front of the cheering masses, led by the bloods in all their finery, he finished a highly respectable fifth out of fifty.

Other interests also competed for Tony's attention most notably the school OTC in which he rose to the rank of sergeant. Institutions like this since their inception in 1908 had often endured a chequered history in peacetime with many of their activities being viewed with indifference bordering on contempt. This all changed, however, in the mid-1930s when the escalation of overt aggression on the continent sent a shiver down the spines of the British military establishment whose preparations for war left much to be desired. Their general state of unreadiness seeped through to Shrewsbury where Tony found the sudden intensification of training and reorganisation rather discomforting. 'The muddle is appalling,' he tartly informed his mother in February 1937. 'We are having so many specialist courses and lectures that we're thoroughly confused.'

Not surprisingly against this background of growing anxiety the coronation of George VI and Queen Elizabeth in May 1937 proved a welcome distraction for the nation. It so happened that Tony and Lorimer were almost the only two boys in the school

---

⋆ Since the School House was twice as large as any other it was (for competitive purposes) divided into Headroom and Doctors. Tony and Robin Lorimer both belonged to the Doctors.

who didn't go home for the three-day exeat they were granted in honour of the occasion. Consequently they volunteered to represent Shrewsbury's OTC at the ceremony in conjunction with 900 colleagues from other schools. The night before they were billeted at Rutlish Grammar School, Wimbledon, later to find fame as the Prime Minister John Major's alma mater. A 3.30 am reveille set in motion the train of events that were to make this day so memorable to all who took part in it.

Having congregated in Eaton Square the six columns of cadets marched down Constitution Hill to the Victoria Memorial opposite Buckingham Palace where they took up their position on parade. With crowds milling everywhere jostling for the most opportune vantage points from which they could readily bear witness to history a touch of improvisation was called for. The cadets had been ordered not to stand on the parapet round the fountain in case the tackets in their boots should damage it, but because neither Tony nor Lorimer were tall enough to see anything they disobediently scrambled up on it, with many other undersized cadets. Their efforts were well rewarded. 'We got a very good view of the King and Queen leaving the palace, and of the princesses who looked very happy and thrilled.' After seeing the Life Guards and the coach disappear round the corner down the Mall they dispersed for lunch, reassembling at 2 pm to watch the royal party's return. Later in the day Tony, now demob happy, met up with some Salopians living in London and clambered aboard the roof of a London taxi to join the thousands of revellers thronging the streets of Piccadilly in carnival spirits. 'The lights and the decorations round Trafalgar Square were very fine,' he observed. 'Selfridges I thought a monumental work of vulgarity.'

If one takes into consideration Tony's duties with the OTC, and his charity work at the School Mission in Liverpool, there was no area of school life, with the exception of music, then a very low priority, untouched by his presence. 'He is bursting with life,' his housemaster wrote in 1935, and, certainly, his letters home tell of a hectic schedule which filled every minute of the day. This energy involving achievement and camaraderie in equal measure gave Tony confidence which deep down he still lacked.

A striking feature of his letters is the frequency with which he seeks advice from his parents on fairly mundane matters such as which books to buy for scholarship awards and travelling arrangements during the holidays. Rarely is there a hint of arrogance born of success or of headstrong adolescence struggling to escape the clutches of parental authority. As he was physically a late developer, his appointment as a house monitor at the age of sixteen brought no sudden projection of confidence, raising doubts with his housemaster as to whether he had the personal authority to be head of house and a school praepostor (the Salopian term for prefect) for his final year.

Hope Simpson's reservations had evaporated by Christmas 1936, when clearly delighted by the way Tony had risen to the challenge, he wrote that 'he is an optimist and looks for the best in people.' As an accurate assessment of Tony's lifelong approach to leadership his housemaster's succinct comment could barely be improved upon but amongst his contemporaries some were less forthcoming in their praise.

The novelist Francis King in his recent autobiography *Yesterday Came Suddenly*, recalls an incident during his first term in School House when all the new boys, seated together at a long table, vociferously dismissed from their presence a bowl of unappetizing cottage pie by tipping the contents of a salt cellar along with some pepper, mustard and sugar into the disdained offering. Reported to Tony by one of the maids all the new boys were summoned to the monitors' room, called the Headroom, where he awaited them with the enamel pie dish on the table and fourteen spoons beside him. Reprimanding them for disgusting behaviour, Tony handed each a spoon and cried, 'Now you can eat the mess you created. Eat, eat, go on, eat.' They ate and afterwards, while the five chief miscreants remained to be soundly beaten, King headed straight for the lavatory where he was sick. To King, a respected contemporary of Tony at Oxford after the war, Tony was 'a supercilious, capricious and cruel head of house', a view at odds with the general consensus but one which came to be held by a vocal minority thereafter.

That such a divergence of opinion should come about requires some explanation. For all his modesty in the company of his peers, Tony appears to have been less restrained when laying down the law to cowering thirteen-year-olds. Lorimer recalls that Tony felt responsible for their moral welfare which, if left unsupervised, would suffer accordingly. An example of this appears in one of his letters when he denounces the recklessness of some in his House for repeatedly exposing themselves to the biting east winds on the touchline, clad only in the scantiest garments. 'Only very strict interference makes them take even the most obvious precautions. The trouble is that a lot of people going out of School disorganises things terribly, and spoils the House's athletic chances among other things. So one has to be very down on people who are just careless.'

King's reference to Tony's cruelty stemming from his excessive beating is certainly instructive in the light of the bitter allegations which later dogged him on this vexed issue. Lorimer recalls Tony complying with a statutory requirement then in vogue that even minor offenses received a standard penalty of four strokes, but never gloating over the travails of his victims. His memory of School House under Tony is of a law-abiding one with very little bullying to report. As a leader Tony was admired by Lorimer for his physical bravery, humour and ability to engender house spirit.

At the same time Lorimer saw how his craving for a quasi fantasy world where mutual success and admiration were uppermost made him oblique under attack and susceptible to having favourites. Silver-tongued reprobates, well aware of the unpleasant fate that awaited them, were able to charm their way out of his censorious grip raising doubts about his firmness of purpose. Such reservations remained chiefly confined to the lower deck. In the company of his superiors Tony was ever the perfect courtier; the less appealing side of his character, apparent to discerning sceptics like King, was rarely apparent to them. Consequently his stock, already high in their estimation, continued to soar ever upwards as advancing maturity brought him more on to their plane.

By the time Tony handed over his duties in School House to his great friend Ronald Prentice in July 1937 he had completely won over the confidence of his astute housemaster who, according to Lorimer, thought the world of him as his final report makes clear:

> Last year I thought we were losing the best head of house I could remember, and now I believe we are losing a better . . . He seems to be aimed at all points to carve a brilliant career for himself and one inspired by the very best ideals. We are most grateful for the way he has tackled the job, and, above all, for his handling of monitors. He should find it a priceless experience.

Hardy concurred in similar vein:

> The Upper Sixth will seem at first a dull place without him next term, but he will leave big gaps elsewhere too. He has fulfilled all our prophecies and will continue to do so. I hope four years hence to see him appointed to some high administrative service though he could ensure an academic

career if he prefers. We are all grateful to him and proud of his success.

Shrewsbury's regret at the parting of the ways with Tony was more than reciprocated. A week after leaving he summed up his feelings in a letter to his parents from OTC camp.

> I am more sorry that I can say to leave Shrewsbury, where I feel so firmly rooted that I had come to regard it as part of myself. But not only is it true of course that one always hates 'uprooting' but it is equally certain that one never comes near understanding how much one likes the place until one is in one's last term. Having in the last few weeks come into contact with a great many 'outsiders' from Oxford etc. one begins to have some idea of the terrific reputation of Shrewsbury in circles not only academic, and of course this heightens one's gratitude to it. I can't say how much the last year has profited me and I'm so glad I stayed on for it. Not only in the academic way in winning prizes etc. which bring a certain amount of temporary 'kudos' but in more ways quite indefinable. I'm sure that one must feel in the long run the benefit of such responsible jobs though in a very restricted sphere as running a House, an OTC company, various societies and editing a school magazine. if only in the knowledge of how far from easy it is. For all of which I feel no small gratitude, as I do for the fact that I've had a very good time.

In the same letter Tony mentions that Jimmy Street had floated the possibility of using his influence with the headmaster to get him a job at Shrewsbury once he had finished at university. 'Very good of him, I thought', remarked Tony, 'and I should very much like to do so if I have a year or so spare between things after Oxford. If not as a permanent job.'

The fact that Tony had exceeded all expectations at Shrewsbury and had seen numerous doors opened to him for the future earned the school, as he had acknowledged to his parents, a very special place in his affections but, in common with others who had blazed a trail of glory at school, the triumphs came a little too easily for his subsequent developing maturity. In Tony's case his effortless charm and brilliance were increasingly too ready substitutes for the more prosaic attributes of efficiency, dependability and self discipline required in high office particularly when resolute action was needed to confront the demands of those under him.

For Tony, the magic of Shrewsbury never deserted him. It remained, in his eyes, a perennial shrine to carefree youth where time stood still, protected from the outside world with all its pitfalls and uncertainties. It is no coincidence that Tony should have been an ardent devotee of A.E. Housman's *Shropshire Lad,* in particular the extract subtitled *The Land of Lost Content,* and that he should have often quoted it to his friends:

> Into my heart an air that kills
> From yon fair country blows
> What are those blue remembered hills
> What spires, what farms are those?
> That is the land of lost content,
> I see it shining plain,
> The happy highways where I went
> And cannot come again.

Leaving the happy highways of Shrewsbury in temporary abeyance, Tony took the high road to Oxford in October 1937 and Christ Church, the largest, most prestigious of all the colleges, founded by Henry VIII in 1546, and a ready home for Old Etonians. In these august surroundings, comprising five quads of differing architectural styles, Tony was comfortably housed in Peckwater

Quad, a fine example of 18th-century Classical architecture, well looked after by the scout (a college manservant) on his staircase who learnt to cope with his untidiness. In contrast to the boisterous antics of the college hunting brigade who habitually smashed windows in his vicinity late at night, Tony led a sober, relatively unostentatious existence during his first two years at Oxford. Regular hours, rowing at Bow for the 2nd VIII, cycling down the High Street, homely tea parties, trips to the theatre, evensong at the Cathedral and entertaining friends all bore the hallmarks of a more reputable university lifestyle. As would be expected for someone of Tony's cultural pedigree the history and beauty of this ancient city were not lost on him. His letters home convey glowing descriptions of the Deanery with its priceless array of antiques, and of college evensong with its invigorating choral singing. The arrival of summer only enhanced his appreciation of Oxford:

> It is very good down on the river in this weather: the backs of Merton, Corpus and Christ Church look too good for anything, and the Meadows full of sun are at their best. There's no doubt that Oxford in sunshine is a dream city — made to be seen in summer.

As he gradually immersed himself in university life Tony began to build up a loyal circle of friends fashioned around Christ Church and Balliol, the majority of whom, like him, were reading Mods. Aside from the ever-present Salopian coterie, in which Lorimer and Robin Prentice, a freshman in 1938, predominated, there was Dick Hare from Rugby and the Etonian trio of Charles Fisher, Henry Head and David Macindoe, their nostalgic yearnings for their old school rivalling that of their friends from Shrewsbury. Elected to an elitist Christ Church debating society, the Twenty Club, brought Tony added contacts including the historian Hugh Trevor-Roper.

Other friendships had stemmed from more bizarre origins. Tony recalled how one morning soon after arriving at Christ Church, he lost his way and entered the room of a slumbering fellow undergraduate who, mistaking him for the scout's boy, muttered, 'Nothing, thank you. Would you be kind enough to draw the curtains?' This Tony did and then withdrew. Their next encounter was to be on rather more equal terms on the Scholars' table in Hall when a scion of the aristocracy expressed great surprise and embarrassment for his *faux-pas*.

Shunning the Union, mainly on grounds of expense, and the University Dramatic Society, because of constraints on time, Tony saw his main priority as getting a First: his view was sustained by the presence of three other Salopians from the Classical Sixth invested with similar ambitions and by his tutor, the distinguished Senior Mods tutor, John G. Barrington-Ward, a former Westminster scholar and staunch apologist of the Oxford tutorial system. He was a bluff, friendly man given to massive outpourings of conceit, never desisting from mentioning his numerous compositions, which included *The Times* crossword every third morning, something Tony expected to complete in under ten minutes. When one of Tony's fellow scholars, Michael Watson, a distinguished cricketer, met Barrington-Ward for the first time, only to be greeted with a sarcastic, 'Oh, you're the cricketing Watson, I suppose?', implying that his work was quite secondary, a nettled Watson much to Tony's amusement answered, 'Yes, Sir, and you're the golfing Barrington-Ward, are you not?', a telling riposte at one of the best Latin prose scholars in Oxford.

Although Tony's exceptional ability was soon plain enough to convince Barrington-Ward that here was something special, his aloof mien and exacting standards meant immediate praise wasn't forthcoming. 'I find Barrington-Ward slightly trying as a tutor,' wrote Tony in mild frustration to his parents, 'as he will never commit himself or make any definite statement as to how well

or badly you do a composition — consequently it's very hard
to know how you stand with him.' Gradually the clouds lifted,
however, and underneath a guarded exterior lurked a warm,
amusing personality dedicated to his pupils' well-being. Several
weeks later on 11th November, Tony's sense of relief that recognition had finally come his way was palpable:

> A great triumph for me came along yesterday when he
> (Barrington-Ward) actually said a version of mine was "really
> quite good" – extremely high praise for him, and very
> reassuring for me as I had no idea how much progress I
> was making. Usually he gives no judgement at all.

Now that Barrington-Ward had earmarked Tony for the prestigious Hertford prize at the end of his first academic year, he
prepared him with a crash course of Latin compositions that
dominated their weekly tutorial during which Barrington-Ward
would read Tony's efforts and suggest improvements, showing
him his most expert fair copy. Tony's proficiency at composition
increased quickly even though such mindless repetition tended
to blunt his enthusiasm. More stimulating for him were his hourly
tutorials with Denys Page, a profound humanist, 'for whom the
ghosts did drink and live with a fierce clarity', enabling his pupils
to glean a proper insight into the mores of the ancient world.

Despite the rigours of Tony's preparation for the Hertford,
and Barrington-Ward's high hopes for him, the results, as Professor
Page's letter reveals, were to prove disappointing.

> Dear Chenevix-Trench
> I have to bear the sad news that you did not qualify for
> appearance on the Hertford but, I am delighted to tell you,
> you were sixth on the list and that your claims were very
> seriously considered to the last. You made an impression
> on all your examiners and it was only an unfortunate lapse

on one paper (Latin Verse – bad luck) that stood between
you and recognition. I congratulate you on a splendid effort
in a year when the rivals were quite unusually strong.

'As far as I can see,' wrote Tony to his mother, 'the only
dissatisfied one is myself, who has little cause to be. But it is
very annoying that the one paper which should have been my
best and, had I been up to form, would have got me something,
should have let me down!' In private, Professor Page acknowledged, 'the absurdly high standard' set by the Eton Classicist,
D.P. Simpson, in the Hertford. But, while in no doubt that Tony
had laid the seeds for a serious challenge a year on, he was moved
to remark that, 'he was not yet very mature'.

Fortified by some gentle study on a Salopian reading party at
Quatford Castle in Shropshire, hosted by Roger Bevan, Tony
resumed his studies in October, determined to improve on his
first year's standing. Although still prone to occasional excesses
of gusto when something more technically solid was called for,
his efforts now bore fruit.

First, in April 1939, he gained a First in Honours Mod with
twelve alphas in his fourteen papers, and second, in June, he
won the De Paravicini Scholarship (awarded to the runner-up
in the Hertford), the first Salopian to gain anything of the sort
for some time. The Hertford, it is true, still eluded him but the
great faith that Barrington-Ward had continued to place in him
had at last been properly realised. 'Thank you very much for
getting us (and yourself) another Varsity honour and just in time
for the Speech Day programme at the eleventh hour,' chortled
Hardy from Shrewsbury. Others wrote to congratulate in more
personal terms. Few seemed particularly surprised.

As Tony beavered away at his studies the war clouds began
to darken ominously over Europe as Hitler's Nazis went on the
rampage violating the rights of small nations. Undergraduates

returned in October 1938 in the immediate aftermath of the Munich settlement which had witnessed the Czech Sudetenland cravenly handed over to Germany under threat of naked force. It so happened that a standard by-election in Oxford, a traditionally safe Conservative seat, now assumed an added significance as it promptly turned into a national referendum on appeasement. All those hostile to the Conservative-dominated National government's policies rallied to the banner of the Popular Front candidate, the socialist Master of Balliol, A.D. Lindsay, ensuring full student participation in the contest.

Tony, although he had become increasingly perturbed by Nazi advances over the years, nevertheless, as a staunch member of the University Conservative Club, campaigned loyally for the government candidate, Quintin Hogg who, as Lord Hailsham, later held high office in a succession of Conservative governments. Out canvassing in the distressed area of St Ebbes with Charles Fisher, Tony found that the poorest households were either apathetic to the result or staunchly Conservative, the self-perceived symbol of respectability. Come election night, and Tony enjoyed the unseemly spectacle of witnessing crusty dons casting their dignity to the winds as they jostled and argued with one another in the streets, doubtless settling a few old scores in the process. To angry cries of 'Heil Hitler!' from the most vocal of his opponents, Hogg retained the seat for the government with a much reduced majority, and wrote to thank Tony for all his help. In retrospect, this election appeared to be one of those political occasions when the opposition lost the vote but won the argument. Neville Chamberlain's predilection to tie Hitler to diplomatic pacts soon proved to be a policy of illusion as the Nazi cavalcade continued to trample its way across Europe. As undergraduates relaxed over the summer vacation, the German invasion of Poland on 1st September 1939 finally brought matters to a head. The British declared war on Germany on 3rd

September and for Tony, as with all his contemporaries, the idyllic world of Oxford soon became but a vanishing dream as dangerous new challenges lay ahead.

CHAPTER 3

PARADISE LOST –
THE RAILWAY OF DEATH

Within a week of war beginning Tony began the great
transition from Oxford OTC amateur to professional soldier
for King and Country by applying to join the Royal Regiment
of Artillery on the grounds that it would offer more intellectual
satisfaction than the infantry. His oath was witnessed by Hugh
Trevor-Roper. On 28th September, 1939, Tony was posted to
Aldershot for training as Officer Cadet No.121, a member of a
squad of highly qualified civilians with no previous military experience such as Territorial service.

Amidst the mud, the duckboards and pitch pine of Aldershot,
the cadets on two shillings a day paid serious attention to the
lectures on organisation and gunnery technology. They also enjoyed gun drill but parade ground and dress regulations were for
the most part successfully ignored. A Guards sergeant, trying to
instil discipline, mixing standard epithets interspersed with the
statutory sarcastic 'Gentlemen' or 'Sir', received a very ribald
reception. Thinking better of it, he decided henceforth to join
them for drinks and became a friend who gently shepherded
them occasionally round the parade-ground. In these pre-Dunkirk
days, work finished at five o'clock and everyone went home for
the weekend.

Having passed through A Battery (the Baby Battery) to B and
C Batteries and thence to a field unit in England, Tony was
commissioned on 1st March 1940 as a second lieutenant, Royal

Artillery. He and his colleagues were asked whether they would like to go as replacements for service in India. With his earlier associations with that country still rich in his memory, Tony leapt at the opportunity, and on 15th March, in the cool, grey dawn, he left Southampton on a voyage which was to transform his life. Landing at Le Havre, Tony was responsible for escorting forty rough licentious gunners around the local sights, reminding them that bières, *brunes* and *blondes* only meant beers before they caught the train to Marseilles. There they embarked on a luxury liner which carried them to India.

In Bombay, a large selection of postings was on offer. There were four vacancies in a Mountain (Indian Artillery) Regiment, the 22nd, based in Singapore, and Tony, the expert on all things Indian, persuaded three of his friends from the OCTU, Dick Hare, Richard Wilcock and Rawle Knox to join him in taking up the vacancies, believing quite rightly that the Indian Army was not only more interesting but also better paid than the British regiments. Leaving the others to make their own way, Tony then boarded a series of trains and arrived a few days later at the Mountain Artillery Training Centre in Ambala, in northern Punjab.

The Training Centre took all the recruits for the Mountain Artillery, irrespective of race or religion, whether Sikhs, Punjabi Muslims and certain classes of Hindus, and put them through their paces before posting them to batteries on the frontier. Because of a grave shortage of officers Tony found himself in charge of a training battery where very few spoke English and only a few spoke Urdu. Fortunately, he possessed the ability to master Urdu quickly and within a fortnight he was able to converse fairly fluently with the native Indians on parade. A nostalgic link with the past was renewed when Tony acquired as a bearer, Abdullah Shah, who had previously served his father in a similar capacity. Abdullah accompanied Tony out to

Singapore and remained with him until the onset of hostilities convinced Tony it would be fairer to send him home.

For all the harmony that prevailed between British officers and Indian men Tony found organising a multi-ethnic battery, with its different religious customs, a taxing business. Two quite separate sets of cookhouses, water taps and canteens were needed. It was difficult for Tony to inspect the Sikh cookhouses, as the Sikhs were always cooking. 'If the British Orderly Officer enters,' he wrote, 'it's ritual pollution and the whole meal has to be cooked over again.' Away from his instructional duties, Tony was persuaded to play polo and go pig-sticking. Both sports were adventures which, in the extreme heat, left him exhilarated, exhausted and more than a touch relieved to have escaped serious injury when an attempted thrust at a pig with his spear caused him inadvertently to somersault into a bush.

From Ambala, after a month's stay, Tony began to make his way to Singapore where the 22nd, to which he had been seconded, was stationed. As he proceeded on his leisurely journey across South-East Asia, via train to Calcutta and slow boat to Rangoon, 'a remarkably vicious town', Tony had plenty of time to reflect on the dangers facing his countrymen back home as they faced up to Hitler unaided. 'The sky grows darker yet and the sea rises higher', he wrote in forbidding tones to his family, drawing poetic comparisons with King Alfred's sanctuary in Athelney away from his Danish pursuers. On arrival in Singapore he was relieved to hear that they had emerged unscathed from the German bombs raining down on Britain. He could now turn his attention to the task of defending this vital British base at the foot of the Malayan Peninsula adjoining the Indian and Pacific Oceans. His regiment, which had been in Malaya since 1939, consisted of four batteries, each of about 180 men with four British officers to a battery.

Tony was posted to the 4th (Hazara) Mountain Battery, Frontier Force, first raised in the Punjab in 1848, with a proud record of service in numerous frontier operations and, during the First World War, in East Africa. Recently it had given up its screw guns in favour of 6-inch howitzers, which were far less manoeuvrable than mountain guns and totally unsuitable arms for a mountain regiment.

As a senior subaltern in the battalion, Tony was able to escape some of the more tedious chores in pursuit of more interesting duties such as acquainting the more intelligent gunners with the fundamentals of maths and teaching morse signalling to others. He was alternately fascinated and perplexed by the majority's inability to read or write and the necessity of converting them from Punjabi-speaking to Roman Urdu, an undertaking greatly facilitated by his quick mastery of the two Urdu grammars, Munshi and Saighal. 'Now I've got the knack of making myself fairly well understood,' he informed his parents, 'I find them very responsive and very eager to learn any new thing.'

Tony's intimacy with his Jawans wasn't simply the result of linguistic understanding. It was based largely on a deep and abiding mutual respect. Besides warming to their courage and *joie de vivre*, Tony admired their commitment to the Allied cause. They, for their part, according to Edward Sawyer, Tony's battery commander, loved him for his friendly charm and total devotion to their well-being.

Together they appreciated many lighter moments, particularly when training in the jungle. On one occasion when tropical rain had reduced the country to a leech-ridden swamp the path they were marching along disappeared under two feet of water. No sooner did Tony step confidently forward claiming to have found the path than he would repeatedly vanish to the hoots and cheers of his men.

Another time, to lessen the monotony of trudging the narrow jungle tracks, Tony taught his men to march to the stirring classical couplets of the Shrewsbury school song when, by the most complete of coincidences, they came across another Salopian leading his platoon in the opposite direction. Not surprisingly the vision of a battery of Sikhs lustily bellowing the refrains of *Floreat Salopia* in the density of the Malayan jungle strained his mental faculties to breaking point.

Tony's year in Singapore was spent in relative comfort, sailing his pram dinghy during his hours of leisure when not writing a translation of Ovid's *Fasti*. Every Saturday morning the battery went for a route march for exercise before its officers repaired to the grandeur of the Adelphi or Raffles Hotels to gorge themselves on *Rijstafel*. A meal at the airport was the scene for one of Tony's notorious pranks on an unsuspecting Sikh officer, Davinder Singh Bedi. Dick Hare remembers how, having ordered oysters, brought in from Sydney, Tony warned Bedi off, 'You must be careful to nip the oysters with your back teeth before swallowing them because they are alive.' Bedi turned an ashen white and put down his fork leaving his companions to finish the oysters.

In contrast to his opinion of his Indian troops, Tony was scathing about the local inhabitants. 'My opinion of Malaya's civil white population goes down daily, and I think Noel Coward was right when he called this "a first-class place for second-class people". A more money-grubbing, unpatriotic set I have never seen. When you think that there is no income tax, and though we are fighting for our lives, the war fund of this, the wealthiest area in the Empire, is only 3,200,000 dollars, or just £400,000, it gives you an idea of the unspeakable meanness of these dollar millionaires, of which there are all too many here.' He was equally censorious of the Singapore Chinese: 'a pretty grim lot of people', he concluded; an opinion he would surely have revised in the light of later events since the Chinese were the only people in Malaya who fought effectively after the fall of Singapore.

During the summer of 1941, Japan's expansion in the Far East increasingly imperilled the Western colonial powers. Since 1938 Japan had been waging a full-scale war for the control of China. In August 1940, she had announced her intention to create a 'Greater East Asia co-prosperity sphere'. This aimed to subjugate East and South-East Asia under the guise of economic co-operation and colonial liberation, a camouflage to obtain the oil and essential minerals which Japan lacked.

In June 1941 while the Western powers were pre-occupied by the German invasion of Russia, Japan moved into Indo-China. In May, to counter such aggression, the 4th Hazara Mountain Battery joined the 11th Indian Division in Kedah, in north-west Malaya, and in September moved to Jitra amidst the rubber plantations, close to the Siamese border. The 11th Indian Division had the offensive role of crossing the border to meet an invasion, with an alternative of holding an uncompleted defensive position around Jitra to cover the Alor Star airfield.

Tony, promoted to battery captain in July, wrote to say that a major part of his duties now consisted of reconnaissance of jungle paths to see what tactical possibilities they afforded. 'This is very hard work. It is carried out among deep clefted hills of 1,500–4,000 feet, densely forested and in places so tangled and thick that one progresses at about half to one mile an hour cutting a path with a parang.' He found it fascinating to imagine an opposing army of tiny individuals patrolling their territory just across the valley shrouded in the same close mysterious jungle. 'If war comes here,' he predicted, 'it will start with a fantastic game of hide and seek.'

Despite the limited use of artillery in jungle warfare, the month of August, Tony reported, passed with some successful battery practice firings. Marvelling at the ability of his Sikhs to master complex new skills such as truck driving and wireless operating, Tony radiated confidence. 'We now feel ready for anything,' he bullishly declared. In October he and several other officers penetrated the steamy interior of a grade-2 jungle, to learn survival techniques. He returned 'very fit and full of beans', his mood further buoyed by a surprise visit from General Wavell, 'very much the idol of the Indian troops'.

With the benefit of hindsight this optimism seems cruelly misplaced. Did Tony genuinely believe his own hype or was it something of a charade to uplift the spirits of his family? His own subsequent reminiscences, although tinged with hyperbole, would surely point to the latter. 'My chief memory of Malaya,' Tony recollected in 1979, 'was how totally psychologically unprepared for war it seemed to be. Right up to the Japanese invasion we were getting intelligence reports saying that the Japanese fighter planes were made of bamboo, and couldn't fly at more than 150 mph, and these were official intelligence reports.' In reality the opposite was the case. Not only did the Japanese achieve superiority in aircraft, ships and tanks, they, unlike their allied counterparts, were properly prepared for the type of war in prospect.

The phoney war in the Far East finally ended on the night of 7th–8th December 1941 when the Japanese successfully landed forces on the eastern coast of the Malay Peninsula, either side of the Siamese border, hours before their surprise attack on the American Pacific Fleet in Pearl Harbour. The opposition was minimal with the obsolete British air force wiped out in a couple of days. This was the prelude to the Japanese sinking of two prize British capital ships, the *Prince of Wales* and the *Repulse* off Kuantan on 10th December, giving them complete control of the sea.

On 11th December, Tony's battery, supporting the 1st battalion of the 14th Punjabis from their defensive position on the Jitra Line, north of Alor Star, was obliged to withdraw after coming under heavy enemy attack. The force had been part of a plan called Force Matador which was to have advanced into Siam at the start of hostilities in order to secure the Kra Isthmus. When it reached the border, however, it was opposed by the Siamese Police and stopped in its tracks by orders from above. The Allies were now most anxious not to jeopardise Siamese neutrality. Compelled to fall back on the sodden defences of Jitra in heavy rain the Allies were psychologically deflated, especially the Indian troops, who preferred attack to retreat. From then on it was retreat all the way to Singapore.

The string of depressing setbacks associated with this ignominious campaign should not obscure the doughty part Tony played in its rearguard action. Although a bit inclined to foster favouritism, he was, according to Dick Hare, 'a very good officer'. As the trumpets sounded for battle Tony, resembling a latter-day Hannibal, lined up his Indian troops beseeching them in Urdu to do their duty and inspiring them thereafter by his own example, a Newboltian voice of the schoolboy rallying the disheartened ranks. When the rearguard of his battery was attacked on 11th December, causing the separation of the two sections and in the temporary absence of the battalion commander, Edward Sawyer, fortunate to survive a landmine, Tony managed to extricate the Punjabi Muslim Section, withdrawing under cover of darkness to Tanjong Pau.

On 26th December, the battery was in action at Kampar, half-way down the Malayan peninsula having received two 3.7-inch howitzers to replace those lost with the Sikh section. On New Year's day 1942, Sawyer rejoined his battery having spent a brief period in hospital in Seremban. Five days later he wrote to his wife in Singapore. 'I felt like a new boy when I rejoined, chiefly I think because the chaps had gone through pretty good hell since I left . . . Tony Trench has been a tower of strength though and has done remarkably good work.'

Years later Sawyer paid tribute to Tony's extreme professionalism throughout the campaign not least his great attention to detail. 'One small incident concerning myself well illustrates this. In the early days of the fighting at a particularly tiresome moment when I was with the C.O. in his HQ bunker, Tony turned up with an orderly bearing my lunch — hot chapattis wrapped in a spotlessly clean white napkin plus a silver tankard, and a can of ice-cold beer. I was the envy of the Punjabis.'

In fact, thanks to his hard work, the battery was never in want. Tony's praises were also sung by his colleague, Major Sopper, who told a mutual friend, Nina Steele, that 'he had done exceptionally well up-country'. He singled out his part in the battery's repulse of the first Japanese landings at Kuala Selangor, north of Kuala Lumpur when they forced a temporary halt to the Japanese advance.

After briefly holding a line from Mersing through Khiang, and along the line of the Muar River between 11th and 28th January, the 22nd Mountain Regiment was ordered to withdraw over the causeway to Singapore Island where they supported the 28th Infantry Brigade in a sector west of the causeway. Returning to Singapore after a six-month absence during this period of extreme danger, the regiment was struck by how unaware the local population was of the impending crisis engulfing them all.

This ignorance seemed neatly to encapsulate the sheer lethargy of the overall British war effort in the Far East, already suffering from the understandable decision by the High Command to give other theatres of war priority. Inadequate air defences to protect the colony, especially from sustained bombing attacks, alongside declining food supplies, meant that surrender was only a matter of time once the Japanese had crossed the causeway.

On the evening of Sunday 15th February 1942 the British
Empire lived through its darkest hour when the white flag flew
from the ramparts of Singapore and 85,000 imperial troops
marched out to confront their victors. Edward Sawyer recalls
one of his Punjabi Sikhs on his first encounter with the Japanese
turning to him and saying. 'Sahib, how came we to be beaten
by those bastards?' Captivity in Changi would provide plenty of
opportunities to address such questions.

Divested of their Indian troops by the Japanese, who hoped
that such a separation might sow seeds of discord, all that remained
of the Mountain Regiment was a compact, close knit group of
about twenty British officers accompanied by four British signal-
lers, free to pool their talents in their quest for tolerable comfort.
The European elements of the 11th Indian Division were allocated
an area and obliged to wire it in. The Mountain Regiment found
a derelict Chinese house and contrived to have it included within
the perimeter fence. The house had an orchard filled with many
varieties of fruit trees which they were able to pick and was
separated from the rest of the 11th Indian Division by a hedge.
Here for the time being they lived in splendid isolation offering
hospitality to many other Indian Army officers they had become
acquainted with in Malaya.

Tony took control of the catering and continued the sterling
work he had shown on manoeuvres by serving up a range of
appetising rice dishes. Each unit had been allowed one lorry
before being ordered to march to Changi and Tony had the
presence of mind to pack the lorry with all the tinned food he
could find in a nearby supply dump, which eased their lot
considerably over the following few months. Not all Tony's
domestic habits met with such acclaim, however. Rawle Knox
recalls him being easily the untidiest of the officers and, in the
sparse room provided for sleeping, his fellow prisoners drew lots
to see who would have to bed down next to him.

During the idle hours in front of them much time was spent analysing the failures of the recent campaign attributed by common consent to poor fighting and inadequate strategic resources. Tony pursued the polemics of the partition of India, a topic which had absorbed him since his new-won facility in Urdu had enabled him to find out much about the personalities involved. He also sustained himself on Kant's *Critique of Pure Reason* and a beautifully bound anthology of English poetry, compiled by himself and decorated with his personal book plate. The book survived the war and has since become a prized family possession.

Tony's bibliophile instincts made an abiding impression on John Durnford, a fellow prisoner-of-war who met him for the only time in his life in Singapore. 'One morning a month after capitulation,' he later recalled, 'I wandered out of my own hut in Canning Camp at Changi to visit my friends in the 22nd Mountain Regiment, who lived in a disused villa on the edge of the camp. Tony was sitting there in the sun, alone, reading Homer's *Odyssey* in the original Greek. We sat and talked for a while as he gently quoted passages and reminded me that others had faced trouble. Like all great men he ignored captivity and read a book.'

From April 1943 this philosophical detachment that Tony had discovered in captivity was to be severely tested as he became one of many to join the great trek northwards, helpless pawns in their captors' imperial designs. For their invasion of Burma in 1942 the Japanese used the one road that was possible for motor traffic in dry weather in addition to several jungle tracks. After occupying Burma they realised that in order to preserve their forces in that country and maintain any further military operations there, they needed a better overland line of communication. Consequently they decided to build a line linking the Siam and Burma railway systems from Bampong 54 miles west of Bangkok to Taar Besar 30 miles south of Moulmein, a distance of 282 miles, much of it through mountainous jungle country. An earlier attempt by the British in 1912 to construct something similar had been mooted and abandoned because of the dire effects the inhospitable terrain would have imposed on a native labour force. Such reservations were brushed aside by the Japanese in their quest for urgency. The Emperor himself was said to be behind the command that the project be driven through in the minimum time regardless of the human cost. Work began from both ends and the first parties of POWs began arriving in Siam, direct from Sumatra, in June 1942.

Early in 1943 the Japanese gave notice to senior British officers in Changi that they would be required to send 7,000 men north to Siam. When the British protested that their number of fit barely exceeded 5,000, the Japanese blandly assured them that their transfer to Siam was in their best interests not only because of the greater abundance of food there, but also because the hospital conditions were superior.

That April, two large forces, F Force and H Force, consisting mainly of British and Australians with some Dutch in attendance, left Singapore in overcrowded freight trains, the beginnings of an extremely uncomfortable five-day journey to Bampong. On arrival at Bampong any illusions that the Allies might still have entertained about the benevolence of Japanese intentions were soon rudely shattered when the Japanese adopted the most blatantly contradictory of stances. A gruelling march to their various destinations in the wilds devoid of the great bulk of their medical supplies was only the prelude to later misadventures.

As the Allies traversed the wild jungle terrain, the monsoon broke transforming much of the track into a sea of mud. Attempts to spare the sick this ordeal were scandalously brushed aside. The strong helped the weak to struggle along at cost to their own health. In contrast to their comrades in F Force, who had been allotted a stretch of fifty miles south-east of the Burma-Siam frontier, H Force was closer to Bampong, based at Hintok, a low-lying swamp back from the River Kwai. Now that the dry season had ended the jungle appeared a ghoulish grey as gaunt trees wilted in dripping rain. By the middle of May the elements had become so unsparing that the bedraggled troops had water-logged tents, sodden bedding and overflowing latrines, awash with stinking excreta, to contend with also. No wonder the health hazards, already profuse, multiplied in these dreadful conditions.

Because the Japanese were determined to push on at all costs with the building of the railway — which was already behind its completion date of Spring 1943 — a punishing schedule awaited the ragged army. No concessions to humanity or common sense were in evidence. During Tony's six months at Hintok, the consequences of his membership of H Force, his daily pro-gramme was to follow the same chilling routine without a single day off. From 5.30 am, when they appeared on parade, to their return to camp at 9.30 in the evening, they worked with one hour's break living on plain rice subsistence and going for weeks on end without seeing their camps in daylight. Their return late at night brought little respite from their tribulations. The twin tasks of removing the thick grime from their bodies and examining their ailments by firelight gave way to a grim ritual of burying the dead. In the lice infested squalor that passed for their accom-modation even the soothing sustenance of sleep was denied to many as throbbing ulcers and chronic diarrhoea condemned them to confront the agonies of the night.

Ever anxious to ensure the required quota of men for the daily workforce the Japanese rarely exempted the seriously sick from the daily rigours ahead. A reading of Sue Ebury's *Weary, the Life of Sir Edward Dunlop*, the legendary Australian surgeon on the railway, gives ample testimony to the appalling depths of inhumanity to which the Japanese authorities descended. Sickness to the Japanese was a breach of discipline and a sign of cowardice, a shameful undermining of the war effort of their Imperial Army. Prisoners of war in their eyes had no rights in any case. Their capitulation at Singapore had seen to that.

The work was exceptionally heavy even for fit men. With the accent as ever on speed the POWs were driven on with blows from fists, rifle butts and bamboos by sadistic guards. Tony later recalled that he had only one encounter with the Japanese 'Gestapo'. 'They thought I knew something I didn't so I couldn't tell them'. He did, however, witness the distressing spectacle of one colleague being crucified against a tree with bayonets, when attempting to escape. It was a scene that continued to haunt him for the rest of his life.

On the railway, where officers in H Force were treated no differently from their men, Tony performed a variety of tasks from stone breaking to chiselling out tracks from huge limestone gorges. A more unusual assignment was to walk behind an elephant for days on end with a barrow to pick up its manure so that Japanese officers could use it on their gardens. Because of their deprivations in clothing and footwear, all prisoners in this prickly scrub were easy prey to lacerations that went septic. Tony was spared the worst of the ghastly tropical ulcers which afflicted so many of his compatriots, but suffered from bouts of malaria, dysentery and beriberi, a nutritional disease caused by lack of Vitamin B. Indeed, in order to help compensate for the food he never received he was reduced to sporadically eating snails and cooking insects.

In June, a serious outbreak of cholera emanating from the Tamil coolies' camp nearby broke out in Hintok causing blind panic amongst the Japanese as they resorted to the wearing of masks. An isolation area was set up but all the doctors could do to contain the cholera was to inject a saline solution made from rock salt and boiled creek water. On the railway those who collapsed with cholera could expect no mercy from guards desperate to avoid contamination. One guard even attempted to bury a man and his infection alive before he was rescued by his friends. In the camps, a more traditional Japanese method of coping with cholera victims was to shoot them from outside the tent such was their fear about entering. The British quarters were particularly at risk. The number of dead grew so alarmingly that they were denied a dignified burial. Unable to gather enough fuel for the pyres, the survivors buried their comrades in graves too shallow to withstand the rains. Sue Ebury paints a lurid picture of 'men walking to work through a skeletal undergrowth of limbs and rotting flesh'.

Faced with this catastrophe within, Tony was disposed to take the advice of several of the Australians under his command, who explained that cholera travelled over the ground and that a prime cause for this rapid transmission came at night when hungry people were prone to touching the ground as they slept. The only way to avoid this danger, they contended, was to ensure that every man's hands were tied behind his back so that he couldn't suck his hands during the night. Once implemented, these precautionary measures proved their worth in lives saved. Their survival rate compared most favourably with other groups in the camp.

Hugh Lyall Hoppe of the 18th Division had reason to be grateful to Tony during the cholera epidemic. He recalls how in the aftermath of the first fatality he asked Tony to explain the disease to him and suggest any cures in case it ever came his way. Tony informed him that cholera was dehydration of the body and that the one salvation in sight was to drink as much water and lick as much salt as possible. Lyall Hoppe thought of this advice a few days later when his nightmare scenario duly became a reality. Before the doctors left him in the isolation tent his first night he asked them to leave a huge petrol tin of water and his little Marmite pot of salt evaporated from the sea, by his side. They did the trick and saved his life.

On another occasion, an Edinburgh doctor remembers Tony offering a similar solution to a malaria and dysentery victim, persuading a Japanese guard to get some salt. The victim survived.

Aside from maltreatment and disease, desolation was the other spectre that cast an ominous shadow over the captives in Siam. To rise above the stultifying monotony of everyday life and the feelings of despair that accompanied it was the supreme challenge facing each and every one of them. In their many empty moments the temptation to stop and question was immense. For every Rupert Brooke who entered a jungle a Siegfried Sassoon might emerge the other side. Didn't the sheltered worlds of Shrewsbury and Oxford with their hallowed ideals and cast iron certainties seem something of a shallow irrelevance now that Tony had seen the wider world in all its nakedness? The answer was very much a resounding 'No'. His family, his friends and his education acted as his sturdy shield as he sought solace in the serenity of his past, central to which were his literary pursuits. He summoned up his awesome powers of memory to translate all the poetry he knew into Latin and Greek. A particular occupational therapy was translating *A Shropshire Lad* into Latin while stone-breaking on the railway — a very Salopian thing to do, one of Tony's friends later remarked. Fragments of his effort were sent to Hardy, his former headmaster, and published in the *Salopian* in June 1946. 'Not often can Latin verses have been composed in such untoward circumstances', the magazine concluded with understatement. Drawing on his Classical gifts, Tony also entertained his fellow prisoners to a series of talks on Greek literature without recourse to books or other materials. Such resourcefulness helped raise camp morale and drew people to him in their hour of need. Rawle Knox recalls Tony as a man who never uttered a complaint — a heroic attribute in such brutally degrading conditions.

His bravery too was unquestioned. A holder of the VC recalled the time when Tony went through the wire of his camp to barter a watch for food, knowing that the person who had tried something similar before him had been caught and tortured. Later, Tony was to say that his experience as a POW taught him many things not least that almost every man has an automatic safety-valve in his mind which adjusts to make terrible conditions tolerable and that 'the human spirit is a great deal stronger than most people realise even in an ordinary chap like me'.

Meanwhile as Tony endured captivity his family underwent months of agony, ignorant of his fate. Their last communication from him had been a telegram on 1st February 1942, three days after the Japanese had breached the Johore causeway to Singapore Island: 'Safe and well - full of beans. Love to all. Tony Trench.' Thereafter nothing official had arrived for nearly a year. To try to dispel the doubts his parents placed a brief announcement in *The Times* on 13th April. It read:

> Chenevix-Trench: Missing. Capt. Anthony Chenevix-Trench, R.A. 4th Hazara Mountain Battery F.F. 22nd Mountain Regiment. Any information gratefully received by his parents, Ebbor House, Near Wells, Somerset.

It brought the family many letters of sympathy, comfort and, from those who had known him in Malaya, informed speculation as to his whereabouts. Hardy wrote from Shrewsbury, 'Missing is a foul word yet it contains hope.'

Tony's parents continued to enquire energetically for news from the War Office, the International Red Cross and the Vatican Information Bureau. On 19th December 1942 a telegram was received from the Under-Secretary of State for War: 'Official report received that Captain A Chenevix-Trench, Royal Artillery, is a prisoner-of-war. Letter follows shortly.'

This news was confirmed on 8th January 1943 by the British Red Cross Society. Tony's location was not stated. 'Beloved Tony,' his mother wrote to him on 19th January, 'Now that news of your captivity has come through at last, you can imagine how thankful and happy we are. Nothing matters but this, that we shall have you back again in the end.' Relief at his being still alive was, however, mingled with concern about his treatment in captivity. Oliver Quick, a member of School House at Shrewsbury during the war years, recalls the dismay with which J.R. Hope-Simpson informed the House that Tony had been captured at Singapore. His parents were immensely cheered to receive in July 1943 Tony's first postcard, written on 19th June 1942. It read, 'Dearest Mother. I am alive and well. Tell Susan not to worry. All my love, Tony Chenevix-Trench.'

The phrase 'Tell Susan not to worry' so perplexed his parents that they advertised in *The Times*. Two replies from parents of Japanese POWs reported similar inexplicable phrases. A third postcard from Tony was addressed to 'Sir Ganope Chenevix-Trench', Sir Ganope being an anagram of Singapore. (All his three subsequent cards were written from Singapore in 1943 and 1944, thanking his parents for their letters and assuring them of his good health.) They, for their part, under the correct impression that their letters had been reaching Tony, kept up a regular correspondence regaling him with news of the home they had moved to near Taunton, the family and the local wildlife. 'Well, my sweet Tony,' his mother rounded off one such letter in July 1943, 'All my dearest love goes with this. You are constantly in the prayers of many, night and day; and are always remembered in the Church at the Communion. God bless you and bring you safely back.'

On H Force's return to Singapore in November 1943, once the railway had been completed, Tony was briefly deposited in Syme Road Camp. Here, in one of the better camps, the inmates, according to Hugh Lyall Hoppe, with Tony to the fore, had hilarious fun and games. Then it was back to Changi in early 1944 for the remainder of the war.

In Changi the officers were housed just outside the main camp in much the nicest of the Atap huts, the good insulation ensuring adequate protection from the heat. Barbed wire surrounded the perimeter but inside they were free to do what they wanted. A copious array of books helped to keep them stimulated. Tony, besides occasionally exchanging Greek and Latin verses with Dick Hare, followed his friend's example in learning both Persian and Mandarin. So taken was he by these new languages that on release he gave serious thought to reading them at Oxford. Cooking, gardening, bridge and poker were other recreations that kept the inmates occupied, even on occasions amused.

Hare recalls Singapore being 'not too bad', particularly for the officers who weren't housed in the jail and were exempted from working on the airport; 'better than fighting in the Burma jungle'. Their only major deprivation during their final months in captivity, when the Allied blockade began to bite, was the shortage of food, condemning prisoners to subsist on a paltry 800 calories a day.

Although the war dragged on in the Far East for another four months beyond the surrender of the German armies in Europe, the successful deployment of the two atomic bombs on Hiroshima and Nagasaki finally broke the back of Japan's resistance. On 14th August the Emperor Hirohito formally surrendered to the Allies but because there was no guarantee that all Japanese proconsuls would abide by these terms, it was decided to treat the reoccupation of Singapore and Malaya as a formal military operation.

It was as part of this plan that HMS *Cleopatra,* with Tony's brother Godfrey on board as navigating officer, in addition to the Commander-in-Chief, East Indies, entered the Malacca Straits bound for Singapore. After preliminary formalities with the Japanese the Allies landed a powerful force in Singapore on 5th September without any enemy interference. A week later Lord Louis Mountbatten took the formal surrender of the Japanese troops in front of the ecstatic local population in the middle of the city. 'The arrival of our troops in Singapore,' Tony observed, 'was the most moving thing; after three and a half years of incredible oppression under the Japanese whips and scorpions the population was crazy with joy and showed it. The main difficulty was to protect the Japs, blow them. Starvation, death and hatred are all the Japs had left from their Dai Toa' (their subjugation of South-East Asia).

Godfrey Chenevix-Trench, forbidden to land during his first trip to Singapore, was granted permission to go in search of his brother two days later when the ship returned to port. Making enquiries at one of the emergency organisations for the repatriation of POWs, set up the previous day, he asked tentatively for Captain Chenevix-Trench. No sooner had he mentioned Tony's name than an officer who knew him well exclaimed that he had just departed and was expected back later that evening. 'The whole thing was like a fairy story,' Godfrey informed his parents. Tony heard about his brother's presence and within an hour not only had they managed to meet up, but Godfrey was also able to take him back to his ship for the night. There, Tony enjoyed the luxury of a bath and a soothing sleep after a major heart to heart with his brother in which they both relived the war through their own particular experiences.

'We had a terrific talk that night,' Godfrey reported, 'and I came to the conclusion that he must have been very tough indeed to have survived the living conditions in Upper Siam . . .

23,000 British prisoners died during this work and some 70,000*
Malays but our Tony managed to survive. I was so pleased that
he had managed to remain just the same Tony as ever, charming
and amusing as always, and this particularly impressed me as
many prisoners seemed to have suffered a psychological blow
which made them listless and almost unaware of their changing
circumstances. I don't think you will find him changed to any
great extent, Mum, and I am quite happy that for the rest of
his short time in Singapore he will be well looked after.' He
concluded his despatch by remarking on Tony's good cheer when
they parted. 'I don't think there is any cause for anxiety from
now on.'

On that same day, 19th September, as Godfrey was writing
home, Tony was composing his first proper letter for over three
and a half years. The contents are extremely moving. 'Before
anything else,' he tells his parents, 'I want to say God bless you
both for the wonderful letters you wrote in the mere faith (for
a year at least) that I was alive to get them. At first almost twelve
to fifteen came through and a few later, though the Japs let
practically no mail in this year or last. I can't tell you what they
were to me in Siam on the now notorious (I hope) Bangkok-
Moulmein railway. I think I know them all by heart. Thank you
a thousand times'. He then went on to give a brief but vivid
description of his time on the railway rounding off with a tribute
to those who didn't survive. 'I feel very grateful to be on my
way to you both again. I hope the Government will do what it
can about those poor chaps' graves up there — we built cairns
where we could — but the jungle grows so quickly again.'

Tony was free now to return to Britain but he felt honour
bound to escort his Indian troops, with whom he and his fellow

---

* Not many ethnic Malays were employed on the railway. Asiatic coolies were
mostly Tamil Indians.

officers had been joyfully reunited on release safely back to their villages. He therefore decided to delay his homecoming, sailing instead to Calcutta. The voyage did him enormous good as it helped him to shake off the remains of beriberi and quickly recover the weight lost during captivity. Returning to the gentle warmth of Ambala, he paid a final glowing tribute to his men:

> I dare say you'll have heard a lot of POWs going direct from Singapore to the UK and may wonder why I've not done so too, but I know you'll understand. I needn't say how I longed to be with you as soon as possible but after all my men have been through and their magnificent behaviour under shootings, beatings and starving by enemy propagandists, I feel the least I can do to thank them is to see them all happily home to their villages. They deserve far more than that and I'm very fond and proud of them, bless them. So I knew you'd agree with me in counting a few days delay in getting home worthwhile and you wouldn't have liked me to choose otherwise. As it is, I hope to be with you in a month at the most and I can't tell you how excited I am.

Mission safely accomplished, Tony began the final stages of his journey home via Karachi, Bahrain, Tel Aviv, where his plane had a minor crash, and Malta. After the misadventure in Tel Aviv, Tony became rather nervous of the RAF and Rawle Knox has recollections of him wandering around the plane in Malta as the pilot was discoursing on safety. With his discerning eye Tony had the sharpness to notice that one of the tyres was flat and so another delay was endured while a new wheel was flown out from England. Finally, on 29th October 1945, some five and a half years after setting out on his travels, Tony, like a latter-day Odysseus, returned safely home into the arms of his beloved family who, through all the doubts and dangers, had continued to hanker for this moment.

When Tony duly appeared before the Board of Selection for the India and Burma Service in May 1946 to relinquish his commission he was, in the words of Gordon Neale, one of the commissioners, 'outstandingly the best of the three hundred candidates before them, not only on his scholastic record but on his army record.' Apart from the wonderful references from his commanding officers the Board were most impressed by the way Tony remained behind with his Indian troops to escort them back to their homes.

Those then are the bare facts of Tony's war and his time in captivity. It is an inspiring tale of one man's battle against overwhelming odds. What then were to be the effects of such an ordeal? The answer must surely be 'considerable', although more glaringly so in the longer than the shorter term. We have already noted the favourable first impressions of Godfrey Chenevix-Trench after his brother's release, a view which was broadly in line with later contemporary observations. 'Everyone imagined that he (Tony) had had a tougher war than most, building railways for the Japanese', his Christ Church friend, Christopher Pemberton, later recalled. 'You could say it showed in his face and in little things like feeling the cold — he is the only person I know who brushed his teeth in warm water — and in his tenacious cosiness, always a pipe and fire in those rationed days, but basically he was fit.' Certainly, aside from the fleeting effects of malaria, which reduced him to outbreaks of shivering, Tony appeared to regain all his old physical stamina, so much so that he was able to lead an ultra-energetic life, surviving on the minimum of sleep.

If the war had taught him anything, it was curiously by way of reinforcing the deep-seated attachments of his youth — his family, his books, his love of nature and delight in simple things.

Even his unswerving faith in human nature remained remarkably untainted. He, unlike some others in his position, was spared the brutalisation of the mind, brought about by constant exposure to unalleviated cruelty and degradation.

On the contrary, Tony drew strength from the bravery and camaraderie of his colleagues, which shone out like lights in the darkness. It was the essence of the team spirit that he had been brought up to espouse at Shrewsbury as a boy, and which he subsequently, as a master, would proselytise with renewed fervour. Many of the normal dictates of life became, as a result, insignificant. Thus lax teenage standards of dress and of punctuality which could drive colleagues to distraction simply passed him by. Even the more serious offences of pupils which merited a firm response were rarely allowed to linger in his consciousness such was his continuing capacity, even need, to forgive.

It would probably be an exaggeration to say that his experiences in the war left him without a trace of bitterness, but very seldom did Tony look back on the lost years and cast aspersions on his tormentors. Sometimes among his close friends or sixth-form classes he might refer to some of the more amusing incidents that took place in captivity. Otherwise, like the vast majority of his fellow prisoners, these were memories he'd undoubtedly prefer to forget.

Francis King recalls frequent walks around Christ Church Meadow at Oxford in the immediate post-war era when lengthy stints of carefree conversation would invariably give way to contemplative gloom, causing King to wonder whether his company offered Tony enough stimulation. The mystery was finally solved one day when Tony requested a new route for their wanderings because a circle of Christ Church Meadow resembled a circle in his prisoner-of-war camp. 'I used to walk round and round the camp day after day,' he confided, 'longing for my freedom and wondering if I'd ever survive.'

For the next couple of decades whilst he lived out his life in the sunshine, Tony could afford to let bygones be bygones, but from the time he went to Eton dark clouds began to hover menacingly. 'Age shall not weary them nor the years condemn'. These words, alas, don't always apply to the survivors of great conflicts as they do their fallen comrades. As the years rolled by and the pressures multiplied, the defence mechanisms that Tony had built up to cope with his war began to break down. Physically, the legacy of malnutrition and dysentery increasingly troubled him while medical investigations revealed substantial damage to his liver. Gradually the malaria attacks returned and a ready supply of pills became the norm. Psychologically, too, the past returned with a vengeance, its bitter memories an eerie curse upon the present.

An invitation to Tony by a Fettesian governor to give a talk to the school on Japanese prisoner-of-war camps was met with a polite refusal, and attempts by the college chaplain to get his headmaster to preach on Remembrance Sunday repeatedly came to nothing. 'I can't do it,' protested Tony, 'because a colleague of mine was crucified.' For those who witnessed an ailing headmaster in his later years struggling to contain some of the more wayward streaks in his personality, the internal scars he carried, which his outward character might conceal, but which were never totally healed, invite both compassion and tolerance.

CHAPTER 4

PARADISE REGAINED–
OXFORD AND SHREWSBURY

A MIDST THE MULTITUDE of conflicting emotions that engulfed Tony on his return to Britain, relief vied with uncertainty as to his future plans. His parents had moved to Norfolk and his brothers, now all married, or about to be, were embarked on their various careers: Christopher in educational administration, Richard and Godfrey in the navy. The question now was whether Tony could come to terms with the upheavals in his own life.

Philippa Tooth remembers Tony contacting her family to arrange a lunch at which he could pour out his thoughts. 'What do I do now?', he wondered. Philippa's mother advised him to confide in his father who realised he remained rather disorientated. 'Would it be a good idea to have your inheritance now?', Jack sympathetically inquired and Tony agreed that it would. He bought a car, went to Scotland, and there amidst the isolated grandeur of the glens he began to rediscover his bearings. He returned, resolved that Oxford and the Classical world were again for him.

In July 1945 Britain had taken a giant leap forward with the election of Clement Attlee's Labour government committed to extensive social change, but the Oxford which Tony returned to in January 1946 was little different from the privileged world he had vacated over six years earlier. Austerity, it is true, gripped the university like the rest of the country, with the rationing of food and the lack of fuel bringing unappetising meals and cold rooms. The reappearance of many war veterans also bred a more serious work ethos than had been prevalent in the 1930s. Yet in other ways it was essentially the same privileged, exclusively male world of bachelor dons at High Table, and obliging scouts, the very model of civil discretion that many had left behind six years earlier.

Back in this familiar milieu Tony soon found his niche again as he embarked on Greats. Although still surrounded by Salopians and Etonians his status in college brought him into an ever expanding circle of intimate companions. Some pre-war friends, such as Henry Head and Charles Fisher, had been killed on active service. Others, such as David Macindoe, Ronald Prentice and Peter Stuart, survived to be joined by new ones, among them Cim Mellor, Christopher Pemberton, Geoffrey Rae-Smith, Roger Young and William Gladstone, a number of whom later followed Tony into the teaching profession. Owing to a shortage of space caused by the abundance of senior undergraduates, sharing in college was commonplace. Housed in a palatial set of rooms in Kilcannon Quad, between Tom and Peckwater Quads, Tony shared with Cim Mellor, Geoffrey Rae-Smith and Christopher Pemberton respectively. Here in these elegant quarters he paid court to all and sundry. Christopher Pemberton recalls him as a model of hospitality. 'His natural friendliness led him to invite in, usually for a glass of sherry, more casual acquaintances than I was able to handle.' Even if interrupted at an inopportune hour, Tony would always feign pleasure although his unfailing bonhomie might not survive their departure when the unflattering cry of, 'Gosh what a bore', would frequently pass from his lips.

After serving as secretary of Christ Church Junior Common Room during the Hilary (Easter) term of 1946, Tony was elected its president for the following academic year. In October 1946, he, along with Christopher Pemberton as secretary and Cim Mellor, Captain of Boats, was presented to King George VI, the

College Visitor, and Queen Elizabeth on their visit to com-
memorate Christ Church's quatercentenary. In these prominent
positions Tony played his full part in helping the college to
return to normality after the upheavals of the war, his genial
personality a powerful bond between ex-servicemen and freshmen
as well as between the Senior and Junior Common Rooms. It
wasn't only his practice of hosting a sherry party to all the
freshmen on his staircase that marked him out. Complaints about
facilities or discipline which came to his attention were taken up
with the authorities with great tact and all the more sympathetically listened to as a consequence.

Despite the stringencies then in fashion Tony helped reintro-
duce the Guest Table whereby members of the Junior Common
Room could entertain in some style. Such hospitality became
the envy of other colleges although Tony's notoriously bad memory meant that many more guests of his turned up at Christ
Church than often he would bargain for. In the opinion of Cyril
Little, the esteemed college butler, he was 'without any doubt
the most outstanding of the senior undergraduates who came
back after the war', words faithfully echoed by R.H. Dundas in
his Christ Church report of 1950.

In addition to his presidency of the Junior Common Room,
Tony's other main contribution to Christ Church was his part
in reviving the College Boat Club which had lain moribund
during the war. With Peter Stuart, he chivvied their fellow
colleges into joining and soon they had the makings of a competent crew. After years in closed captivity Tony found the daily
diet of afternoons on the river, followed by muffins and tea,
extremely therapeutic although a malaria sufferer like himself had
to be dissuaded from taking to the water in freezing temperatures.
Back at oar Tony weighed in at 9st 7oz, exactly his pre-war
level, and won selection to both the 1st Christ Church Torpids
and House VIIIs in 1946. In the words of his coach, Stephen

Kemp, he was 'a good, neat oar well taught at Shrewsbury, if not big enough for a top-class crew.'

Very much to their satisfaction the Torpids were to the fore in the March Bumps — the Oxford convention whereby one college's boat overhauls another's on the river and bumps it in order to replace it in the league table. They 'scored' each day of the week, a feat which earned them their oar. At their first Bumps supper for twenty-one years the wine flowed freely, speeches were delivered and Tony made a presentation to the coach. It was a convivial evening with all the hallmarks of a Varsity Students' Rag, not least its parting shot.

As the revellers were dispersing they noticed the gates of Tom Tower had been left open. In a trice they scaled the heights of the tower in their dinner jackets to release the chimes of the cathedral clock and get them booming away. The mission was no sooner accomplished than the forces of authority converged upon them, their torches identifying the majority of the pranksters on the roof. Tony and Peter Stuart, managing to avoid detection, returned to base unscathed, unlike the others who once rounded up were forced to face the music. The next day, feeling somewhat remiss for their part in the frolics, the two of them reported to the head porter's office to make their confessions and offer their apologies.

'Don't worry,' replied Joe Borritt, the head porter, 'It was our fault for leaving the door open. Besides it is nice to see some fun coming back into the place without any damage being done'.

Further accolades came Tony's way on the river when he and Cim Mellor won the Open Pairs in the Pengwern Regatta at Shrewsbury, the cox weighing more than Tony. A chance to impress in the rarefied atmosphere of Henley went begging, however, when the Christ Church VIII made a speedy exit from the Ladies Plate, a competition for schools and university colleges, beaten by Bryanston in the opening round. Granted honorary membership of Phyllis Court country club Tony raised a few disapproving eyebrows amongst its august clientele when summoning an ice-cream boat so that he could indulge his fancy for an ice-cream. It wasn't to be the last time that he flouted the decorum of Regatta week. The highwater mark of Tony's sporting career proved to be 1946. The following year his weight began to tell against him and he was demoted from the 1st to the 2nd VIII. All was not lost, however. A change of roles saw him take up the cudgels of coaching and enjoy a quick return for his efforts when his crew, the 2nd Christ Church Torpid, won their oar in Bumps week.

As a humorous, accommodating figure of some repute Tony was in constant demand as Oxford drew a veil on the immediate past and got back to enjoying itself. Getting him to a party was a hazardous business because he invariably forgot an invitation but once present he proved to be the life and soul of the gathering, often being the last to leave. Entertaining friends with his fund of stories was always one of his favourite pastimes; participating in some of Oxford's arcane social rituals was another. Members of one small dining club he belonged to were instructed to invite to one dinner the greatest bore they knew. The next time they convened they focused their discussions on deciding which of their guests had ultimately topped the bill.

With his much prized membership of Vincents, the prestigious club for sporting bloods at Oxford, by dint of his Junior Common Room credentials, his membership of the Christ Church Beagles and his possession of a car, a rare luxury in those austere days, Tony led the life of a privileged if not totally extravagant undergraduate. During the summer of 1946, he, Peter Stuart, and Cim Mellor took off in his Ford 8, affectionately christened Diomede, for a tour of the Continent on a £25 foreign travel allowance. Forced to exist on minimum resources they slept rough in barns or even in the open, without even the luxury of a tent, but they were able to inject a modicum of style to their holiday by changing for dinner each evening in their local bistro. Having journeyed down through France to the Pyrenees, they veered eastwards along the Mediterranean coastline and then up to Grenoble before heading back via Geneva and Paris. Blessed by six weeks of unbroken sunshine and idyllic scenery Tony was able to continue his path back to renewal which Oxford had already begun.

Because he appeared to be so much the hub of activity the casual observer could be forgiven for thinking that work occupied a lowly position on Tony's list of priorities. When asked at dinner by Sir Isaiah Berlin, the eminent Oxford philosopher, which lectures he attended, Tony replied, 'None except yours.' Such insouciance, however, was like much of Tony's exterior, a veneer for more serious traits. Blessed with great stamina, he would labour well into the night or arise before dawn, breaking only to make Cyril Little a cup of coffee when the butler appeared at 6 am. Aside from his assault on the Ireland, the blue-riband Classics scholarship open to undergraduates at Oxford, which necessitated a return to linguistics, Tony's course in Greats focused entirely upon literature, ancient history and philosophy.

As at Shrewsbury, Tony again struck gold with the quality of the tuition he received. Leading the field in ancient history, though not the most intellectually able, was the best known of all the Christ Church tutors, R.H. Dundas, a gruff, austere bachelor whose large, untidy set of rooms in North-West Quad, once occupied by Lewis Carroll, was a frequent meeting-place for generations of Christ Church undergraduates. Here Dundas would pontificate on a host of subjects, his astringent, amusing remarks finding a receptive audience in Tony who zealously stored them away and repeated them *ad infinitum* over the years. Partnering Dundas in ancient history was Eric Gray, a Rhodes Scholar from Adelaide, while the philosophy tutors, Gilbert Ryle,

Jim Urmson and Maurice Foster were all part of the celebrated Oxford School of Philosophy which led the world in their field.

From a perusal of college reports the reader is struck by the ease with which Tony settled back into the academic groove and how much his tutors appreciated his return to their midst. 'First-rate and as nice as clever, and all in an effortless sort of way,' observed Foster in July 1946. 'Absolutely first-class,' concurred Urmson. 'I had forgotten how nice and able he is,' commented Denys Page at the end of the following term. In philosophy, a discipline with no set answers, enabling an able undergraduate to meet his tutor on a level playing-field, Professor Urmson recalls that tutorials with Tony were fun because he was very interesting to teach. He has recollections of the occasion when, after one particular discussion on Aristotelian ethics, he turned to Tony and said, 'Well, I agree with you. What shall we talk about now?' - the only time he paid anyone such a compliment in over forty years of teaching.

With his flair for argument, Tony's presence was much in evidence at the reconvened Twenty Club debates, in particular when he led the opposition to such motions as 'Mortality is Anti-social,' and 'This House Prefers Foolish Adventure to Bourgeois Security'. He also successfully combined with Hugh Trevor-Roper to defeat Professor Ryle's motion, 'This House Endorses Oscar Wilde's Description of Fox Hunting as the Unspeakable in Pursuit of the Uneatable', the famous occasion when Ryle accused Trevor-Roper of suffering from a bad dose of talihosis.

Losing nothing of his pre-war appetite for academic excellence Tony, at a time of fierce competition, was well placed for further honours. Professor John Dancy, later Master of Marlborough College, and Principal of St Luke's College, Exeter, remembers his heart sinking outside the Examination Schools for the Ireland Scholarship when Tony, wearing a red rose in his subfusc buttonhole was pointed out to him as one of the favourites. In the event, Tony had to be content with joint *Proxime* with Hugh Lloyd-Jones, later Regius Professor of Greek at Oxford, their consolation being that the winner, Kenneth Dover, later Provost of Brasenose College and Chancellor of St Andrews University, became the nation's pre-eminent post-war Classicist.

Disappointed but not downhearted by his near miss Tony bounced back the following year. Having been awarded the Slade Exhibition, awarded annually after an examination in Greats for those taking the Schools that year, his Oxford career concluded on a triumphant note in December with an exceptional First in Greats including alphas in every paper. His tutor is reported to have informed him that it was the best Classics degree at Oxford since Gladstone but, as Professor Urmson explained, even if such a tribute was paid there is no means to corroborate its validity since no official records exist to render such a judgement possible.

What we can affirm is that in the opinion of those who taught him Tony ranked among the very best. Urmson never knew anyone so completely in control at tutorials and Denys Page was moved to write in 1946, 'I have learnt much from him — the best Latinist I have ever had as a pupil.' The only inkling of doubt emanated from his contemporary, Hugh Lloyd-Jones. 'Certainly he was a very able man,' Professor Lloyd-Jones conceded, 'but he was more interested in passing exams and in winning prizes than in literature or culture. I remember him going over facts and dates with several of his friends in an efficient and entertaining but rather soulless way.'

Even before Tony's final results were known his future was attracting maximum interest from various parties. His father wanted him to go into business and John Bett, an engineer entrepreneur, offered him a business partnership. Tony gave it some thought but confessed to his prospective employer that he didn't think he would be able to care enough about the half-pennies. In any case his mind was really set on teaching, a career which had first appealed to him when still at Shrewsbury. During his final year a flu epidemic had incapacitated several members of the Classics department and Tony had so revelled in the opportunity of filling in at short notice that ideas began to germinate for the future. Nothing during the next decade gave him serious cause to reconsider. John Dancy recalls how, when discussing at Oxford their respective futures, both Tony and he were inclined towards teaching, setting their sights on headmasterships. 'When I am a headmaster,' Tony declared, 'the first thing I shall do is to sack the bursar.'

Once Tony informed his father of his preference for teaching over business, Jack was quick to relent. 'Forget what I ever said,' he reassured his son. The question Tony now had to address was where? Robin Lorimer recalls being invited by Tony to Vincents and being quietly informed that he had been offered three jobs — at Christ Church, Eton and Shrewsbury respectively. When Tony expressed doubts about which one to take, Lorimer suggested the Fellowship at Christ Church but strongly cautioned against returning to Shrewsbury feeling such a move would be retrograde and contrary to his interests. 'Why not?' replied Tony indignantly, his affection for his alma mater unalloyed. Once he discovered the Eton job offered no prospect of sixth-form teaching, the choice became a mere formality.

With the blessings of the Classics department, Tony was one of a number of young appointments made by Shrewsbury's new headmaster, Jack Wolfenden, as part of his campaign to reduce the average age of the Common Room. Taking up his post in January 1948 Tony spent his first two terms in bachelor accommodation with Michael Charlesworth, a fellow Old Salopian and exact contemporary. Together their verve and vigour helped pour new wine into old bottles, for otherwise the school to which they were returning was broadly the one they had known as boys.

As might be expected from a proud Old Salopian, whose journey through adolescence had been enhanced by the world of the public school, Tony remained true to its fundamental ethos. His devotion, however, wasn't born of a blind compliance. As befitted a man of some prescience he espied the hidden cracks that lay within an edifice of fading splendour. Imaginative restoration would be needed if the glories of a former age were to be preserved in a modern setting.

Tony felt that public schools had become too uniformly regimented in their approach with the result that the individual spark necessary for moral and intellectual self-discovery had been reduced to a flickering ember. Such reservations applied to teachers too. Well aware that the word 'school' derived from its Greek counterpart '*schole*', meaning leisure, he thought it essential that a teacher should find time amidst the busy life of a boarding school for academic renewal. For it was only by constantly drinking at the cup of fresh learning that his thirst for his subject remained assuaged; this was crucial if the taste for learning was to catch on amidst his pupils.

With time at a premium Tony was keen to see schoolmasters forfeit some of their supervisory responsibilities. Not only would it give them greater opportunities for reflection it would also unleash the ever encroaching fetters of compulsion in the life of the boys, providing them also with scope for self-discovery. Although uncompromising in his commitment to certain basic imperatives he was well aware of the dangers of filling the pupils with moral indigestion. In a speech to the United Ushers, a public schoolmasters' dining club, at Marlborough in May 1953, he laboured this point quite forcibly. 'We have to resist the temptation to be forever teaching out of school as well as in, for ever advising, appealing, explaining in our enthusiasm to hurry on the improvement of mind and character. I have known masters who made it their aim to get as close to their pupils as they could, to share, as it were, their lives in an intimate sympathy: they dominated their boys.' He went on to quote William Johnson Cory, an Eton master in 1860, who warned against exhortation to adolescents. 'Do let them alone sometimes: trust them to the sun and air and their chosen companions. Give them their heads a little while.'

Preferring an open school where the majority of boys kept the majority of the rules most of the time rather than one which stifled individual vitality, Tony, however close to the boys he became, was always prepared to give them their heads. It was not for nothing that he always basked in the description of himself as something of a risk-taker. It was this roaming unorthodoxy that set him apart from his colleagues, making him such an arresting schoolmaster.

As a teacher Tony took his cue from the celebrated pedagogues of the nineteenth century like Benjamin Hall Kennedy whose lack of method and decorum in the classroom was more than offset by his burning ardour for the Classics, combined with his magnetic personality. Such fervour found ready echoes in Kennedy's Salopian pupils, seventy-two of whom subsequently were elected to Oxbridge college fellowships. Even though Tony rarely found time to act upon the wisdom of his words concerning academic renewal, the striking presence essential to great teaching never deserted him in the classroom. Lessons would begin with a theatrical flourish as he would sweep in with a determined stride after the bell had sounded, gown virtually touching the ground.

Thereafter, the tempo rarely slackened as Tony paced up and down the classroom with a terrier-like intensity expounding a point with great lucidity or overseeing a myriad of unseens at once, refining phraseology where appropriate. In more formal assignments with the lower forms, those who slipped up in oral translation laid themselves open to a verbal ribbing and those

who erred foolishly in written compositions were branded with
a design of a crab. The penalty for exceeding three was a trip
to the study for the ultimate sanction. Equally, a modicum of
bribery was not unknown and laggards would invariably be prevailed upon to greater efforts with the lure of financial induce-
ments. When their preps met the required standard Tony would
proffer out of his own pocket the promised shilling or half-crown
with congratulations to match. With so much at stake a certain
frisson was injected into the lessons which, along with Tony's
natural wit, could elevate even the rudiments of Greek grammar
from the mundane to the exhilarating.

In the sixth form Tony's presence was a breath of fresh air;
not least his propensity to treat them as adults either by taking
them into his confidence or with the humorous, slightly *risqué*
banter he entered into. Shunning the shackles of a syllabus,
whenever possible, Tony would often begin a sixth-form session
with Housman or Swinburne, two of his favourite poets, before
he branched out into Ovid, Thucydides or Homer, quoting reams
of their lines verbatim. Indeed such was his phenomenal memory
for Thucydides that he rarely needed a text when covering his
works in class. Although much of his teaching was typically
Salopian with its stress on linguistic purity, since Tony knew that
it was essential grounding for understanding the literature, he,
according to Colin Leach, a sixth-form Classicist under Tony
and the most recent historian of the school, broke new ground
by introducing them to textual criticism mixing literature with
history and philosophy. For unlike a number of his colleagues
who clung to the time honoured tradition of linguistic techniques
ad nauseam, Tony felt greater emphasis should be given to
exploring the meaning of ancient texts. He found himself in
complete accord with Housman's remark that, 'In general, if a
man wants really penetrating judgements and really illuminating

criticism on a Classical authority, he is ill-advised to go to the Classical scholar to get them.'

Language and philosophy set books and maverick poets could all blend together in one lesson as Tony constantly ventured into new territory with dramatic unpredictability stretching the critical faculties of his students to the full. Humour, too, was never far from the surface, especially when Classical study gave way to personal reminiscences based on the lighter moments of his own educational and wartime experiences. The pending visit one term of the Reverend A.L.E. Hoskyns-Abrahall, a former school chaplain, to preach, fuelled recollections of previous encounters. Amongst the unflattering pseudonyms handed out to this unfortunate cleric Tony had weighed in with Foreskin-rubberballs. To the mirth of his class Tony let slip this soubriquet and although beseeching them not to dwell on it when listening to him in chapel his plea was duly ignored as the Classical sixth sniggered the whole way through his sermon from their prominent position in the front row.

In addition to his efforts in the classroom Tony would see many a sixth-former at odd hours out of school on a one-to-one basis in conditions closely akin to an Oxford tutorial. Here in the relaxing confines of his study over a drink he would touch upon a few rough edges providing his own translation for fair copies. Alternatively he would be as likely to take the trouble to simplify some quirk of grammar to a struggling O-level candidate, often with the aid of personally typed sheets for each topic covered.

A desire to be constantly in the company of others made the marking and prompt return of work a low priority. A failure to meet deadlines for report writing also taxed the patience of his head of department but whatever reservations Stacy Colman harboured of his young protégé's efficiency, there was no doubting his boundless admiration for Tony's pedagogic gifts. His views were corroborated by former pupils. To Colin Leach, one of ten

members of the Classical sixth who gained open awards to Oxbridge in the vintage year of 1950–51, 'he was a gifted schoolmaster
of an unusual kind.' To Richard Raven, later Second Master at
Shrewsbury, 'he was more adventurous than the schoolmasters of
the day', while to Richard Ingrams, later editor of *Private Eye*,
'he was a very good teacher who played on the idea that I'm
one of you.'

In the years to come as his duties multiplied, Tony's reliance
upon his scholarship and memory became all the greater whenever
he turned his attention to teaching. Occasionally the mask would
slip and his lack of preparation could be detected by a top-flight
pupil as he bluffed his way through a searching question. That
such instances were rare says much for his formidable powers of
native wit. Even when the rigours of headmastership began to
sink home he could always find solace in a classroom where the
sheer joy of bestowing his largesse on others remained complete
to the very end. By then, of course, the Classics had seen a
dramatic reversal in fortune, becoming by the 1970s an endangered
species even in those establishments where once it had reigned
supreme.

That the Classics became the victim of a revolution in educational philosophy which gave prominence to vocational subjects
cannot be denied. Whether the Classical lobby had contributed
to its downfall by refusing to countenance change is a moot
point. Looking back in the 1970s over a scarred battlefield Tony
evidently felt so. Whilst accepting that the integrity of mind and
accuracy, so beloved of 19th-century Classicists, shouldn't be
sacrificed, he felt that the cut-and-dried Oxbridge approach had
failed to make the discipline interesting or relevant enough to
its students. He declared:

> At present, conservatism and a certain pride in what was
> once an aristocratic tradition maintained a steady if decreasing

trickle of able boys on to our Classical side, but those very boys are beginning to feel that all is not quite what it should be, and to succumb not always, as is generally supposed, to the lure of science but often (perhaps too often) to that of history, economics or English. I believe that the study of ancient history and the ancient tongues have still a great value if only because they are both ancient and also in a real sense fundamental for European civilisation.

But if that study is going to endure it will need the injection of a new approach. The basis of that new approach must be that technique is not an end in itself but a means that makes possible the appreciation of a civilisation that still has much to say to us today.

There is no doubt that Tony practised what he preached, always relating what he taught to life both as the ancients lived it and how his pupils should live it today. The lines of the Greek poet Pindar, 'What is man, what is he not? Man is the shadow of a dream', were quoted to illustrate the Greek view that men are little more than clay and yet, with gentle nurturing, capable of so much. Plato's *Republic* was often cited to remind those in authority that they had responsibilities as well as rights. Aristotle was invoked to press home the maxim that virtues are acquired by practice.

Out of the many pieces of Classical literature which left a special mark on Tony's affections both for their towering language and pertinence of message, two in particular stand out. The first was the Chorus Ode from the *Antigone* of Sophocles which considers man's strange paradoxical nature with his potential for both order and destruction. The only real safeguard for him and his city against his whims, the Chorus cautions, is the rule of law. If this was violated, the individual is ruined no less than the city. The second was The Funeral Speech of Pericles in

Book II of the *Peloponnesian War* of Thucydides which Tony
rated as fine a piece of prose as any in the Greek language. In
it, Pericles, the celebrated Athenian commander, pays eloquent
testimony to the greatness of his city, asserting how the government's concern for the rights of each and every individual had
induced great loyalty and self-sacrifice in return. This paean to
the ideal city community was Tony's mission statement and he
proselytised its moral well beyond the confines of the classroom.

Away from his teaching Tony threw himself into the life of
the school with complete abandon, giving generously of his time
and talents. House Tutor of School House, officer in the Cadet
Corps, rowing coach and Fives coach were amongst his principal
responsibilities. He also renewed his links with the school mission
in Liverpool, organising holiday camps for underprivileged
children in Shrewsbury when he would think nothing of treating
his volunteers to a beer in their off-duty moments. Adopting
such a high profile enabled him to become acquainted with
Salopians of all ages and to communicate with them on their
level. Although a stickler for discipline when the occasion demanded it, Tony liked, when possible, to throw off the inhibitions
of his profession to become a relaxed, engaging and eccentric
companion. One of his earliest admirers at Shrewsbury recalls
how he was infinitely more accessible than other adults. 'It was
through him that I learned that the relationship between master
and pupil could not only be interesting and agreeable but also
quite natural on the level of equals and enormous fun!'

Part of Tony's great appeal stemmed from his lack of ceremony,
particularly evident when a victim of life's minor misfortunes.
Only he could laugh off the indignity of entangling his gown
in his bicycle while cycling to class, rendering him totally im-
mobile until released by sympathetic boys.

This sparkling cocktail of spontaneous wit and unbridled self-
mockery was very much to the fore on Michael Charlesworth's

skiing trips to Scheidegg in Switzerland each Easter holiday. Undeterred by his indifferent performance on skis, with his outdated equipment and camouflage trousers, Tony amply compensated for his limitations by instigating some ferocious snowball fights. During *après-ski* Herr Tronk, as he would be addressed in these surroundings, would unveil all his gifts as a raconteur, letting slip a number of gentle indiscretions about his colleagues in the process.

'Tony was at his brilliant best on these occasions,' recalled Charlesworth, 'talking a kind of German to the French which they then disliked, French to the Americans, which they didn't understand, and Urdu to the Swiss, who were more than puzzled. Late at night he was heard discoursing to a puzzled Frenchman on the origins of his name but explaining gravely that Chenevix-Trench was in English pronounced 'shoe-trees.'

In September 1948 Tony was invited into School House as House Tutor by the new housemaster Major Tom Taylor. Peter Holt, then Head of House, remembers Tony as 'a man of great charm and charisma, someone it was exciting to be with'. At his happiest when in the company of boys, Tony made himself readily available to tend their needs, inviting groups of them to his quarters for tea or drinks. Even their tiresome displays of juvenile tomfoolery rarely discomfited him. One evening Tony was discovered by a friend sitting in his study nonchalantly correcting a prose with an open umbrella to protect him from a leaking roof, courtesy of a water fight in the School House bathroom above him.

As Tutor, Tony placed a great emphasis on the academic life of the House, something which hitherto had been a rarity. Not content with the existing practice whereby housemasters or their deputies only bestirred themselves concerning bad reports, Tony set out to positively redress this situation by making himself available to those under duress. 'Top Schools', as prep was known

at Shrewsbury, would see a constant flurry of activity in the
vicinity of his study as boys went in search of that spark which
would unleash the logjam in their minds and enable them to
meet the expectations of their masters. Given his initiative Tony,
in return, felt justified in waging war against the shirkers who
didn't reciprocate in kind. When they duly appeared in his study
to request a piece of blue penal, a ringed sheet on which shoddy
work would be repeated, Tony warned them that three such
penals would earn them a beating since they hadn't bothered to
seek his help. This carrot-and-stick approach had its desired effect
in implanting a more fertile work ethic in the house. Initially
some masters complained that School House boys received preferential treatment compared to other Salopians because of the
oracle in their midst. But in time other houses followed suit as
tutors began to act out the true meaning of their titles.

When Tony became a housemaster the priority he gave to
work was in no way diminished. Boys, knowing that the stakes
were high, would stand in breathless awe as Tony, puffing his
pipe, carefully scrutinised their fortnightly reports. It wasn't only
the idle who were prevailed upon to elevate their sights. Nicholas
Barber recalls how during his first term in School House, Tony
with one eye on the trophy board, persuaded him to enter the
Latin Elegaics Prize for the Removes, and for good measure
offered him some assistance, a gesture which ran counter to the
regulations of the examination. Great was his surprise therefore
when an undistinguished Classicist in Churchill House was later
declared the winner. As Tony licked his wounds he began to
suspect that he had been beaten at his own game. The Head of
Churchill's was none other than Peter John Ingrams, Richard
Ingrams's elder brother, and an outstanding Classical scholar. Years
later at an Old Salopian reunion, Tony's suspicions were borne
out when Ingrams confessed to his part in the plot. Erroneously
thinking that the competition was open to all comers he decided,

on realising his blunder, to foist his efforts upon a junior boy in his house.

Within months of Tony leaving Oxford, Dundas had been trying to mastermind his return to Christ Church, telling him that his gregariousness and bonhomie were sorely needed not least when recruiting Classicists from the public schools. In 1950 Denys Page was appointed Regius Professor of Greek at Cambridge thereby creating a vacancy for a Mods don. Many assumed that Hugh Lloyd-Jones, then teaching at Cambridge, would be Page's successor but despite Lloyd-Jones's exemplary qualifications he missed out to Tony thanks to the machinations of Professor Roy Harrod, the Senior Student (a Christ Church term for the Senior Fellow). Christ Church had paid Tony a singular compliment. The question was — would he accept?

Not for the first time during these years he was torn between Shrewsbury and Christ Church. As he pondered the latter's entreaties he was alive to the dangers of missing the opportunity to ride with the tide of fortune. To an aspiring academic, Shrewsbury, for all its eminence, might seem something of a cultural backwater compared to Oxford which throbbed with intellectual vitality. Christ Church and Dundas, in particular, managed to convince Tony that only by returning to his old college would he be making the very best use of his talents. Their joy when he finally accepted knew no bounds. 'Next autumn,' opined Dundas in the 1950 report, 'we have secured as our new permanent Mods don, in succession to his old tutor Mr Page, the one man we thought of as a worthy successor.'

Welcomed back with open arms in October 1951, Tony was thrust straight into the limelight. In addition to the twelve first-year undergraduates he was assigned to tutor he was constantly inundated with invitations to speak to various university and sixth-form societies. Within weeks of his return he gave the Bodleian Oration in Latin in front of the Vice-Chancellor and other dignitaries from the university. Opportunities like this to operate on a public stage might have appealed to someone of greater vanity, but to Tony the honour barely compensated for the time and trouble involved. Aside from his academic commitments he spent many hours on the river helping to coach the College VIIIs and he ran the university's Old Salopian club which necessitated a series of individual meetings with the umpteen number then present.

To his tuition Tony brought his usual passion for the subject but despite teaching some of the ablest freshmen in the college, their lukewarm interest in their studies, particularly their failure to read for pleasure, served to disillusion him. In addition, the rather arid lifestyle of a university don wasn't to Tony's liking. He missed the opportunity to cultivate close relationships among his students and shape their future destinies.

To Richard Raven, a Classicist under Tony at Shrewsbury and Oxford, his mentor remained a schoolmaster at heart, given his reluctance to partake in the serious academic research that accompanied university study. (His only book was a *History of Ancient Rome*, jointly written with Jimmy Street, which was published in 1960.) Even the aura of Oxford and the congeniality of High Table couldn't entirely compensate since, for all the undoubted pleasure he drew from the company of his colleagues, their sedentary lifestyle left him a trifle unfulfilled. 'I could see myself getting pickled in port in the SCR by the age of forty and never getting married because it was so comfortable,' Tony later recollected.

In this mood of self doubt it is perhaps not surprising in retrospect that Tony was prey to lurking suitors but nobody then, least of all Tony himself, would have staked any money on the tables being turned on Christ Church quite as rapidly and acrimoniously as they were. In his recent autobiography, *Behind the Headlines*, Michael Charlesworth recalls betting

William Gladstone, a colleague at Shrewsbury in 1950–51, that Tony wouldn't be headmaster of any school before 1965. Others clearly begged to differ. The headmastership of Charterhouse was about to fall vacant on the retirement of George Turner and both he and most of his governing board were adamant that Tony should be his successor. Why they were so set on Tony isn't entirely clear but there are a number of positive clues.

The world of the public school is a small, enclosed one and Tony's name would have been familiar already to influential figures inside it. In 1949 Tony, much to his delight, had been elected to the Ushers Union, the élite schoolmasters' dining club. In this august company he would not only have renewed links with H.H. Hardy, his old headmaster and one of his most fervent admirers, but would also have become acquainted with both George Turner and Robert Birley. Birley, in addition to being Head Master of Eton, was also a governor of Charterhouse, the school he had previously led with distinction.

As Turner and Birley contemplated the succession to Charterhouse they would have been party not only to Hardy's views on Tony but also to those of J.C Masterman, Provost of Worcester College, Oxford, and a renowned kingmaker with his inexhaustible list of contacts. Tony had been a favourite of his ever since their paths first crossed at Christ Church before the war when Masterman had been a history don there. From then on Masterman had taken Tony under his wing and had quietly been grooming him for a life on the Olympian peaks.

In February 1952 both Turner and Birley wrote to Tony impelling him to stand and their chairman, Geoffrey Fisher, the Archbishop of Canterbury, even paid an unannounced visit to Tony's rooms in Christ Church bearing the same message. Flattered, if somewhat bemused, by these overtures Tony agreed to brood on the matter taking soundings from Christ Church colleagues. Their unanimous advice to him was to stay put. Apart from his value to Christ Church the extra years of experience would be a worthwhile investment for any future ambitions. With these strictures ringing in his ears, Tony as requested met the sub-committee of the Charterhouse governing body.

He later recalled how he was ignored by the other candidates as they congregated in the antechamber, believing him to be a humble outsider. Inside, however, he lived up to his advance billing and became the clear favourite to succeed Turner when the full governing body met on 10th March to make their final selection. Already undecided between Charterhouse and Christ Church Tony's conflict of loyalties was further compromised when fate dealt him one of its most crushing blows.

At the end of February, during a game of Fives, Tom Taylor, the energetic housemaster of School House, suddenly dropped dead from a heart attack, throwing the whole community into a state of shock and confusion. In these harrowing circumstances, with such an important position vacant, and with no obvious successor to step into his shoes, the temptation for Jack Peterson, the headmaster of Shrewsbury, to appoint Tony was irresistible. Not only had Tony lived up to expectations when tutor in School House, his bachelor status would enable Taylor's widow Mary to stay on there as housekeeper.

Forewarned as to what was in the offing and with Charterhouse on hold, Tony travelled to Shrewsbury on Saturday 9th March to discuss his future with Peterson. He was resolved by now to leave Oxford but still uncertain as to where his future destination lay. Becoming housemaster of his old house held out enormous attractions but his enthusiasm was tempered by misgivings about such a sudden return to Shrewsbury, especially since his promotion might prick the sensitivities of his more senior colleagues.

For such a mild person Peterson proved uncharacteristically ruthless in his determination to get his man, playing on any lingering doubt Tony still harboured about becoming a headmaster at a relatively young age. He also sought to reassure him that his homecoming would be greeted with open arms. Certainly the symbolism of returning to Shrewsbury in the school's 400th year to answer a cry for help by running his old house wasn't lost on one of its most devoted alumni. Thus, duty and personal preference combined to destroy Charterhouse's hopes. The next day Tony contacted the Archbishop and Birley to tell them of his decision to withdraw his candidacy for the headmastership. A despairing letter from Turner, imploring him to think again, was to no avail. Twenty-four hours later Charterhouse bowed to the inevitable and appointed Brian Young, a youthful Classics master from Eton, as Turner's successor.

The reaction to Tony's decision from the respective parties ran along fairly predictable lines. A section of the Shrewsbury Common Room, sensing a whiff of Old Salopian nepotism, felt suitably aggrieved, but amongst the establishment the chorus of joy was near universal. 'You have a genius for getting on with boys,' declared Peterson, 'and you should certainly not miss out the housemaster stage. I think it would have been a mistake for you to get enmeshed in the administration at the age of thirty-two. For you do not have the same contact with boys as headmaster.' And just to labour his point, Peterson proceeded to describe the pupils' reaction when they learned the identity of their new housemaster. 'You should have been there when I told the School House. When I mentioned your name, there was first an audible intake of breath then the widest of grins on all faces and finally when I got out of the room pandemonium of excited and happy chattering.' 'I suppose I will have to call you, "Sir", again,' quipped one pupil now on Christian names with Tony, 'but it will be very difficult. The whole house is very pleased.'

At Charterhouse they accepted their loss with good grace, Turner reassuring Tony that, 'It's better to be a good friend than

a successful young headmaster,' but at Christ Church the distress
was obvious. Ray Harrod, so prominent in bringing Tony back
to Christ Church, spoke for the college when he wrote to Tony
on the 11th March, airing his reservations in the strongest possible
terms:

My dear Tony,
I have heard your news. First may I express my sympathy
for all the mental distress it must have caused you and my
conviction that you have acted from the best of motives. I
feel that I must make a comment as my reaction is both
strong and clear. We have not had close contact here perhaps
but I have a vigilant eye. While I have never supposed that
you would be with us for many years, I had hoped that
your time with us would make its contribution to your
ultimate career.
Next, may I say, still by way of preliminary, that I am not
actuated in what follows by a sense of the interests of Christ
Church. These are indeed affected, but the college goes on
and I feel this aspect less strongly than perhaps some of my
colleagues do.
What I have to say is just this. I think it was not right to
come to a conclusion in a few days in circumstances of
distress and that your so-called 'decision' has no moral validity
whatever. I certainly think it most wrong of the authorities
at Shrewsbury to accept any such decision. You would be
perfectly justified in sending a wire now, and it is what I
think you ought to do, saying that you need a further ten
days before you give your final decision. I say ten days
because you need a week of quiet thought after the hurly-
burly of our term is over . . .
I don't say that you won't necessarily reach the same conclusion at the end of the ten days. Good luck to you if you

do. But a decision reached as yours has been has no pre-
sumption in favour of it being right . . .
There is something about the way this has been done that
shocks me. I have a terribly strong sense that it is wrong.
I apologise for the intrusion in what is not strictly my
business save that what one observes becomes one's business.
Yours
Roy H

Tony went to great pains to explain to Harrod and others the
reasons for his departure, but they cut little ice with the likes of
Dundas who could still barely contain his dismay some nine
months later when compiling his *valete* in 1952 in the Christ
Church report:

> Mr Anthony Chenevix-Trench whose imminent return here
> in 1951 as Mods Tutor I celebrated with great delight in
> the 1950 report, has, to our consternation, left us to return
> as housemaster in the School House at Shrewsbury; the
> sudden death of Mr Taylor there and Mr Trench's deep
> affection and pride seemed to override even the claims of
> the House . . . the loss to us is irreparable.

At least Tony could count on the total support of his parents
during his week of agonizing choices:
'Just a line to assure you that I am as well satisfied with your
revised plan of action as I should have been if you had gone to
Charterhouse,' wrote his father on 11th March. 'It is a great
thing that your affections and your interest are so bound up in
Shrewsbury and work that you love and a peaceful conscience
are worth a great deal.'
'Bless you, my sweet — you have our undivided support and
sympathy,' concurred his mother. 'This is a great comfort to

me,' Tony replied to his father . . . 'I don't know how I'd have got through the last forty-eight hours without you.'

The truth was that once Shrewsbury had thrown their hat into the ring they were always likely to win any contest for Tony's services. Had fate not intervened it remains a tantalising question as to whether or not he would have accepted Charterhouse. The chances are that he would, but given his reservations, most notably handling the Common Room, it is just possible that the massive pressure which Christ Church orchestrated in persuading him to stay might have paid off.

Tony's impending return to Shrewsbury raised great expectations. Michael Hoban, who arrived there as a young Classics master in May 1952, found him already to be a legend. 'There was quite a buzz,' he recalls, 'when it was known that he was coming up for a couple of days. Stacy Colman and Jimmy Street were urgent in their anxiety for me to meet him.' When Tony duly appeared for the school's quatercentenary celebrations in June he spoke to over two hundred separate groups of parents during his visit. It was as if he had never been away.

Once back in residence he wore his promotion lightly when socialising with his colleagues in the Common Room. David Main, a newcomer to the staff in September 1952, recalls Tony being the one housemaster he could approach and feel at ease with. 'He had time for you.' He also had time for other newcomers, such as Arnold Ellis, Michael Hoban, Robin Moulsdale and Peter Gladstone. Already a member of Trimmers, an exclusive Common Room dining club which periodically met in some secrecy, Tony continued to be a pillar of the Clwydog, an informal walking club under the auspices of Jimmy Street, which penetrated the hidden delights of the Welsh marches. Here on these expeditions, Tony and Street would happily lay wagers to see who could outdo the other in their recitation of poetry.

Rumour had it that Street won by virtue of knowing the whole of Homer.

Two events dominated Tony's first term back. The first was the visit of the Queen and the Duke of Edinburgh to Shrewsbury on 24th October to mark the school's quatercentenary. It was ironically six years to the day since Tony had been presented to the new Queen's parents at Christ Church when they had attended the college's quatercentenary celebrations. Now in commemoration of the same landmark at Shrewsbury here he was rubbing shoulders with royalty again as he dined with them in School House.

A month later after this auspicious occasion, the school once more was in the news but this time for the wrong reasons. A routine meeting of the school debating society became a night to remember because of the motion debated and the antics of its proposers. Old Salopians, Julian Critchley and Michael Heseltine, then both undergraduates at Oxford, en route to political eminence, wangled an invitation to speak at the Debating Society on the motion that 'This House Deplores the Public School System'. Neither Critchley nor Heseltine had seen entirely eye to eye with authority during their time at Shrewsbury and, as Critchley recalls, a packed house heard home truths fly like confetti. Heseltine, the honorary proposer, dressed in fancy waistcoat, found much to criticise about the system, not least its monastic existence, its social exclusiveness, its addiction to corporal punishment and its favoured status for muscular morons. His speech went down well, attracting increasing laughter and applause from the audience, particularly from its younger members.

It fell to Tony and Michael Hoban, later Head Masters of Eton and Harrow respectively, to deflect the withering barbs coming their way. Tony admitted that life at a public school was somewhat monastic but countered by suggesting that children at co-educational schools spent so much time falling in and out of love that they had no time to work. He conceded that public schools were exclusive but reckoned that this wasn't so much their fault as that of the age they lived in. He defended the concept of corporal punishment, asserting that the proposer's alternative system of constructive punishments would merely give boys a hatred of domestic chores they would have to perform later in life. He concluded by stating that privileges were neither childish nor silly since they enshrined traditions.

After what the *Salopian* called 'the most good humoured but also the most controversial debate for some years', during which both Heseltine and Critchley ridiculed Tony's penchant for corporal punishment, the division and the result, declared amidst scenes of wild pandemonium, was carried by 105–95.

While Tony, according to Critchley, departed in a huff without so much as a word of farewell, and Heseltine went off to stay with his old housemaster, Critchley himself, flushed with victory, contacted the Press Association to alert them to his triumph. In his memoirs he recalls how the tabloid papers, in particular the *Daily Mirror*, who had rung up the headmaster in the middle of the night, led with the story the next day, giving a defiant Heseltine an awkward breakfast to negotiate before Critchley took him back to Oxford, leaving Shrewsbury in a state of high dudgeon.

The whole incident carried an ironic sequel when nearly thirty years later Heseltine, by now a Cabinet Minister, made an appointment to see Hoban, by now headmaster of Harrow, with a view to sending his son there. 'We haven't met before', exclaimed Heseltine when they met.

'Oh, yes, we have,' replied Hoban and proceeded to remind him, somewhat to Heseltine's embarrassment, of their previous encounter.

As housemaster of School House, Tony not only had one hundred pupils under his care but also the catering arrangements to contend with. He was fortunate that the pressures of such a position were somewhat eased not only by his past associations with the House but also by his harmonious relationship with his dedicated deputy Freddy Mann. The two complemented each other nicely. While Tony made no secret of his dislike for administration, Mann was adept in this department bringing a shrewd eye to the accounts. He also continued the emphasis on academic matters which Tony had instigated, his specialisation in mathematics neatly contrasting with Tony's in the Classics.

Although spared some of the administrative excesses to which housemasters of today are now subjected, housemastering for a conscientious person like Tony was, nevertheless, a full-time occupation. While mornings would broadly be devoted to teaching, Tony would spend most afternoons prowling the games fields or the river bank in support of his boys when he wasn't turning out on the Fives courts or playing host to prospective parents. Evenings after supper, when not taken up by confirmation classes, would consist of an endless procession of boys repairing to his study during Top Schools, to seek help on academic or personal matters. These deliberations would sometimes continue after house prayers, an occasion at which Tony would always use the Prayer of Newman. By the time he had finished corresponding with parents or caught up with overdue marking, another day had beckoned. So consumed was he by the House and its affairs that Tony's concentration could waver even when in conversation with his trusted deputy. His commitment was typical of a housemaster who wanted genuinely to know his boys and be amongst them whenever prudence dictated. As far as he was concerned the green baize door, the traditional barrier behind which housemasters retreated whenever they needed respite from the daily treadmill of communal life, was something to be done away with.

This breach of convention stemmed from Tony's fondness for teenage company. Still captivated by the gilded innocence of his own youth, Tony continued to find in this age-group a ready outlet for his unabated enthusiasm and carefree simplicity which paid scant attention to the more mundane chores of adulthood. Humour was particularly important to him. Not only did he relish holding the stage by making others laugh, he appreciated the bonds which could be built by it. These held Tony in good stead when he was called upon to soothe ruffled feathers. Many boys felt able to share with him their problems knowing they would receive a sympathetic reception from someone who understood the teenage mentality. He spent much time, for instance, consoling those who were particularly upset by the death of one of their friends from cancer.

Tony was well aware that the role of a housemaster was to help his charges grow up to the point where his own position became superfluous. 'Never, never should we need children,' he cautioned a group of fellow schoolmasters at Oxford in 1954, and yet in the same breath he was honest enough to admit that he found such advice easier to preach than to practise. Tony's willingness to put himself at the disposal of his boys was entirely genuine yet simultaneously it served an inner need for security by keeping him at the hub of institutional life. Once he saw himself as superfluous to requirements, as was rather the case at Christ Church when tutoring, Tony felt somewhat bereft and unfulfilled.

This open informal style which rapidly became his trademark, was in evidence from the moment he introduced new boys to their new surroundings. At the new boys' tea in School House he would fill their pockets with éclairs and get them to play raucous games like 'Are You There Moriarty?', a gesture designed to curb homesickness. His infectious zeal was again to the fore when he demonstrated the house fire-drill procedures. Tony then took great delight in launching himself out of a top window on the escape pulley. If any boy seemed reluctant to follow his example he gave another demonstration just for that boy. Never happier than when entertaining an audience Tony wasn't above a touch of acting as he roared around the site gesticulating to all and sundry. A particular pleasure was showing off his boys to visitors, investing each and everyone with a special quality peculiar to them. Ever happy to receive good news, his ready retort on hearing it was 'simply splendid' or 'absolutely glorious, fellows', phrases which soon resounded to repeated schoolboy mimicry.

Some of his stories did the rounds too. One he loved to relate was the occasion he had been sent by his father to a Savile Row tailor to get fitted for a decent suit. 'And it was only then that I had remembered that I had forgotten to take off my pyjamas that morning' was his punchline. Never a stickler for sartorial exactitude himself Tony didn't make it a high priority for his charges. Humphrey Ward recalls how their housemaster actually encouraged them to get all their clothes in order the night before so they could dress in the minimum of time for the first lesson, which began at the anti-social hour of 7.45 am. Another memory that remains with him is of Tony demonstrating in the dormitory how he was locked in confined spaces as a Japanese POW by climbing into the 'coffins' all boys had at the end of their beds.

Tony's talent for showmanship was never better demonstrated than at the School House concert at the end of each Christmas term when housemaster and tutor would combine as lyricist and pianist respectively. Charles Shelton-Agar recalls entering Tony's study just as rehearsals were on the point of beginning and finding him hammering out on his typewriter the verses which were to be practised that night. 'He had an astonishing facility for doing this sort of thing in great haste and yet quite superbly.' The end result was invariably hilarious.

For all the informality and the relaxation of certain restrictions such as the constant checks on pupils during their free time, there were few departures from the hierarchies and expectations of the School House Tony had known as a boy in the 1930s. He continued to support fagging, for instance, because he felt that the young with less pressures placed upon their time were best equipped to carry out the numerous community chores associated with a large boarding house. Content to let the monitors get on and administer day-to-day discipline Tony concentrated on more serious breaches of protocol. An individualist in discipline like so many things, Tony's leanings in this area were later to land him in trouble, but at the time his uncompromising approach, when he felt the need to act, certainly served him well.

Younger boys, in particular, were kept on a tight rein. Charles Shelton-Agar recalls one particular evening when his older brother, in conjunction with a friend, missed the school concert, which everybody was supposed to attend. Tony, who happened to be in the house, heard noises and footsteps upstairs. Closer investigation led him into one of the dormitories where he strode down the aisle between the beds. Having reached the far end he turned about and was on his way back when the lid of one of the boxes at the end of the bed lifted.

'Oh, I was just going to ask you, Sir', stammered Shelton-Agar's brother.

'I never discovered what he was going to ask me,' said Tony afterwards, recollecting the incident with great amusement, 'he got what had to be done on the spot!'

Such youthful innocence and resourcefulness in an impossibly tight situation always appealed to Tony, enabling him quickly to wipe the slate clean. Shelton-Agar recalls another occasion which brought the best out of his housemaster when during a game of

French cricket he succeeded in injuring Tony's dog, Offley, named after the chairman of the governors of Shrewsbury, Sir Offley Wakeman. 'I had not seen Offley, and the flick of my bat caught him a dreadful blow — which, as it turned out, put his eye out. I had never felt so awful, and remember wondering how on earth I could tell Tony what had happened. The poor dog yelped around in fearful pain. I went to see Tony later that afternoon in the private side of School House with great anguish. No one could have been more forgiving or understanding.'

This ability to let bygones be bygones was one of Tony's most agreeable qualities. Bill Williams recalls how he was on the point of being dismissed when Tony took over in School House. 'I'll forget about these things if you do,' he reassured him and Williams in time went on to become Head of School.

Not everyone found Tony's character or his sense of justice so accommodating, however. Paul Foot, later to become a leading radical columnist and author, was one such person. A member of a distinguished family with non-conformist roots he swiftly made his mark at Shrewsbury as a popular crusader for justice. It was here that he merged his talents with those of Richard Ingrams, William Rushton and Christopher Booker to transform the school magazine from a pedestrian record of sporting events into a satirical send-up of all things Salopian. Out of such modest beginnings was the later *Private Eye* formed.

History doesn't relate the precise cause of Tony's *contretemps* with Foot but we can safely assume that the latter, with his sophisticated, mildly subversive views, was less receptive than most to Tony's bouncy conventionality and exuberant verbosity. He in turn treated Foot with scant sympathy and for a person whose dislike of corporal punishment was such that he never beat when Head of House under Michael Charlesworth, his treatment by Tony left a bitter taste thereafter. An article in *Private Eye* many years later, when Tony was at Eton, entitled

'Jolly Beating Weather' made few concessions to the passing years as Foot looked back in anger:

> From 1952–1955 Mr Chenevix-Trench was housemaster of the biggest house at Shrewsbury School during which period beating by the housemaster, previously rare, became quite common. Trench developed the theory of the punishment alternative, offering those who were about to be beaten a choice between the cane (with trousers on) and the strap (with trousers off). Beatings with the cane normally took place in Trench's official downstairs study, while beatings with the strap took place in the more informal surroundings of his drawing-room, or, on some occasions, a bedroom. During the beatings, the door was locked and the boy would be required to lie on the couch or bed to receive his punishment.

When similar charges of compulsive beating arose in Tim Card's book *Eton Renewed* in 1994, with the lurid publicity that this generated in the press, the case against Tony seemed to be cast iron. The truth is rather more complex. To begin with Tony's early days in schoolmastering coincided with an era when beating was still a legitimate form of punishment in society and particularly prevalent in boarding schools where it had reigned unquestioned for the best part of two centuries. By the end of his career the practice had largely run its course, its ways discredited, and its passing largely unmourned. In this context Tony, representing a whole generation of schoolmasters who wielded the cane at random, stands condemned by their children for, as Charles Moore rightly observed in *The Spectator* on 7th May 1994, when mulling over the controversy, 'there is nothing harder to sympathise with than fashion just discarded.'

Like every schoolmaster Tony saw punishment as a necessary and wholesome element in discipline although he drew a firm line between two different types. First, the Kantian retributive view of moral disapproval and, second, sanctions as a deterrent. In a public school where a boy grows into manhood Tony, drawing on Robert Bridges's *Testament of Beauty,* believed there must be a progressive notion of discipline from the thirteen-year-old's 'must' to the eighteen-year-old's 'ought'.

For younger boys, still not capable of conceiving of a moral duty to conform, Tony reckoned passionless censure and hurt moral remonstrance to be out of place. He used to quote the example of Sir Henry Sidney's epistolary admonition to his little Philip during his first term at Shrewsbury that a wound given by a word goes far deeper than one given by a blow. Thus, beating, in Tony's opinion, was a quick conventional sanction to a breach of social discipline readily understood by the offender and rarely the cause for lasting resentment. For older boys Tony was more inclined to resort to reason, trying to hold out to them an idea. He knew every boy to be different, particularly in their growing levels of maturity which necessitated, in his opinion, a different type of response to each individual.

Much of Tony's outlook on beating was tacitly accepted by the majority of pupils, particularly younger ones, who could see the rationale behind their punishment and appreciate the lack of animosity involved. For Tony, ever anxious to keep on terms with the world, invariably tried to make amends quickly, a shake of the hand, perhaps even a glass of wine, tokens of his reconciliation. But for every ten who accepted their lot with equanimity there was one who heartily disapproved and the bitterness such a boy felt towards his former housemaster wasn't effaced by advancing years as he looked back over the charred landscapes of turbulent youth. At issue wasn't only the frequency or the severity of Tony's beatings, but the way he reduced a solemn occasion to a degrading spectacle.

This was the nub of Paul Foot's polemic and he had a point. For whatever the theoretical merits behind his defence of corporal punishment there can be no denying the fact that Tony often approached it with an unhealthy exuberance. Shortly before taking over at Eton he gave hostage to fortune in an interview with the *Scotsman* by cheerfully invoking the name of Dr Keate, his early 19th-century predecessor, a man of similar diminutive stature and well-known for his flogging tendencies. By then Tony had acquired the unflattering soubriquet of 'Whacker Trench' and in a more permissive age the public voice of dissent began to eat away at his reputation on this most sensitive of subjects.

Why then did this essentially humane individual who never once beat his own children develop this blindspot? Was it the sense of physical power previously denied to a man of his size or was it the consequence of his years in captivity when iron entered his soul? The answer to the first question is, possible, and to the second, unlikely. For however superficially plausible the theory about captivity may sound, it doesn't explain why, first, the same reservations about Tony were being aired at Shrewsbury even before the war and, second, the remarkable absence of bitterness that accompanied Tony's return to civilian life. We can only conclude that his fervent belief in the purifying effects of corporal punishment released forces within him which he couldn't always contain.

It was during Tony's first year as housemaster that he took Shrewsbury by surprise with the news of his engagement. He had never previously expressed a great interest in girls, but as he confessed to Peter Stuart, 'when I fell, I fell like Lucifer'.

Elizabeth Spicer, an attractive auburn-haired primary school teacher, was born into a family of worthy Sussex dignitaries whose desire for worldly success was tempered by a well developed social conscience. Elizabeth's brother Peter was a contemporary of Tony's at Christ Church and it was through him that she met her future husband. By June 1953 after Elizabeth had won the affections of everyone at Shrewsbury on Speech Day, Tony felt moved enough to write to her in rhapsodical terms. 'I cannot tell you how I look forward to your next visit, but I think that by this time you must know yourself how much I love you. I no longer feel that I want or need anything in the world but to be with you and that my deepest joy will always be in surrender of myself to you.'

Two months later on 15th August they were married in Chichester Cathedral. Peter Gladstone has recollections of the dress rehearsal the evening before. When the bishop asked for the best man to step forward both he and his brother William, much to their mutual surprise, obliged. It emerged that Tony had asked them both, so they tossed and William won. Afterwards during a carefree stag night on a neighbouring farm, a hay stack set on fire as a jape brought an impromptu visit from the local fire brigade.

The following day in brilliant sunshine the wedding ceremony went off without a hitch. The reception was held in the Bishop's Palace and Tony, standing on a chair, made a dazzling speech to their guests which included a sizeable component of the Shrewsbury Common Room all of whom had been invited. 'I did enjoy the wedding,' remarked Tony to his mother from honeymoon in Switzerland. 'I hope you had a chance to see some of the lovely presents we've had at the Spicers . . . We long to see you at Shrewsbury.'

Once Elizabeth was in residence, she took on much of the domestic organisation of School House from Mary Taylor, who had moved elsewhere. The School House *Study Fasti,* a termly record of achievement in the various studies compiled by the study monitors, commented on an immediate and marked improvement in the standard of food. This was no coincidence. Apart from her passion for gardening and music Elizabeth was a superb cook and hostess. She was also methodical and practical in day-to-day family matters, a useful corrective to her husband's shortcomings in this department. For not only was Tony no businessman he was hardly an asset in the home with his habit of scattering the remains of his pipe over the carpet. On one occasion when their car sustained a puncture it was Elizabeth not Tony who came to the rescue by changing the wheel. But for all his domestic limitations Tony amply repaid his wife's tolerance by his unfailing gratitude and good cheer. Together their contrasting characters and mutual affinity to people of all types made them a formidable partnership for their life together in the public eye.

In October 1955, to the amazement of all, including her doctor, Elizabeth gave birth to twin daughters, Laura and Jo. 'Six cheers,' was Dundas's enigmatic message of goodwill from Christ Church. 'Yes, very virile', was Tony's reply as he accepted the congratulations of his colleagues. School House was informed of the joyful news by their proud housemaster and thereafter were treated to the spectacle of both parents each feeding a twin on the dining-room table propped up by a Latin primer. Two boys, Richard and Jonathan, later completed the family after they had moved to Bradfield.

With a young family now to contend with, exotic holidays were rarely embarked upon, Cornwall or Norfolk being the preferred options. Tony also greatly enjoyed his winter shooting sorties with the Gladstones and Michael Ricketts, either at Holbeach in Norfolk or at Fasque, the Gladstone ancestral home in Kincardineshire.

At Holbeach the shooting party stayed in a pub on the Wash from where they would sally out before dawn in search of geese. With his short legs Tony had great difficulty traversing the muddy creeks in thigh boots. Peter Gladstone recalls the occasion when he mercilessly exploited this handicap and Tony's shortsightedness by leading him repeatedly over the same creek, much to Tony's amusement when Gladstone finally owned up to his deception.

At Fasque, Tony and Ricketts once caused their hosts much merriment by arriving at Aberdeen airport dressed in fishing coats and waders to avoid exceeding the weight limits on luggage on their flight. On the shoot Tony struck up an amicable relationship with an ancient Scottish gamekeeper who used to call him Dr Dench, changed by the others to Dr Drench. Butts for shooting are generally designed to conceal people of some height. Tony couldn't see over the top when the birds were coming. 'Shoot, shoot Dr Dench', would come the cry. Long after the birds passed Tony would shoot. He didn't hit much but he laughed a great deal.

Although Tony had rejected powerful suitors to return to Shrews-bury in 1952, he found, like the Roman general Cincinnatus, that a yearning for a simple life down on the farm wasn't something others were prepared to accept. It so happened that Bradfield College in Berkshire were looking for a new headmaster to replace the controversial figure of John Hills, who had ruled with a rod of iron since 1940.

During his years at the helm Hills had achieved much but his imperious style had found few takers in the Common Room. Led by the Second Master, John Moulsdale, they had positively quashed any ideas that the Council, the school governing body, had entertained of extending Hills's tenure beyond the previously agreed fifteen years' limit. Their overriding wish was to seek a fresh beginning in the form of a new leader who would open a few windows and clear away the oppressive atmosphere that had built up in the Common Room. A further priority in the eyes of Sir Guy Garrod, the chairman of the sub-committee

responsible for drawing up a short list of three, was to appoint
someone of academic distinction to raise standards in the classroom. With these criteria in mind, the Bradfield Council set to
work in the autumn of 1954 to find Hills's successor.

Tony originally wasn't one of the 140 candidates who let their
names go forward for the vacancy but from the start he was the
name bandied about as the ideal person, if he could be persuaded
to stand. Chiefly on the promptings of E.E.A. Whitworth, a
former headmaster at Bradfield, and one of the leading members
of the selection panel, the Council made its pitch. Whitworth
didn't have far to go in search of support.

Jack Wolfenden, headmaster of Shrewsbury between 1944 and
1950, and the man responsible for appointing Tony to the staff
in 1948, was now a member of the Bradfield Council by virtue
of his new position as Vice-Chancellor of Reading University.
Moreover R.H.Dundas, Tony's great patron at Christ Church,
was also a close friend of Sir Guy Garrod. When news first
reached Tony of Bradfield's wish that he should submit his name
for serious consideration he went to Peter Gladstone to discuss
his response. Gladstone recalls Tony's pleasure at being asked,
feeling such a move might save him from a possible rut, a familiar
fear of his. Yet there were countervailing arguments. Not only
did Shrewsbury remain close to his heart but he wondered what
Jack Peterson's reactions would be to his departure so soon after
taking over at School House. It was only after Peterson's assurances
that he had no objections that Tony agreed to be interviewed
by the sub-committee on 4th January 1955. Safely through this
stage he found himself on the final shortlist of three as the front
runner. The meeting of the whole Council to determine the
future of Bradfield was set for 17th January 1955 at 23 Carlton
House Terrace, London. Sir Eric Faulkner, then chairman of the
finance committee, recalled the bizarreness of this encounter in
the 1979 *Bradfield Chronicle*:

The tradition at Bradfield is that a committee of the Council considers all candidates for the headmastership, interviews as many as it considers necessary, and then recommends two or three for final interview. It is also a tradition that this final interview and selection is undertaken by the whole Council meeting together, and that all the finalists are seen before the sub-committee reveals to the rest of the Council any collective preference it may have.

On this occasion the whole Council met in London to interview three strong candidates: one at 11 am, Tony Trench at noon, and the third candidate at 2 pm. A light lunch had been arranged in a club for 1 pm; and it was assumed that discussion and decision would be completed by 3.30 to 4 pm, and the members of Council, busy men all, could hope to return to their offices thereafter.

All started according to plan, but at 11.30 a telegram was received from Shrewsbury saying that on arrival at the station Mr Chenevix-Trench had found that the train of his choice was not running. He would be late but he hoped to be with us by 3 pm.

This was highly irritating; it was impossible to change the order of the candidates, the Council would have an hour to waste before it could lunch, and proceedings in the afternoon would necessarily be inconveniently prolonged.

There was some feeling that express trains from Shrewsbury to London are not usually cancelled without notice, and that perhaps the candidate could have taken a little more trouble to ensure his punctual appearance. When, therefore, Tony Trench entered the interview room at about 3 pm there was evident a certain air of irritation on the part of the Council – which was not noticeably reduced by his apologies. The sub-committee (which had been unanimous in its preference for him) felt that

his chances of selection had been materially reduced. They were
not increased either by the fact that his collar was disarranged,
his tie badly off centre, and his suit in need of pressing; while
his shoes had clearly not been polished for some days.

The first question posed to candidates on such occasions is
always one they have previously been asked at their interview
by the sub-committee; after that it is open to any member of
the council to raise any matter or ask any question at all. The
first question was asked and answered concisely, clearly and firmly.
Then from a quite unexpected quarter came an unanticipated
question: 'Mr Chenevix-Trench, what do you think of cricket?'
'I cannot see the questioner,' said A.C-T., 'he is sitting in the
window against the light.' 'I always do', said the member of the
Council. 'Ah,' said A.C-T., 'then I must be talking to an Admiral
of the Fleet. Well, sir, as a way of keeping twenty-two boys out
of mischief for a substantial period of time, I would say that
cricket has much to commend it as a school game. I have to
admit, however, that perhaps because I'm no good at it; I detest
the game, and that's why I've always been a wet bob.' There
was a roar of laughter. 'Quite agree with you,' said Lord Fraser
of the North Cape, 'but do just put your collar and tie a bit
straighter, there's a good chap.' An hour later the Council was
unanimous in its decision to appoint Tony Trench headmaster
of Bradfield.' Tony accepted without hesitation.

Ironically enough, one of the defeated candidates was Jim
Pitts-Tucker, then headmaster of Pocklington and Tony's old
House Tutor at Shrewsbury. Years later he recalled how on
emerging from his interview he ran into Tony waiting his turn
last. 'I knew then that I would not be wanted.'

As Tony prepared for headmastership his excitement was tinged
with regret at severing his links with the past. 'Life is a sustained
goodbye', was one of his standard sayings but this time his
departure from Shrewsbury was no temporary *au revoir* but a

permanent adieu. If the school site had meant Arcadia to Neville Cardus it held out something similar to Tony. Sadly for him he was barely to set foot in the place again.

What then was his legacy to Shrewsbury? Through his own irrepressible enthusiasm and charismatic personality Tony undoubtedly created a good house spirit which, for the most part, overrode any fear or misgivings about his predilection for corporal punishment. Although some understandably found his never-ending capacity to praise as smacking of insincerity it provided an undeniable fillip to many. The fact that Tony went to great pains to know his boys and have their best interests at heart was a point much in his favour. Indeed some positively idolised him. Others were more guarded. A few remained totally unreconciled. Freddy Mann felt that Tony ran the house well, a view broadly endorsed by Michael Charlesworth, Tony's successor as housemaster, who recalled a successful, happy community, one easy to take over.

In the Common Room at large the verdict appeared less fulsome. Tony certainly retained a set of loyal, devoted friends but his absorption with School House allied to his general absent-mindedness and singular personality made him an unreliable colleague. The excess of Irish blarney which won him so many admirers on first encounters, and which sustained the majority thereafter, wasn't able to repair every fractured breach of trust. For all those whose relationship with Tony went deeper than mere pleasantries, a considerable degree of tolerance was needed for his idiosyncrasies if the champagne wasn't to lose its sparkle. Fortunately for all at the school Bradfield accepted Tony for what he was. The festivities were set to continue.

CHAPTER 5

BRADFIELD –

HIGH NOON AT CAMELOT

I N AN AGE OF CREEPING URBANIZATION that has reduced vast tracts of Green Belt to soulless anonymity the pastoral oasis of Bradfield has remained a haven of peace, untouched by the clutches of neighbouring Reading. Set amidst the rolling hills and sheltered copses of the Pang Valley that lend a sense of timelessness to this unspoilt corner of Berkshire, Bradfield has, since 1850, been a small part of Britain's educational heritage.

Founded by the Rev. Thomas Stevens, the local rector and lord of the manor, as a school for the sons of clergymen, Bradfield became the preserve of the professional middle-class, its hardy, unassuming character very much the product of its surroundings. Driven to the point of closure in 1877, it had been rescued by the efforts of Dr H.B.Gray who restored the school on firm foundations. Thereafter, as the 20th century progressed, its fortunes ebbed and flowed, with the depression and two world wars throwing its numbers into jeopardy. It needed the enlightened autocracy of John Hills, a former Eton housemaster, to see the school through the rough passages of the Second World War and into the calmer waters of the 1950s. Numbers rose from 280 to 373 and a talented Senior Common Room was assembled, but Hills's inability to sustain their confidence meant a fresh face was needed.

In stark contrast to the imposing presence of Hills, whose dignified bearing of stiff collar, white bow tie, black coat and gown was one of studied reserve, Tony, twenty-five years his junior, cut a figure of youthful gregariousness, his dishevelled appearance and ever-present pipe trademarks of the new regime. In keeping with his past, and in no way amended because of his new found status, the accent remained very much on informality. Bradfieldians, seldom used to setting eyes on their headmaster, now rarely saw a day go by when they weren't cheerfully hailed or stopped and engaged in more extended conversation. Amongst the common sights of these years was the headmaster taking to his rusty old bike, with the faithful Offley in tow, to watch the various sporting activities on view. A favourite haunt was the 1st Xl cricket field where many a happy hour was spent amidst a huddle of boys on the boundary expending his repertoire of jokes and stories.

Such informality wasn't confined to the everyday. At Bradfield the triennial Greek play in the school's Greek theatre retains a special place in the school's folklore. In Hills's time the entry of the headmaster to the packed auditorium would be greeted with a fanfare of trumpets as the assembled company rose in unison to salute the official party. Such pomp sat uneasily with Tony and a more relaxed procedure was subsequently followed whereby he and his guests could slip in almost unnoticed to less prominent seats. One year the intense heat caused Tony to publicly invite everyone to join him in dispensing with their suit jackets. The sight of the headmaster sitting there unfazed in his braces may have shocked the purists but to the perspiring masses the gesture was manna from heaven. Conversely, the image lingers of another year when Tony, again defying convention, was cheered to the rafters by a rain-sodden audience as he entered, grinning broadly, in a pair of oversized Wellington boots to watch a performance of *A Midsummer Night's Dream*.

During Tony's first visit to Bradfield to meet the staff he promised the Senior Common Room that his door at Crossways –

the headmaster's house at the heart of the school – would always be open to those who wanted to see him. It was a promise he had much pleasure in keeping. With Elizabeth the perfect hostess, their home became a mecca for social gatherings, formal and informal alike. Most weekends would see a lunch party which members of the Senior Common Room and their wives would attend. A cosily furnished drawing-room with children's toys scattered under the sofa gave the feel of a family atmosphere that others were immediately made part of.

It wasn't simply the academic staff who were accorded such treatment; the matrons, so often neglected in these male-orientated environments, were taken in from the cold, as were the domestic staff. Children weren't forgotten either. Basking in the joys of parenthood the Trenches went out of their way to open their doors to the families of their colleagues. Elizabeth ran a popular nursery school and was hostess at a series of children's parties which were always eagerly anticipated. While she, as ever, attended to the culinary arrangements, Tony genially presided over the entertainment, conducting treasure hunts through the nether reaches of their home and organising inventive games, the pick of which was 'Are you there Moriarty?' Such outpourings of hospitality not surprisingly placed strains on the purse strings and the school accounts for 1958–59 showed that the headmaster had exceeded his general maintenance allowance by £310. Under stipulations then in operation, Tony was responsible for clearing the deficit but so appreciative was the Council of the warmer climate prevailing at Crossways that it happily forestalled any potential embarrassment by consenting to foot the bill. Furthermore, it decided to operate a newer, more flexible maintenance account in future, although knowing its man it judiciously inserted a ceiling of £300 per annum in respect of wines, spirits and tobacco.

It wasn't only within the college itself that the Trenches gave of themselves. They also reached out to the wider Bradfield community. Villagers were made welcome at school events, and bidden to Crossways for drinks on Christmas morning. In turn, Tony was a regular guest both at the local village school and the Women's Institute where his witty talks always guaranteed a good night out. With the prep schools Tony set out to mend fences that had been broken by his predecessor for, despite increasing Bradfield's numbers, Hills had offended many by lecturing them on their shortcomings when visiting them as their guest. Tony, in comparison when invited into their midst, praised them unstintingly and in returning hospitality at Bradfield treated them like royalty. The upshot was closer links and a further rise in pupil admissions.

Tony also set great store by the old boys, going to great lengths to ensure the crippled and infirm could attend a school function even if it meant a wheelchair arriving after the curtain had gone up. During term time Tony tried to stay close to base but important meetings of the Old Bradfieldians were exceptions to his rule. His speeches at their dinners were invariably well-received whilst those who turned up at Bradfield unannounced could expect the same cordial welcome extended to all comers. Despite his indifference to cricket, Tony would be a frequent participator in Waifs Week held at Bradfield each July, attending the formal dinners and revelling in the after-dinner entertainment before returning to his study in the small hours to write reports.

As befitted his talents for showmanship Tony took great delight in personally showing parents around Bradfield. Not for him the brief, formal meeting in his study before gratefully handing them over to some understudy who would act as official guide for the duration of their visit. Rather he would entertain them either in his drawing-room, often lying in front of the fire, or in his study before escorting them to all corners of the school, keeping

up a running commentary throughout, pausing only to greet a
passer-by.

Flattering though Tony's attention to parents may have been,
these same parents invariably took second place to their offspring.
He immediately put them at ease by stepping off his pedestal
and coming down to their level asking about their interests,
sharing a joke or even racing them around the obstacle course.
These exertions inevitably took up time that might possibly have
been better spent elsewhere but time was rarely a problem at
Bradfield such was Tony's phenomenal stamina. Besides, he rightly
took the view that it was the headmaster prospective parents
came to see and, with the majority falling easy prey to his effortless
charm, the effect could be quite breathtaking.

These early encounters were often the beginning of a long
and fruitful relationship. Greeted like royalty whenever they visited the school thereafter, they couldn't but be impressed by the
depth of knowledge he displayed of their sons and the upbeat
way in which he communicated news of their progress. Being
Tony, there was doubtless a certain bravado in his remarks, which
often stored up trouble as promises were left hanging in limbo
or plans were never implemented. But for every parent irritated
by such flighty absentmindedness, ten would be eternally grateful
for the genuine, deep interest he took and for crafting such
polished end products, often from unpromising beginnings. Their
many letters of regret on his departure to Eton were as heartfelt
as they were genuine.

Declaring a special affinity to the intake of 1955 with intro-
ductory remarks that 'we're all new together', Tony gave notice
of a different type of relationship developing between headmaster
and pupil. During their first few weeks he would repeatedly stop
new boys and check their names, excusing himself to anyone
whose name had slipped his mind. If he was still groping after
a month he told them they could hold it against him for, by

then, he reckoned to know the name of every boy in the school, Christian as well as surnames, rarely letting such previous information seep out of his memory thereafter. Old boys after many years absence could suddenly descend upon Tony and expect their identity to be instantly recalled. Those pupils whose family had personal or regional affiliations with his own were always especially welcome, their connection a useful means of cementing their relationship. Those who were undersize and vulnerable could find ready empathy from someone who still stoically endured such handicaps. Once walking down Bloods Passage he was mistaken in the mêlée for a junior and ignominiously pushed out of the way. 'I don't think that is quite the way to address your headmaster,' Tony cautioned his assailant with a smile.

Unlike most headmasters Tony was often away from his desk in order to be in the company of the boys. It was not unusual to see him down at the gym, during periods, observing the boys at close quarters and how they reacted amongst themselves. Similarly, he would appear at the swimming-pool where he might sit down and help a boy with his Latin prep or lie down at cover-point in a junior cricket match so he could simply be part of the action. Even camps in outlying parts of the country could be graced by his presence. Those who were at Weybourne, Norfolk, in 1961 will remember him at the helm of a leaking assault boat which, after a gallant attempt to complete its course in the teeth of a howling gale, was fortunate enough to touch base some way down the coast.

Given Bradfield's pastoral setting and his own love of nature, Tony liked to see boys engage in rural pursuits, particularly those boys who didn't excel elsewhere. Pupils who fished on the Pang — a chalk stream tributary of the Thames — could expect periodic visits from the headmaster as he toured the furthest corners of his domain. Will Garfit, now a successful landscape artist, remembers how on one occasion he was so preoccupied with his casting that he hadn't noticed Tony come up behind him. At this point, disaster struck, when the unsuspecting Garfit's cast caught the headmaster's pipe with his hook, reducing Tony to a rare display of apoplexy as he frantically sought to untangle himself. 'Look where you're casting', he sternly rebuked his errant pupil. Happily their relationship survived this temporary hitch and Garfit later, as a prefect, became the focus for a typical piece of Trench improvisation when the great freeze of 1963 rendered all normal forms of sporting activity impossible. 'Will, you come from East Anglia near the Fens', Tony declared, 'I'm making you captain of skating.' With that, Garfit was responsible for organising mass expeditions to the neighbouring Englefield Lake in which most of the school participated. Tony himself was a regular visitor and, kitting himself out with skates, joined the hordes on the ice. With his blessing, informal ice-hockey matches were arranged against other schools, helping to give shape to an otherwise frustrating term.

Interesting though it was for the headmaster to observe his boys from the touchline or the boundary it was second best to actually being in the midst of them. The performer in him liked to steal the show and amuse his audience. Many of the stories he told referred to his own schooldays, often depicting him in an unflattering light. Others focused on contemporary Bradfield society by touching on some incident that had come to his attention, allowing him to find particular cause for amusement when the author of a pompous remark or the perpetrator of some botched misdemeanour received their come-uppance from the street-wise member of staff. Such send-ups of the leading miscreants often made great entertainment for the serried ranks of schoolboys particularly when the headmaster, so often the leading figure in these tales of the teenage subculture, acted as the narrator. In various discourses with his charges, be they

personal or collective, serious or amusing, Tony's unpretentious-
ness was a major asset in his quest for closer relationships.

His refusal to talk down to the boys and his willingness to
listen to their opinions earned him much goodwill. Richard
Henriques remembers being reported to the headmaster by the
chaplain for posing a provocative question about religious faith
during a house debate and how Tony dealt with it as an expression
of intellectual curiosity rather than adolescent impertinence. Self-
confidence was, of course, something which he encouraged and
he had no wish to see the system quash individuality. He loved
to repeat the rebuttal Field-Marshal Montgomery received when
visiting Bradfield: 'Do you know who I am, boy?' 'Haven't a
clue, Sir,' came the reply.

Intimate dealings with many pupils helped Tony compile the
same kind of lengthy and perceptive reports that he had produced
as a Shrewsbury housemaster. Forsaking the old single report
sheet, he introduced a booklet which gave a separate page for
each subject and a general report enabling all concerned to have
their full and proper say. Besides neatly summing up the general
consensus, Tony would add his own impressions inclining towards
the constructive whenever possible. Even the unloved were left
in no doubt that they, too, had their place in the kingdom.

Tony's complex approach to discipline, as so clearly witnessed
at Shrewsbury, was evident at Bradfield in an era when traditional
values still held sway. At his first Senior Common Room meeting
he had ceremoniously held up a copy of the school rules and
asked rather theatrically, 'Do we need these?' The numerous
stifling restrictions still in vogue were something of an absurdity
to a headmaster whose regime was built on trust and common
sense. Rules such as that requiring a cap to be worn by all boys
visiting Reading were abolished; some like compulsory attendance
at school matches survived, Tony reasoning that boys on these
public occasions should be seen to be supporting their school.

Although not a pothunter by nature Tony, like any headmaster, knew how the winning of the odd cup or trophy could work wonders for the school's morale and reputation. Martin Marix-Evans recalls the time when the Bradfield cross-country team returned from London, proud winners of the South of England cross-country schools championship. As they awaited the bus at Reading station they by chance bumped into Tony who, when informed of their triumph, exclaimed gleefully, 'Good God, that's marvellous. This calls for a beer', whereupon he took them off to the pub to celebrate before cramming eight of them into his shooting-brake and transporting them back to school.

Because of his dislike of organised meetings the prefects rarely met as a body with the headmaster and even his official briefings with the Head of School could be spasmodic. Essentially, Tony let them get on with their duties expecting them to set the right example. He was happy enough to see fagging as a personal service continue, but took steps to eradicate it as a weird tribal custom full of hierarchical symbolism. In common with some other boarding-schools, Bradfield school prefects still had the power to beat and although this was something Tony reduced he didn't abolish it. An inspection of the records shows that the cane was still employed for such offences as talking after lights out, misbehaviour in the dining-hall and insolence to a prefect.

More serious matters would be dealt with by the headmaster, alongside the more trivial ones brought to his attention and over which he felt bound to take action. When dispensing justice he rarely resorted to any punishment beyond the cane although the number of strokes was tailored according to the boy and the nature of the offence. Bullying, bad manners and smoking were the biggest crimes in his lexicon and when some of his prefects failed to toe the line on smoking, Tony took drastic action. At the end of his first year he caused quite a stir by summarily expelling his Head of School after he was caught lighting a cigarette on the school bus returning from a cricket match.

Was Tony considered an over-zealous disciplinarian at Bradfield? David Blackie, an Old Bradfieldian, felt that, 'the power he was granted to indulge his penchant for administering unrestricted and unsupervised corporal punishment to adolescent boys corrupted him. How much harm he did, even if it were known by his charges themselves, can only ever be a matter of speculation and debate.' Others returned a more favourable verdict.

David Foot, a self-confessed rebel, recalled that compared to some of his colleagues, Tony's beatings were not to be feared, at least physically. 'Intellectually he was a more challenging presence. I can recall a number of interviews with him, lasting several hours in which he showed a real desire to understand my perspectives and debate the issues I raised. He was able to bridge the gap of trust which enabled me to begin to explore with him why I was behaving as I was. I know he resisted calls for my expulsion, calls which were heard soon after Tony left the school.'

Martin Marix-Evans, suspected of being absent at night to indulge in homosexual activities, had also good reason to be grateful to Tony when sent to him for a beating by his housemaster. 'He accepted my explanation that drinking beer and smoking cigarettes was the purpose of the jaunt, remarking that it was, while a breach of the school rules, a more gratifying activity, for "buggery is not only messy, but futile". The physical comfort was temporary and he left my self-respect not merely intact but enhanced.'

These memories which came to light in 1994 are distinctly personal but they probably reflect the wider view of many at Bradfield during these years. Although Tony's efforts to rid the school of homosexuality by engaging in a massive beating spree were seen by many as discrimination towards the non-robust boys, only the minority appears to have been alienated by this addiction to the cane. This tolerance was partly because of the prevailing ethos and partly the headmaster's desire to part on the best of terms with his victim. Will Garfit remembers being beaten for some mundane offence on the day that one of Tony's children was born. As he turned to leave he had the effrontery to congratulate Tony on his good news whereupon he was thanked and invited to stay behind for a sherry. Such cases of instant atonement weren't infrequent.

One of the stories Tony loved to tell concerned a troublesome little boy in his first term who had been granted permission to keep two white mice providing they didn't violate school rules. A month later the boy was sent to Tony by his form-master for breaking the agreement and disrupting the class. Just as he was bending over the chair ready to take his punishment, the boy suddenly piped up, 'Oh, half a sec, Sir,' and after fumbling around in his back pocket continued, 'Would you mind holding Peter, Sir?' Seeing the black humour of the occasion, Tony fell into convulsions of laughter and spared the boy his ordeal.

He found a number of unorthodox ways to teach boys a lesson. Nigel Stoughton, a school prefect, recalls a junior master's life being made a misery in the classroom as he struggled to establish any sort of authority. One day the usual commotion was in progress when suddenly in walked the headmaster to total silence. Without uttering a word, Tony simply took over the lesson, effectively making his point. Another time when dealing with a particular surge in smoking Tony's investigations uncovered one of the smokers' favourite dens in the base of a ruined tower in the school grounds. The boys had posted guards so that a direct approach was impossible. However, Tony climbed on top of a wall which adjoined the tower and looked over the top. The boys were amazed at seeing the sky eclipsed by the face of the headmaster.

Because of its rural location Bradfield was sheltered from the seductive pleasures of city life but, nevertheless, the countryside threw up temptations of its own, especially since the school shooting range actually bordered the neighbouring Englefield estate. A typical ruse at this time was for boys to go out on a Saturday afternoon and set rabbit wires so they could bring game back on Sundays under the cover of the gowns they were obliged to wear.

Will Garfit recalls how on one Sunday when he went to collect his pickings, he noticed all the wires had disappeared. Replacing them in each snare was a small typed note bearing messages such as, 'The early bird catches the worm', 'If at first you don't succeed, try again', or 'Better luck next time'. The following week Garfit was the recipient of a parcel containing nothing but empty snares. To this day he isn't totally sure about the identity of the jester but he strongly suspects Tony because of his extensive knowledge of the estate, as a keen shot himself.

Indeed, despite having to reprimand various poachers to appease the rage of the local squire who, rather inconveniently, also happened to be the Warden of the Council, Tony could see the funny side of the situation and wasn't averse to a touch of poaching himself. Sir Eric Faulkner remembers Tony sheepishly returning home with his gun trying desperately to conceal the unauthorised bag in tow. Any guest attending a formal dinner at Crossways in season could go in the expectation that pheasant would be on the menu.

On the neighbouring estates Bradfield boys would volunteer to go beating on the local weekend shoots if only to partake in the sumptuous hospitality available afterwards. Garfit has recollections of the time he and his fellow beater were under the influence of alcohol. In front of the departing dignitaries which included their headmaster they clambered uneasily onto their bikes only to collide with one another and fall flat on their faces to the evident amusement of all.

Such incidents to Tony could be excused as adolescent exuberance rather than anything more sinister. It was merely an extension of the free spirit in the individual that he admired and encouraged. It was this spirit that he appealed to either in his regular Wednesday homilies or in his Sunday sermons in chapel. Refusing to use Christianity as a lever to buttress the public school system, he rather tried to pose challenging questions for individuals to wrestle with, focusing on such profound matters as man's relationship with God and his relationship with the world around him. A committed Christian himself, his sermons at Bradfield were invariably personal, down to earth, penetrating and relevant. Difficulties surfaced only if he hadn't done his homework and started extemporising, whereupon his line of thought could become diffuse and oblique. This tendency increasingly crept in as the years went by so that the quality of his sermons began to vary but right till the very end of his life he could dream up something special.

For such an informal person, Tony was capable of assuming great dignity when the situation demanded it. One of the richest memories of his time at Bradfield was his sublime reading of the Bidding Prayer at each carol service after a notorious performance his first year when he was stricken by a severe attack of nerves. Given his flair for the public stage this diffidence of disposition seems a curious paradox but colleagues latterly detected a dislike of formal speaking, such was the strain it placed on nervous defences already splintered by the effects of Siam.

Tony's relationship with his staff was little different from that which he encouraged with the pupils. Shunning the isolationist instincts of his predecessor, he enjoyed their company either at Crossways or around the school. His participation in country pursuits wasn't unknown either. With Jo Wilson, Michael Ricketts and Val Liddall he formed a syndicate to shoot, deriving much pleasure from his tramps round the Berkshire countryside close to Sulham. Jo Wilson, sometime head of English, recalls that Tony's sporting activity received a mixed reception. 'A very good little shot' was Val Liddall's flattering verdict but Frank Turk, a senior master, begged to differ. He always maintained that he had been peppered by Tony outside his front door.

If such socialising came naturally to Tony as headmaster it was a revelation to his Common Room. Apart from a couple of old stagers, who resented the passing of the ancient regime, they felt his coming like a breath of fresh air and immediately responded to his overtures. During the week there would be a constant flurry of activity, as colleagues either dropped in for a drink and a chat or came to tax him with a problem that required a prompt solution. To those who felt that the world was against them, Tony poured oil on troubled waters by listening sympathetically to their tales of woe and raising their self-esteem by assuring them how highly he appreciated their contributions to the well-being of the school.

In addition to personal entertainment and counselling, Tony was willing to stand up for the interests of his staff at meetings of the Council. When the teaching commitments of John Moulsdale, his Second Master, were substantially reduced so that he could run the appeal, Tony insisted that his salary should not be diminished in any way. Similarly, when an old retainer had reached retirement age with no home of his own to move into, Tony kept him on in some honorary capacity so that he could continue to live in school accommodation.

A particular scandal that needed addressing was the archaic accommodation arrangements for bachelor housemasters. The three housemasters-in-college couldn't continue in residence during the holidays and if they married they had to give up their houses for want of space. Tony therefore proposed to the Council that living accommodation out-of-college be provided and they duly went ahead with these plans. The Council also agreed to Tony's request to improve housemasters' emolument rates by £100 per annum in December 1958, which he reckoned would bring them more into line with other schools, and to adopt a new salary scale for the Senior Common Room in December 1961.

Although a friend to all his staff, Tony felt a particular leaning towards the younger ones, believing quite correctly that they were the heart-beat of a boarding school with their reserves of energy and enthusiasm. Throughout his years as a headmaster he therefore deliberately channelled fresh blood into the veins of the Senior Common Room with a string of imaginative appointments straight out of university.

Antony Collieu recalls his first two years in teaching under Tony at Bradfield with fondness. Surviving the mutterings of disapproval for deigning to attend his interview in a suede jacket — Tony didn't blink an eyelid — he was quickly taken under the headmaster's protective wing. Appointed out of the blue to be master-in-charge of gym, he made clear to Tony his antipathy to boxing, still then an important part of the sporting curriculum. Boxing had always rather fascinated Tony and he was unconvinced about the arguments to abolish it, but the crucial intervention of the school medical officer gave Collieu's case added weight. In these circumstances, Tony bowing to medical advice, banned boxing as a competitive sport in July 1963.

With Tony on good and often intimate terms with many of his housemasters, such as Basil Johnson, Philip Stibbe and Michael Ricketts, the majority were amenable to his unique way of running Bradfield, whereby any boy could seek out his services in a pastoral capacity. He in turn would appreciate the opportunity of visiting the houses to take evening prayers and do the rounds before lights out, entertaining the boys in the process by showing

them how he could sit on the ground and lift his entire body
with his arms down either side. By the time he emerged from
the housemaster's study after a relaxing drink and chat, the small
hours would be upon him. Still, no matter. Much rather this
type of friendly consultation than the aridity of formal housemasters' meetings, which not surprisingly, were kept to a
minimum.

As with everyone over whom he lorded it, Tony left housemasters to their own devices although he was ever willing to
lend a hand when necessary. Michael Ricketts recalls having a
boy in his house whose parents were at loggerheads with each
other, and living apart. The mother came to see Ricketts to
inform him her husband was returning to take the boy out and
implored the housemaster to refuse his request. When the father
rang to say he was coming anyway in defiance of Ricketts's
wishes, Ricketts went to see Tony, who immediately contacted
the father to give him a piece of his mind.

Combating boorish parents and dealing with troublesome teen-
agers were the most likely scenarios for housemasters seeking out
Tony's advice, confident that his reaction would be tactfully
sympathetic. Having reassured his flustered colleague that he too
had experienced similar problems with the same person, he would
then more often than not mediate to good effect allowing for a
hint of civility to be restored between the warring factions.

Being housemaster of the whole school, as one wag put it,
was a role Tony loved to play but there were limits to the
tolerance of his housemasters when he departed too far from the
official script. A couple, in particular, objected to being kept in
the dark either about the beating of their boys or the granting
of privileges they had previously withheld. Whether dispensing
fear or favour Tony's decisions were often spontaneous and then
forgotten about with the result that they weren't relayed to other
interested parties so that the great communicator on the public

stage could slip up on the more mundane but often vital matters of general administration behind the scenes.

Arthur Sopwith, Tony's Second Master between 1960–63, was informed at forty-eight hours notice, 'Oh, Arthur, could you look after the school next week, I've got to go to the Soviet Union'. Similar absent-mindedness meant that the head of maths wasn't aware of a new appointment in his department and the head of modern languages was caught completely by surprise by an announcement in one Commemoration Day speech that a new language laboratory was to be built. Socially, too, Tony was extremely unreliable in keeping engagements. Val Liddall, the art master, twice made the mistake of issuing an invitation to the Trenches to dinner through Tony, and on each occasion they failed to turn up. The second time Liddall rang Elizabeth and she later used to relate how, after one dinner already inside them, they went along for a second one.

Throughout his career Tony almost prided himself on his administrative shortcomings viewing paperwork as a debilitating clog to a free spirit like himself, who wished to be forever dreaming up new ideas and planning new futures. The chaotic state of his study told of his administrative inefficiency. His secretary, Beryl Embley, did as much as she could by writing all his letters leaving him only to sign them but she couldn't make important decisions for him. Consequently, bachelors could be placed in a three-bedroom house while married couples could be placed in a minute flat. Similarly, one master recently appointed to teach physics in place of a retiring member of staff, received a note thereafter to say that he would have to have a special timetable for his first year as Tony had just discovered the master didn't retire for another year.

For much of the day-to-day running of the school Tony leaned enormously on his two loyal Second Masters, John Moulsdale and Arthur Sopwith. 'Don't talk to me about timetables,' he groaned, 'they make me feel quite ill,' but because of his tendency to agree with the most recent person who lobbied his support on a particular issue, a firm line was rarely held on matters of routine. After a period when the hour for lunch fluctuated with bewildering rapidity an exasperated housemaster was moved to comment, 'Headmaster, can you put up a notice saying lunch is at 1 pm for the next twenty-seven years?' Basil Johnson recalls that at the end of each term Tony used to remark at the Senior Common Room meeting, 'Thank you for catching all the bricks before they reach the floor,' referring to the administrative confusion that often prevailed.

Adding to this uncertainty in the Senior Common Room was Tony's inability to say what he meant. Colleagues soon learned that a promise of intent was a statement of goodwill not a guarantee of action. The result could be chaos and indeed heart-ache when the same promoted post was promised to two different people. Tony also had an extraordinary habit of exaggerating numbers. The thought of the headmaster having written to nine Oxford colleges over a particular boy as he assured one house-master, Murray Argyle, was laughed out of court by his secretary when he referred the matter to her the next day.

Argyle, a pillar of the Bradfield community for many years, was one of those often wary of Tony's pronouncements. He recalls one Senior Common Room meeting when general con-cern was expressed about an upsurge in cheating and Tony, out to quell the unrest, announced that he would expel the offender. Sensing that he would renege on this commitment Argyle, amidst a general hush, asked him to reaffirm this conditional statement on discipline, at which point Tony backed away in alarm, ad-mitting to an element of bravado. On another occasion, Argyle bumped into Tony one Saturday evening in summer after an undistinguished display by his cricket team. 'My word, the 2nd XI played well today,' enthused Tony. Argyle, inclined to the opposing view, simply kept quiet to see if Tony could substantiate. He couldn't.

Hand in hand with Tony's peacemaking went a determination to improve the school's academic standards. These were by no means modest and indeed had progressed quite respectably under Hills but to a first-class mind like Tony's there was something rather lacking in Bradfield's approach to scholarship commensurate with its image as a rural backwater.

As with so many of Tony's initiatives the impetus stemmed not so much through explicit commands but rather through personal participation and example. Kicking against the pricks of prevailing orthodoxy Tony saw no reason why his promotion to headmastership should significantly reduce his teaching time-table even though there would be occasions when he would be unavoidably absent when an emergency cropped up. With two distinguished Classicists in Raymond Hawthorn and David Rae-burn already in residence, Tony's presence merely adorned rather than revolutionised the teaching of Classics at Bradfield.

Aside from the formal lessons in the classroom Tony often taught sixth formers *al fresco* where a gin and tonic might be an added inducement to learning, or in his study reclining in leathered chairs. Robert Sopwith, later a master at Wellington, recalls one such session on Pluto and Aristotle, interrupted by a knock at the door whereupon an Indian pedlar was ushered in bearing his wares on a tray. Tony immediately greeted him like a long-lost friend, striking up a conversation with him in Urdu, and consented to purchase one of his choice silk scarves before politely showing him the door. No sooner had he departed than Tony quietly put his new possession on one side pausing only to observe, 'Best Marks and Spencer, I think.'

Thanks to the lead that Tony gave to the teaching of the brightest boys, Oxbridge became a reality for a number of them. Those who were cruising in the shallows were often personally challenged and impelled to greater things. Richard Henriques, now a successful QC in Manchester, remembers being called in by Tony when underperforming and told that coming from such a distinguished family he should be raising his sights to Oxbridge and beyond. Within fifteen minutes the spark had been lit. In addition to the sixth form, Tony taught Latin, Greek or Divinity to a fair cross-section of the school, lighting many a warm fire in a cold classroom with his scintillating presence. True to form his methods remained unconventional, not least in the manner he rewarded effort and punished idleness. Colin Smythe has recollections of coming top in a Latin test and Tony saying to him, 'Go off to my study and you'll find a man with a face like a wizened old apple. Go and show him Bradfield.'

When the Council once expressed concern about the heavy burden of Tony's teaching programme, he replied, 'That is the way I can get to know my boys.' In the opinion of Sir Eric Faulkner, then chairman of the finance committee, he never knew a headmaster so well informed about his pupils. Whenever the Council was confronted by parents in straitened financial circumstances they could be assured always of the appropriate facts about the boy and his family from the headmaster. Any deserving case that carried a recommendation from him for sympathetic consideration was likely to be so received. Such was the determination of the Council to pay heed to their headmaster's advice.

Teaching wasn't Tony's only contribution to the intellectual life of the school. He was in addition tutor and confessor to a large number of his flock. Those who were the holders of unflattering reports were summoned to the study to account for their lackadaisical ways. Such indolence might lead to an immediate thrashing but these encounters were normally forward looking and liberating in their tone. Because the majority appreciated Tony's concern for their welfare, they would happily comply

with his instructions to return at recurring intervals to submit an
up-to-date assessment of their progress. Those who continued to
struggle might become the beneficiaries of some off-the-cuff
coaching. Housemasters were known to be kept waiting to see
Tony as some fourth former had the Latin gerund carefully
explained to him. By dint of personal rapprochement many of
Tony's geese became swans.

Others who distinguished themselves were commended either
in person or in writing. Will Garfit remembers compiling two
books on fishing for a bottom form assignment during his first
year which so impressed his English teacher that he showed them
to both his housemaster and the headmaster. The upshot was
that Garfit received a note from Tony declaring that if he couldn't
think of anything to say in his sermon that evening it was because
he had been reading his two books all day.

By his own input to academic excellence Tony set the tone
for the rest of the school. Inviting the Senior Common Room
to raise their expectations, appointing fewer school prefects from
the sporting fraternity and exhorting the school 'to go that extra
mile' in the classroom was, in Tony's eyes, the surest way of
turning Sparta into Athens. Of course, refining the inner sanctums
of the mind wasn't in itself enough. Accompanying that, there
had to be surgical repairs to the body. Admissions, teaching and
facilities all needed an overhaul if Bradfield was to meet the
challenges of the post-war world.

Always appreciative of how scholarships had advanced the
educational opportunities of his own family, Tony persuaded the
Council twice to increase their value. He also won Council
approval in March 1956 to develop the science complex, engage
a newcomer at a higher salary than normal to persuade him to
quit industry for teaching, and expand the staff numbers to meet
the greater demands that a broadening of the curriculum would
impose on the Senior Common Room.

One of his innovations that won plaudits from the HMI was the introduction of general study classes in the senior school. By 1958 the new science building had been completed, the number of those opting for the subject had risen and the headmaster was able to report to the Council 'a marked improvement in the general standard of work in the school'. However, to ensure that his assessment wasn't moonshine he requested at the end of the year a full inspection of the school by a team from the Ministry of Education, scheduled for March 1959. In general, their report made encouraging reading: Tony informed the Council when they convened weeks later that the HMI had been most impressed with the rapid development and progress which had taken place since the last inspection ten years earlier. They had been particularly struck with the quality of the religious life of the school as well as the manners and general bearing of the boys. However, reservations had been expressed about the inadequacy of study accommodation in certain houses and the pedestrian nature of teaching in the lower school.

The first criticism was quickly addressed by renovating the worst affected houses with the help of the special appeal then pending. The second merited greater thought. Tony felt that the unadventurous teaching in the lower school reflected the uneven calibre of Bradfield's intake. Try though they might to raise their profile, they still laboured under the handicap of being the poor relation to the likes of Eton and Winchester. A possible solution mooted, now that the need to increase numbers had eased, was to raise the Common Entrance pass rate but Tony felt that this would be a breach of faith to the prep schools. Something more innovatory was required.

Consequently, in 1961, Tony — with the support of his Council and the prep schools — launched a new entry procedure which aimed to enhance the quality of Bradfield's intake. The details were simple. When a pupil down for Bradfield had reached the age of eleven, academic and personal qualifications would be assessed by the school of which he was then a member. Should the report be a favourable one, Bradfield would then guarantee him a place providing the parents made them the first choice and paid a deposit of £20. If the parents continued to subordinate Bradfield to one of the bigger schools only for their son to fail Common Entrance, he would then have to compete for a place at Bradfield on more stringent terms than otherwise would have been the case. Bearing in mind it was quality not quantity that Bradfield was after, the new system had its virtues and has survived intact ever since.

Academic success was obviously central to Tony's most forward-looking scheme: the modernisation of Bradfield. No administrator himself, he could always rely not only on the expertise of his bursar, Dick Darvall, but also on the full cooperation of the Council to put his plans into effect. From the moment he took up office he and Sir Eric Faulkner resolved to develop closer relations between staff and Council and as part of this process Tony and Sir Eric used to meet at Boodles, Sir Eric's London club, to brief each other about recent events and anticipate any possible future difficulties. With headmaster and Council singing from the same hymn-sheet, an exciting new venture, combining the vision of the former and the competence of the latter, could be proposed and implemented.

It was back in December 1957 that Tony invited the Council to consider the setting up of a continual appeal fund for the college similar to those that had been previously followed by Shrewsbury. He was at pains to suggest not an endowment fund but one which would be available to general college purposes as, and when, particular items of capital expenditure became necessary. Accordingly, there would be no target figure and no statement of any specific purpose to which the fund would be applied. He reckoned that such an appeal would depend largely

on the efforts of someone — preferably a retired housemaster
— possessing wide contacts with several generations of old boys
and parents. John Moulsdale was his choice.

Tony's suggestions were accepted in principle and, gradually
over the next couple of years, discussions gathered pace out of
which concrete proposals developed. In 1959 a planning committee was appointed to prepare an appeal brochure. Moulsdale,
somewhat reluctantly, was hauled on board and in March 1960
the appeal was officially launched by the Council for £130,000,
employing the consultants John F.Rich to run the appeal campaign. As old boys and others began to dip into their pockets,
the Council agreed that, following an adverse report from the
college medical officer about the inadequate state of catering then
in practice, the first call on the appeal fund would be to improve
the catering arrangements and enlarge the kitchens. Tony's prize
objective was the building of a school music hall but the Council
insisted that it must take its turn in the queue after other priorities.

Thanks to the generosity of Lord Illife, a member of the
Council, who donated £10,000, the appeal was given a flying
start and with old boys rallying staunchly to the cause the figure
was surpassed within eighteen months. Tony called it a 'staggering
success'. It was, as Moulsdale declared in the magazine *School and
College* in August 1962, another tribute to Tony's leadership and
personality.

By the time of Tony's departure, Bradfield was all the better
for new kitchens, study bedrooms and a new oil-fired central
heating complex in addition to renovated boarding houses and
extra playing-fields, with a new music hall and language laboratory
in the pipeline. 'Now we've gone over to the battery system,'
remarked Tony, 'we ought to lay a lot of eggs.' The headmaster
who had earlier lamented to his Council the somewhat un-
enterprising intellect of the present generation of boys at least
could be consoled by the sharp rise in external exam passes in

1962 and a record number of leavers (fifty out of ninety) winning places at university. Of course, by modern standards, these statistics hardly raise eyebrows but in the context of Bradfield in the early 1960s they were progress indeed.

It wasn't only academically that Bradfield experienced a great awakening during these years. The expansion of clubs and societies, the triumph of the Greek plays, the greater emphasis on Shakespearean drama and the development of art and music all spoke of a festival of artistic endeavour hitherto unknown. Such creativity was partly a reflection of a wider cultural chrysalis then endemic in many schools as the final rites of pre-war philistinism were played out to the sound of muffled drums.

Much of the credit for broadening the vistas at Bradfield cannot be personally attributed to Tony. He, after all, was no cultural *aficionado*. Where his influence can be detected, however, is in the sense of self-belief that he had generated into the community along with his overriding support to those who were making things happen. Sport, although a mite downgraded in importance as a consequence, was in no way neglected. Indeed, these were boom times when cricket elevens, featuring Graham Roope, an England player of the future, were unbeaten for a number of years, football teams held their own and shooting continued to be something of a Bradfield speciality. Finally, to complete the picture of a school on the march, the local Outside Service was established to supplement the work of the Bradfield-in-Peckham mission in east London, skiing parties were organised to Zermatt and dances with local girls' schools became the fashion.

It was during the Bradfield years that the personality cult that Tony had unconsciously fostered within the narrow confines of the public schools and Oxbridge began to penetrate the world outside. In October 1960 the *Observer* in an article called 'Headmasters' Report' referred to Tony as 'a gay, tough, polymath of forty-one' and tipped him as a leading contender for Eton once

Robert Birley relinquished his crown. Further accolades came
two years later in Anthony Sampson's *Anatomy of Britain* when
he discussed the leading headmasters. 'They include heroic and
unusual men: Anthony Chenevix-Trench, the gay young headmaster of Bradfield who translated Housman into Latin while
working as a prisoner on the Death Railway.'

As these words were being written Tony's star shone even
brighter in the firmament with his appointment to the Robbins
Committee on Higher Education, the one headmaster to be
accorded such an honour. Tony was well aware that his duties
would take him away from Bradfield but, as he informed the
Council, he felt that in the interests of the school he should
accept. In the event, his commitments at Bradfield along with a
certain diffidence to deliberate somewhat restricted his contributions to the work of the Robbins Committee even though he
warmly supported their main recommendation of expanding
higher education opportunities in Britain.

Sir Claus Moser, who acted as statistical adviser to the Committee, and accompanied Tony on trips to America and Russia,
remembers him as a magnificent companion. 'Whether in a totally
respectable nightclub in Holywood or walking the streets of
Moscow, he was a man looking for and enjoying new experiences,
constantly being enriched in his outlook by new contacts and
insights, and in return enriching the lives of his friends and
colleagues.' Tony returned from Russia suitably impressed by the
advances in Soviet education, most notably in the teaching of
languages in schools, an ironic sop to the totalitarian lobby from
one of nature's most ardent libertarians.

Tony's experiences abroad gave added strength to his conviction
that the torch had indeed passed to a younger generation. On
9th May 1963, he was one of the top twenty-six leaders from
church, education and industry who signed the Marlow Decla-
ration which aimed to break down barriers between groups and

foster a sense of individual responsibility to society. Such ideals, to the frustrated liberals of the 1990s, may contain something of a hollow ring but although Marlow failed to deliver it helped establish Tony's progressive credentials with the media. It also gave him a public platform to stand on in league with the younger 1960s generation, which he considered to be morally braver than his own.

All the favourable publicity that Tony attracted made him once again an alluring catch for the leading schools as they contemplated new headmasters. Marlborough, Shrewsbury, Tonbridge, Repton and St Paul's — which meant squaring up to Field-Marshal Montgomery, the chairman of the governors — were amongst those that had their advances politely rebuffed before Clifton entered the race in June 1962, placing good money on the table as an added inducement. Tony agreed to meet the chairman but all their efforts passed him by. 'I am not terribly keen to go to Clifton,' he told a friend, 'simply because though a great school it has never appealed to me very strongly.' In any case he apparently had no wish, both on grounds of principle and preference, to leave Bradfield as yet.

Against this background of repeated avowals to stay put, it thus seems somewhat mystifying that Tony within weeks of spurning Clifton should be in contention for a very different type of vacancy — namely the vice-chancellorship of the new University of Kent, inspired no doubt by his brother Christopher who at the time was deputy education officer for Kent County. On 7th August 1962, Tony presented himself for consideration, along with Geoffrey Templeman, the Registrar of Birmingham University. In the event, the university chose Templeman as Christopher's letter to Tony makes clear:

> I thought you might like to know something of the impression you left with the interview panel. They liked you,

one and all, in many ways distinctly more than Templeman. If I may say so, they completely fell for you as a chap and they also thought that your mind showed every sign of having the edge on Templeman. Two things influenced the decision in favour of Templeman. One his enormous and valuable experience in university affairs; second, the expectation that with that experience he would get things moving as quickly as anyone could in the decisive early stages. I think also that you left the impression that you were rather more than doubtful whether you really wanted the job . . . Somebody said, and I think this was really the general view, that probably your destiny and your own estimation of it, was either the vice-chancellorship of a big and well established university or, perhaps even more probably, to turn the public schools upside down.

Within a few months such an opportunity duly presented itself when Tony, in January 1963, was carefully sounded out by the Provost of Eton, Sir Claude Elliott, to see whether he would be at all interested in having his name put forward as successor to Birley. That Birley was due for retirement and that such an initiation might be in the offing was scarcely surprising. Tony's name had been canvassed for months. Although confined to a much more selective audience, predicting the next Head Master of Eton, rather like picking an England cricket captain or football manager, becomes something of a national obsession. The press mull over all the possible candidates and clear favourites are established. Tony, the pundits reckoned, was a front runner along with Brian Young of Charterhouse, Desmond Lee of Winchester and Walter Hamilton of Rugby. Amongst those in the know the odds on Tony were even more generous.

A decade earlier, after Tony had rejected Charterhouse, William Gladstone, then still a master at Eton, had written to him, offering this prophetic gaze into the future. 'You can come and be HM after Birley. Brian Young will be your chief competitor but you will have no difficulty in retaining the lead which you have over him at Charterhouse.' This might have seemed like the wishful sentiments of an old friend but they were also the considered thoughts of a shrewd observer with his ear close to the ground and who ironically enough would have his own significant part to play in the drama as it unfolded.

Brian Young was an old colleger who returned to teach Classics after the war before taking on Charterhouse. Upright, gifted, versatile and articulate he was in many ways a superior figure to Tony and was the personal choice of the Provost. But rightly or wrongly, according to Lord Annan, the Provost of King's College, Cambridge and Senior Fellow, the Fellows felt in a curious way that Young had outgrown being a headmaster. 'I remember thinking,' Lord Annan continued, 'that he was really no longer interested in boys though he had of course a first-class mind and whatever he did later, for example, director of the Nuffield Foundation and director-general of the IBA, he did supremely well.'

There is no doubt that although a number of the members of the Eton governing body may have been lukewarm to the idea of Tony succeeding Birley, he had his powerful backers besides Lord Annan, including J.C. Masterman and the Head Master himself. Masterman, an admirer of Tony for over twenty-five years, wrote to William Gladstone, by now headmaster of Lancing, who knew both men well, asking for his opinion. Gladstone replied at length comparing the two and, assuming the well-or-ganised Eton machine could carry Tony's administrative weak-nesses, explained why he felt Tony should be given the nod. It was a letter he was subsequently told carried some influence, and yet one he came to regret.

As for Birley, we have already seen how he had persuaded Tony to no avail to take the headmastership of Charterhouse. Since then, their growing links during the ensuing decade only served to raise Tony's standing in Birley's estimation. Two incidents stand out. The first was Tony's sensitive handling of an Etonian who transferred to Bradfield in difficult circumstances and the second was an acclaimed sermon that Tony preached in February 1960. 'One of the best sermons we have had at Eton for a long time,' declared Birley approvingly. Others reacted with similar conclusions. Birley later recalled two young masters telling him, 'That's the man we ought to get when you go.' He duly obliged by making it quite clear to the Provost and Fellows that he hoped Tony would succeed him. He spoke for the majority of the masters whose views had been discreetly sought by Lord John Hope, their representative on the Fellows. Hope was also party to the opinion of Hugh Trevor-Roper who, unimpressed by Birley and disillusioned with the kind of idle Etonian who went to Christ Church, felt it high time a non-Etonian such as Tony was appointed Head Master, to rid the place of its academic complacency.

When Tony was first approached by Eton in January 1963 he replied to the Provost in polite but guarded tones:

> Naturally the idea of going to Eton is an attractive one. How not? But there are many questions I should have to consider most carefully, not least my own suitability for this kind of job, even supposing that you and the Fellows wished me to go.

Increasingly it appeared that they did and when the final showdown between Tony and Brian Young took place in London in February 1963, Tony started clear favourite. Once again he proved irresistible at interview, as he dealt with a range of questions from his war record to his views on corporal punishment. Even

his candid admission that he greatly disliked administration and
would attach far more importance to the pastoral duties of the
role, failed to count against him. 'I have never seen anyone
perform more impressively than you did at that interview in
London. You really were splendid,' observed Lord Annan, when
writing to Tony to congratulate him on his success. What really
impressed Lord Annan was his vitality and fund of new ideas
particularly on academic matters, a theme taken up by the Marquis
of Salisbury, another of the Fellows and no obvious Trench
supporter.

John Dancy, by now Master of Marlborough, recalls meeting
Salisbury at a dinner soon after Tony's appointment and, being
asked his opinion about Eton's choice: 'I said something general:
he pressed, telling me that what had attracted them about Tony
was that he was a revolutionary. Did I agree? I had to say that
the nearest I thought Tony got to being a revolutionary was in
thinking up totally new reasons for doing traditional things. "Ah,
Dancy", he said, "but I'll tell you something to convince you.
Trench believes that boys at Eton should work from their very
first term. Now if that isn't revolutionary what is?" He also told
me that at interview, when asked how he would raise the intellectual standard of the school, Tony replied, "By teaching
myself!"

Far from feeling elated at being offered Eton, Tony was placed
in as deep a quandary as he had been over Charterhouse all those
years earlier. This time there was Elizabeth to consider as well.
Her love for Bradfield ran as deep as her husband's and she had
no desire to uproot her young family from the securities of their
much loved home. Delle Fletcher, a cousin of the Chenevix-
Trenches, remembers washing up with Elizabeth in the Reading
Town Hall after a WI county committee when suddenly she let
slip that 'Tony has been offered Eton. We don't know what
to do.'

The crux of Tony's doubts lay in the size of the school. 'Eton's too big for me, I'm not the right man. I like to be involved individually with boys,' he confided to William Gladstone. Agonised deliberations also involved his family. John Chenevix-Trench recalls his uncle being very undecided and his father, Christopher, Tony's elder brother, urging him not to accept. This gut feeling that Tony wasn't cut out for Eton wasn't confined to his family. Sir Eric Faulkner remembers that when his name first kept cropping up, he warned off several of the Fellows who had sought his opinion. 'He wants to know and teach every boy in the school,' Sir Eric remarked, 'I don't think Tony is the right man for you. You won't be happy with him and vice versa.'

Given these deep-seated reservations, what finally then forced Tony's hand? He knew he couldn't stay at Bradfield for ever, reasoning that no headmaster worth his salt stayed longer than ten years. He had a wife and four young children to support. If he kept on turning down offers they might begin to dry up, leaving him to rue missed opportunities. Eton for their part were nothing if not persistent, Birley writing to express his staunchest hopes that Tony would accept and Lord Bridges, a Fellow who Tony warmed to, giving a disarmingly frank account of the taxing remit awaiting the next Head Master. It was this challenge of going to Eton, specifically to change the academic culture, that finally convinced Tony his future lay downstream. Once the die had been cast, there was no turning back although his replies to his sceptical friends remained rather defensive. When told by one of his Bradfield confidants that Eton wasn't the place for him, he countered, 'There is nothing I can do about it. This is tantamount to a royal command.'

Duty then played a part in his momentous decision but it would be wrong to suggest that Tony was simply doing Eton's bidding. Throughout his professional career his own horizons had remained close to shore but he wasn't averse to sailing beyond the sunset and the stars. For all the rough passages ahead, Tony, like countless others, in whatever capacity, was attracted by the pull of Eton. To be its Head Master was, after all, the ultimate in one's profession and a mark of respect in the country. Richard Chenevix-Trench recalls how some time later, when his father was cautioned for speeding in Norfolk, he gave his name and address as the 'Head Master of Eton College'.

On Monday, 4th March 1963, the world was alerted by the BBC to the identity of the new Head Master of Eton and for the remainder of the week, while Tony fielded a glut of letters warmly congratulating him, including the most graceful of notes from Brian Young, the press descended on Bradfield to acquaint themselves with the thoughts of a person who was about to become one of the nation's opinion formers. It appeared that they liked what they found. 'In choosing this most unrevolutionary, most empirical and most pragmatic teacher of boys to be Head Master of Eton,' wrote George Gale in the *Daily Express*, 'the Fellows of Eton may well have elected a man who will help to effect a quiet, but most necessary revolution. Chenevix-Trench is a man who could help eliminate caste from education in England. There is no caste in his mind at all, so far as I could discover. There is simply a love of teaching boys.'

From a Bradfield perspective Tony's good news was greeted with pride merged with consternation. It was no small achievement to count the future Head Master of Eton as one of their own but his departure would leave a huge void which would not be easily filled. In the Senior Common Room the news wasn't a total surprise. They had heard the rumours and they knew their headmaster's price-tag. Most accepted that he was due a move. Like that of many brilliant men, Tony's interest began to wane after a certain period, and now that he had placed Bradfield firmly on the map, it was time to seek out fresh pastures, leaving his successor, Micheal Hoban, his old friend, to effectively tie up the loose ends. The question they asked was the one he had asked himself. Should his destination be Eton?

Some, such as John Moulsdale and Murray Argyle, who knew their man, had grave doubts from the start. Argyle recalls being sceptical about the rumours, thinking it most unlikely that Eton would appoint him and even when the rumours became fact he bet Michael Ricketts £1 that Tony would never set foot in the place, convinced that as the full truth about Tony's unreliability seeped out, Eton would have second thoughts. No final hitch cropped up, of course, and Argyle paid up. With the school full to capacity, modernisations galore and work going from strength to strength, the skies over Bradfield shimmered in brilliant crimson as the Chenevix-Trench era began to close. On 7th November 1963, 276 Old Bradfieldians crowded into the Connaught Rooms in London to say their final farewells and present Tony with a beautifully inscribed silver inkstand alongside a specially requested portrait of Elizabeth. After thanking them for their generosity and conducting an upbeat assessment of the school, Tony ended with a heartfelt appeal for future unity.

> We must have positive ideals and make sure we protect the good and the beautiful. It is better to light a candle than go on shouting at the dark. The young and the progressive must join with the old and the wise, the scholar with the athlete to work together to achieve 'the Good'.

A month later, at the end of the Christmas term, having emotionally parted company from his boys, the same scenes of sadness and gratitude, past memories and future hopes were played out at the final Senior Common Room dinner. Humour too had its place as even the Trench's pugnacious Jack Russell was sent up in verse.

> Bradfield dogs are safer now
> Offley Trench is off to Slough.

The overriding mood was, however, one of sadness. On this occasion as the cheers rang out in his ears Tony's heart was too heavy to allow him to make a speech. He just walked out of Big School with his arm round Elizabeth's shoulder.

And so closed an invigorating and purple epoch in the school's history still ingrained in legend for many who passed through it. 'It is difficult to write about our Headmaster without using superlatives,' declared the *Bradfield College Chronicle* in its *valete*. 'His eight years of responsibility for our welfare have been years of wonderful success and development.' In a more personal vein, Sir Guy Garrod, Warden of the Council, was equally effusive: 'I need not tell you,' he wrote to Tony, 'how greatly you will be missed by us all nor of my deep sense of personal loss. You and Elizabeth fit so perfectly into the Bradfield scene and have become so quickly its guiding light and inspiration that it will take time to imagine Bradfield without you.'

As Tony wound up his affairs he was already gripped with pangs of nostalgia clearly evident in his final report. *O mihi praeteritos referat si Jupiter annos.* 'If only Jupiter could bring back the past years to me.' From now on the green pastures and still waters of Bradfield eclipsed even the happy highways of Shropshire in his affections as Tony turned his back on this rural Utopia to brave the great unknown.

In retrospect this parting of the ways with Bradfield was the point of no return. To the Trenches these were always the golden years and with good reason. Distance in no sense dulls their lustre. An educational thinker ahead of his time Tony's vision for Bradfield proved both bold and enlightening. By opening up vast tracts of unexplored territory he gave his pupils a broader more rounded education than that which was then in fashion.

In addition to setting the standards Tony was dynamism personi-
fied helping scholar and dullard alike to take the next step forward.
Some may have found the folksy charm rather too ingratiating
but the majority were enraptured and became converts for life.
It is perhaps no coincidence that the Chenevix-Trench era of
Bradfieldians have gone on to make good in the outside world
without losing their traditional down-to-earth sobriety.

For all Tony's great work, however, the felicitations were by
no means exclusively his. Blessed not only with a dependable
wife and a competent Council, he also inherited a dedicated
team of housemasters tolerant of a headmaster whose triumphs
with individuals couldn't disguise real administrative shortcomings.
Left to his own devices Tony's style bode ill for Eton, unless as
a gesture to the new dynasty in residence they were prepared
to meet him half way.

CHAPTER 6

ETON –
THE CROWN OF THORNS

'YOU WILL FIND MANY THINGS AT ETON that will surprise
you; most of them (the Beaks) are not really in touch with
the great world at all, being intent on their own jobs – and how
they do work at them! But it is a great school and the boy-master
relationship could scarcely be bettered.'

So wrote Jack Peterson, a former Master-in-College at Eton
to Tony on hearing of his appointment. His balanced assessment
stands somewhat at variance from the welter of contrasting opinions that abound about Britain's premier school. For good or ill
its image looms large in the public consciousness, its fascination
for the general public fed by a constant diet of tabloid tittle-tattle
or trivia. But galling though much of this publicity is to the
college, the distance between perception and reality isn't quite
as glaring as many Etonians would have it. For Eton with its
aristocratic bearings and international renown is a world apart
even from the likes of Shrewsbury and Bradfield — not to
mention less well-known establishments.

Founded in 1440 by Henry VI as an ecclesiastical institution
to provide a free education for seventy poor scholars it also
opened its doors on payment of a fee to Commoners, known
in Etonian parlance as Oppidans. Unlike the scholars who lived
in College the latter were lodged in boarding-houses scattered
around the town. Despite troubled periods in its history
the numbers continued to burgeon particularly during the

Ready for battle.
Tony (left) and
Godfrey (right) at
Simla, India, 1923

The budding
Salopian, aged about
seventeen, in
thoughtful pose

The Chenevix-Trench clan out in force for Christopher, Tony's eldest brother's wedding, 1936. Godfrey is second from the left and Christopher is on the right, next to Tony

Tony (front row, fifth from right) with the Moslem section of 4 Battery on their return to India from the POW camp, October 1945

Tony (at the back), as coach of the successful Christ Church 2nd Torpid, March 1947

The Shrewsbury Common Room in J F Wolfenden's last year as headmaster, 1949–50. Tony and Michael Charlesworth (third and fourth from the left in the front row) were among the pick of Wolfenden's youthful appointments

Halycon days. Tony (front row, third from the right) with Michael
Charlesworth (back row, fifth from the right) at Scheidegg, April 1952

Tony's marriage to Elizabeth Spicer at Chichester Cathederal, August
1953. Next to Tony is his best man William Gladstone

With Elizabeth and the
twins, April 1958

'The Guns Fall Silent'. Tony with Peter Gladstone (left) at Fasque, 1960

'Master of all he surveys'. Tony at Bradfield, 1962

The guest of the day. The headmaster of Bradfield presenting the prizes at a prep school sports day, 1962

Tony as Head Master of Eton in 1964. He was the first Head Master to dispense with the traditional black cassock. 'Actually the cassock was jolly cosy in winter and awfully nice in the summer because you could wear a bathing suit underneath and nobody knew'

Eton Recessional. Tony receiving the traditional Head Master's send-off from his colleagues, July 1970.

'Like father like son'. Two generations of Fettesians discuss the school with the headmaster, 1975

'At the end of the day'. Tony's valedictory pose in the company of the faithful Scampy and the Fettes Common Room, June 1979

19th century as its fame spread. By the time Eton basked in the glow of the charismatic leadership of Dr Warre, Head Master between 1884–1905, the school had become the fashionable establishment for the sons of the upper classes, its liberal education providing them with an essential grounding in leadership, commensurate with their position in society. It is no accident that by 1963 the college boasted twenty British prime ministers and countless other luminaries in church and state amongst its alumni. Even in the more meritocratic 1990s many of the nation's leaders still hail from Eton.

As befits a famous school standing in the shadow of Windsor Castle, its stately environs are a constant reminder of the historic links between Crown and College over the centuries. It isn't only the fact that the Provost and Head Master to this day remain formal Crown appointments or that a sizeable section of the court circle boasts Eton pedigrees. The generous endowments provided by Henry VI still enable the Foundation to pay, fully or partially, the fees of the seventy King's Scholars and maintain facilities which in range and quality are unsurpassed. Particularly striking is the elegance of the original College buildings, the Cloisters, School Yard, College Library and the magnificent Gothic pinnacled Chapel, built between 1440 and 1480.

Blessed with such an exquisite heritage it is perhaps no wonder that at various times in its history while the world has moved on, Eton has dragged its feet continuing to pay court to its own noble traditions. Tails and stiff white collars, medieval classrooms, the Field Game, an idiosyncratic vernacular, a series of self-perpetuating schoolboy oligarchies, chief of which is Pop, Eton's nearest equivalent to the prefects of other public schools, and a dynamic tutorial system all told of a school with its own unique identity. But cushioned though they may have been from many of the ills of the outside world, the very nature of Eton's self-electing oligarchies created intense rivalries and pressures which the aspiring office-holder had to overcome as he struggled to win the approbation of his peers. Those fortunate enough to be elected to Pop, their exclusiveness denoted by their colourful waistcoats and sponge-bag trousers, not only enjoyed a certain cachet; they wielded enormous authority within their own particular domains. Even those who failed to reach the ethereal heights were still given every opportunity to exercise substantial responsibility over their lives so that the natural self-confidence for which Etonians are rightly renowned, was embraced at an early stage in adolescence.

The Eton of 70 Collegers and 1150 Oppidans that Tony inherited was in the final throes of a bygone era. It is true that under the magisterial leadership of Robert Birley (1949–1963) A-levels had been introduced, science had received greater prominence and an energetic programme of college renovation had been successfully undertaken, but in its bare essentials this was the Eton of an earlier vintage with some sixty per cent of pupils still sons of Old Etonians and nearly half of its twenty-five housemasters educated at the college. Rooted as the school was in a world of cherished traditions and comforting familiarities the need for change seemed unproven especially when in the world outside the general populace reached new heights of prosperity under three consecutive Etonian Prime Ministers.

But despite the reassuring presence of Harold Macmillan and Sir Alec Douglas-Home the leisurely calm of the affluent 1950s had been shattered in the early 1960s by a series of high society scandals and national strikes. The general drift which accompanied economic and imperial decline helped foster a mood of dissatisfaction verging on contempt within educated circles towards the *status quo*. It wasn't only the government and the Conservative party which felt the sting of these attacks, best demonstrated in satirical programmes like *That Was the Week that Was*. It was established institutions in general. Thus Eton inevitably became a sitting target in this new alien climate, causing much internal soul-searching as the college slowly came to terms with the new realities. These doubts about what the future held surfaced unmistakably in a leading article in the *Eton Chronicle,* the influential college weekly periodical, entitled the *New Head Master,* on 31st January 1964.

> The Head Master comes to us at a difficult time. The past decade of Conservative government has been a comforting one for the school as an institution. It has provided opportunity for necessary internal reform without altering radically the structure and composition of the school. Such a drastic reform it is not for the *Chronicle* to urge but we cannot be blind to the fact that it will be urged. The whole problem of privilege, and the question of integration with the state system of education will inevitably become a political issue arousing vehemence and bigotry in equal proportions . . . In short, with a general election and more than usually hungry press, Eton has seldom been more precariously poised and the Etonian has never been so vulnerable.

The realisation that the winds of change were blowing through Eton was one of the reasons why Tony had been appointed and within days of taking up residence (after an interim of six months when the Lower Master, Oliver Van Oss, later Headmaster of Charterhouse, deputised) he was sharing his vision of the college with the nation. Playing on his non-Etonian connections — for he was the first Head Master of the college neither to have been educated nor to have taught there – in an interview with William Hickey in the *Daily Express* of 17th January 1964, he expressed his hopes of integrating Etonians more into mainstream society. 'Before my time is up here, perhaps Eton won't be Eton any more. It may become a college for clever boys drawing on areas where there are not enough grammar school places, giving a first-class sixth-form training to fit them for university.'

If this was ambitious stuff the change of style seemed to give credence to Tony's expectations. In contrast to the Olympian austerity of the Birley years, the Cloisters, the Head Master's home at the heart of the college, became less forbidding as the Trenches strove to recreate the family atmosphere which had characterised their time at Bradfield. Richard and Jonathan Chenevix-Trench recall how their father would spend many a Sunday afternoon playing with them in his study, building a house out of uprooted furniture and rugs in which they would all take tea, oblivious to any official appointments he might have arranged. When the Trenches were hosts at cocktail parties their children were encouraged to attend, their presence often bringing a lighter touch to the proceedings.

Besides the formal dinners for distinguished guests, there was the ever familiar round of lunch parties for masters' families, tea parties for selected groups of pupils and informal suppers for bachelor masters, all immaculately prepared by Elizabeth, who survived on the minimum of domestic help. In addition to all this entertainment she ran another nursery school, instituted cookery classes for the older boys and started the Jane Shore Society. This society was named after Edward IV's mistress whose benevolence helped save the college during hazardous times in the Wars of the Roses and for the first time it made the ladies of Eton into a coherent body by bringing together on social occasions representatives from both town and gown. The fact that the society still thrives today is a handsome testimony to its founder whose loyal and tireless work on behalf of the Eton community made her a universally loved figure.

Outside their home the same informal unassuming style from Eton's new Head Master prevailed, be it entertaining the Winchester cricket XI of 1964 when they played bowls on College

Lawn after dinner or in College Chapel where he broke with past form by taking Communion with the boys rather than be set apart from them, or even at Henley where a picnic with his family in the car park could assume a higher priority than entertaining dignitaries in the Head Master's enclosure. 'Off duty' he was happier accepting simple homely hospitality as opposed to the grander dinner parties the Head Master was expected to attend. John Elwick, who was appointed to the staff by Tony, remembers meeting him in a local Indian restaurant, dining alone, during his first night in residence at Eton and being cheerfully bidden for a drink the next day. Tom Holden, now Lower Master, recalls how, as a junior member of staff, he and his wife invited the Trenches to dinner with other close friends only to discover, much to their embarrassment, that they had run out of cutlery. 'We'll go and get ours,' offered Tony unabashed.

Sympathetic to those who struggled to find their feet in this forbidding institution, Tony was on particularly good terms with the junior masters many of whom were appointed by him. First impressions often in the light of later events turn out to be wide of the mark. Not so with Tony. Jerry Jarrett, then an assistant master in modern languages, recalls how his interview with the Head Master of Eton was conducted by an apologetic figure covered in mud and gardening clothes. Interviewees expecting some torrid questions were treated instead to a spirited monologue from Tony, one eye fixed on them intently, as eloquent cadences rolled effortlessly off his tongue. Tom Wheare, now Headmaster of Bryanston, appointed as an assistant master at Eton by Tony, recalls him saying with a chuckle at interview 'My dear Tom, one thing sticks out a mile – your deplorable degree result', implying he wanted the man and not his paper qualifications.

Under sufferance to increase the number of masters to cope with the expansion of new subjects Tony broke new ground

not only by appointing (with the permission of the retiring
Provost, Sir Claude Elliott) Eton's first Roman Catholic master
but also recruiting a significant number of staff with minor public
school or grammar school backgrounds. The odd illogical choice
apart, which owed more to kindness than sound judgement, most
of Tony's appointees proved highly imaginative, their talents still
clearly visible to Etonians three decades on. 'You'll be worked
harder than ever before but as an assistant master you'll be listened
to more than in any other school in the country,' Tony informed
Michael Meredith, now College Librarian, at his interview. He
was as good as his word, always receptive to sound ideas and
unstinting in his support of those who put them into practice;
Meredith and Tom Holden, struggling to establish the new
departments of English and geography respectively against the
resistance of certain Classicists, found they could count upon
Tony's backing which meant, among other things, further
specialist appointments in these subjects.

Meredith also received ample encouragement from Tony in
his efforts to modernise School Library since Eton's heritage was
a cause close to Tony's heart. Jerry Jarrett recalls a bedraggled
Head Master on the roof of College Library, clearing the gutter
during a terrific thunderstorm, desperately trying to prevent the
water from seeping inside. Now when the newly appointed
School Librarian expressed his dissatisfaction with its existing
architectural design, Tony suggested that Meredith go and look
at all the recently constructed octagonal and circular libraries in
England. He duly did and eventually the architects used many
of his suggestions for the design for School Library which was
opened by the Queen Mother during the year after Tony had
left. By then the library had undergone a complete metamorphosis
from being underused and out of date to becoming the leading
one of its type in the country. Meredith's ambitious programme
to modernise and develop its resources as well as beginning a

20th-century rare-book collection was fully championed by Tony who fully descried the rich dividends of such an investment.

Gavin Roynon, a junior modern linguist at the time, was another master who had cause to be grateful for Tony's support when he approved of him visiting America on an exchange programme and Peter Lawrence, likewise, with his Tibetan refugee scheme which gave two Etonians the opportunity each year to work in Tibet on behalf of the refugees. Another group to benefit from Eton's more catholic feel during the Trench years was the Rowing VIII. Their ambition, previously unrealised, to compete overseas was realised in 1967 when they won the Youth World Championships in West Germany. Back home, the arts were not neglected with the introduction of music circle concerts, enabling budding musicians to perform in more informal surroundings; nor were the clergy when their pleas for the restructuring of religious worship at Eton were sympathetically received. Finally, to complete a broad based picture, Tony placed his authority behind the introduction of social services, followed later by Eton Action, a new school holding company for charitable activities. As part of their campaign to raise money Tony backed Jerry Jarrett's suggestion, against the reservations of some, for the staging of a masters' play, even wishing to participate himself; something Jarrett successfully cautioned against, thinking that the Head Master's dignity might be impaired by such a venture.

This burst of creative activity, constituting something of a Prague spring, made Eton an exciting place to work in during the mid to late 1960s. Masters' salaries were increased by 12½ per cent in 1965, a switch to the state pension scheme, fully supported by Tony, improved their future security, and greater flexibility was shown towards staff who wished to be absent from Eton for special personal or professional reasons. Another of Tony's concessions, not universally approved, chipped away at the foundations of the tutorial system. Private business, an opportunity for a boy to talk to his tutor about current affairs, had always been compulsory on Sunday. Now it was made voluntary to enable younger masters in particular to have more time to themselves at weekends.

When not paying court to official guests Tony remained accessible to those who happened to be passing or to those who needed a shoulder to cry on. *Ad hoc* visits in a larger establishment like Eton were much less frequent than at Bradfield but often welcome all the same. Even the more formal delegations rarely stood on ceremony in Tony's company. Nigel Jaques, an assistant master in Classics, recalls meeting him in his drawing-room with the Lower Master to discuss exam results and listening to the Head Master expound from the floor lying on his stomach. Those who met him in his study might find him distracted by his affections for Squidge, the family West Highland terrier, whose basket resided there. Tom Holden recalls the formal letter he received from the Head Master confirming his permanent appointment to the Eton staff. At the bottom of it he added 'How stuffy this sounds. It is just for the record and you'll know how happy I am to be able at last to resolve this long suspense. Good luck to you both!'

The gentle drift towards modernisation, begun under Birley and accelerated under Tony, found immediate favour with the media who in this more open era had, all of a sudden, developed a fixed obsession with the school. Duff Hart-Davis, an Old Etonian journalist, in a major feature article for the *Sunday Telegraph* of 17th January 1965 wrote:

> But what makes the present situation especially interesting — and for Eton promising — is the presence of a new Head Master fairly fizzing with energy and ideas.

A month later the *Sun* columnist, Jack Lucas, called Eton 'this extraordinary happy school' and ended his article with the words

'*Floreas* Chenevix-Trench'. A BBC documentary of Eton later that year portrayed the school in a fairly flattering light and members of the Newsom Commission, which visited Eton in November 1966 as part of the Labour government's unrealistic plans to reform the public schools, found much to commend about the place, not least the avenues of opportunity available to each boy. For all his fear of the media Tony, in contrast to Birley, dealt assuredly with them appreciating the benefits of getting his bit in first. Consequently, scandals and gossip detrimental to the school's reputation were given scant coverage and his own stock remained high.

But for all the rave reviews, appearances could be deceptive. The very qualities of friendliness and familiarity which had won Tony acclaim from afar were already the cause of much disquiet in elevated quarters as he struggled to stamp his authority over a community in which other formidable powerbrokers resided, chief of whom was the Provost.

The position of Provost is unique in that unlike his fellow chairman of governors in other schools, he and his Vice-Provost live on site in the Cloisters next to the Head Master. By statute a Crown appointment and invariably a figure of some repute, the Provost directs his gaze at the college estates and endowments, chairing many of these committees. At its best the work of the Provost helps lighten the load for the Head Master, enabling him to concentrate more on educational matters but, conversely, the presence of his nominal chief could be a daunting prospect for a Head Master with different priorities. It was Tony's misfortune that he came into conflict with Lord Caccia, who succeeded Sir Claude Elliott as Provost in May 1965.

Harold Caccia was formerly Permanent Under-Secretary of State at the Foreign Office and prior to that British Ambassador in Washington. A tough, no-nonsense administrator, full of energy and ideas, he was determined to consign Eton's more obsolete

ways to history. Parts of Caccia's forward-looking agenda, notably
his desire both to attract more Etonians into industry and to
abolish the school's antiquated dress code, had much in common
with Tony's desire to modernise, but thereafter there was rarely
a meeting of minds. For although their personal relations were
reasonably civil their characters and interests were poles apart.
Caccia's brisk, hard-headed approach to life unsettled Tony and
he never felt able to unburden himself in his presence. It didn't
help that Caccia's background in the Civil Service conditioned
him to instant decision-making, courtesy of a large and well-oiled
administrative machine, something which Eton patently lacked.
Underestimating the physical demands of the job, Caccia expected
more from his Head Master than Tony could deliver, particularly
since administration was never his forte. This scope for dis-
appointment and misunderstanding was only compounded by
Tony's reluctance to speak his mind or defend his corner. Finance
was a case in point. For such a well-heeled establishment Eton
wasn't overtly generous to its employees. The Head Master's
salary of £4,000 per annum was certainly larger than the equivalent
at Bradfield but a fair percentage of it was swallowed up by his
lavish entertainment costs and salaries for domestic help. The
anomaly became a running sore with Elizabeth and in the end
it was she who alerted the Provost to their quandary because she
knew her husband never would. Similarly, Tony's reluctance to
take on the Provost and Fellows on behalf of his housemasters
over their request for supplementary pensions only strengthened
their suspicions that he was too deferential to his governing body,
a view later borne out by the painful ramifications of the 'Neal
Affair' a year or two later.

Ill at ease in the company of his employers Tony found many
of his august clients equally intimidating to deal with, particularly
those with Etonian backgrounds themselves. The fact that more
than one grandee visiting him at the Cloisters mistook him for

the butler accentuated his sense of inferiority in the company of such people. Tony later recalled his encounter with one distinguished colonel who had reluctantly obeyed a headmagisterial summons to Eton following the disappearance of his son. Having listened to Tony's obvious concern and his desire to inform the police the aggrieved colonel, who up to then had said little, suddenly expostulated, 'Dammit, Trench, you've got me worried now. It's like when one of your Jack Russell's goes to earth!' Nigel Jaques recalls another occasion when Tony fared little better in this type of company. Sir Douglas Busk, a crusty benefactor of the school, became so exasperated by Tony's excessive deference at dinner that he could contain himself no longer. 'If you go on calling me "Sir",' he exploded, 'I'll clock you.' 'Oh, don't do that,' replied Tony, 'I'm a very clockable man.'

The masters as a body also presented problems since Tony was dealing with no ordinary band of complaisant subordinates but, in the words of Elizabeth, a collection 'of brilliant minds and interesting personalities that he both likes and finds exasperating.' Their constant flow of ideas, initiatives and intrigue, resembling the inner workings of the Hapsburg Court, called for a smack of firm government to maintain some order and cohesion, something Tony was ill-equipped to provide. All his life he had set out to please everyone seemingly unaware of the irony that he could only play Mother Bountiful to some by acting Mr. Scrooge to others.

A headmaster, like any really effective leader, must be prepared to stand in judgement over his peers and deliver unpopular pronouncements. This was something Tony never fully grasped and in a highly politicised institution like Eton his reputation suffered accordingly. Particularly debilitating was his tendency to cave in to masters he had originally overlooked when handing out House Lists, the Eton way of appointing a housemaster, because they had refused to abide by his decision. Equally baffling was his habit of promising the same job, including the prestigious position of Lower Master, to several different aspirants and his less than subtle explanations for his change of heart. The burning residue of resentment from the aggrieved parties requires little imagination and it remains a deep mystery as to why such a highly intelligent man should have continued to have committed these elementary errors in man-management.

On the public stage Tony failed to make amends. As a speaker he now often lacked power and conviction while even his prowess hitherto as a teacher and academic failed to impress his critics. Snide remarks about the paucity of his blackboard jottings compared to Birley's pearls of wisdom began to emanate in certain quarters. Charles George, a boy at Bradfield under Tony and then a master at Eton between 1967–1972, recalls how Tony felt overawed by the intellectual calibre of Eton masters, a number of whom would pass each other little notes in Greek. 'They're really different from Bradfield,' he once confided to George, 'they're great men.'

Thrust into this unforgiving arena Tony, like the early Christians in the Colosseum, was apt to struggle. It was as a committee chairman that his shortcomings were really exposed. According to Michael Meredith, he was very amateur compared to his successor Michael McCrum: 'He always took endless votes and always lost'. Neither methodical enough to plan a clear-cut agenda nor calculating enough to organise his support beforehand, Tony was no match for the serried ranks of entrenched interest groups invariably lined up against him.

The mood could turn nasty as it did during the infamous meeting called in 1966 to discuss the plans for a new theatre. Feelings were already running high between the differing factions when a haggard-looking Tony arrived very late and rather the worse for wear. Immediately he came under withering assault from the theatrical lobby who, wanting a theatre exclusively for drama, objected to his plans for a multi-purpose building and Tony, irked by their querulous partisanship, gave as good as he got. It was an unedifying spectacle all round, widening the gulf which had been growing between him and a section of his staff. A few months earlier, under the heading, 'What Eton Means to Me', an assistant master had used the columns of the *Chronicle* to express his opposition to much of what the school stood for. Such effrontery brought a stinging response from Tony in Chambers - the masters' assembly each morning - who pointedly reminded his staff that 'assistant masters are expected to assist.'

At the apex of the masters' pyramid at Eton stood the twenty-five housemasters, often enshrined in Eton folklore as a 'state within a state', fiercely protective of their independence. Tony later added to their mystique by depicting them 'as barons in the days of Henry VI with their swords half drawn and very intractable.'

By dint of its immense size Eton had in many ways to operate as a federal rather than as a unitary system and certainly the housemasters did enjoy greater authority than their counterparts in other schools. Up to 1939 they owned the contents of their houses before selling them on to their successors. All masters hoped to become housemasters which was their passport to financial security since they ran their houses for profit. After the Second World War their financial powers were clipped from on high; otherwise buoyed by the system of House Lists, which gave them the opportunity to recruit their pupils, they continued to rule their roosts as they saw fit. To suggest, however, that they always acted as a united body against the centralising tendencies of the Head Master would be wide of the mark. As with any group of twenty-five individuals they had their own particular priorities reflecting their differing temperaments and philosophy.

Attitudes on freedom and authority varied enormously as did the level of respect they elicited from their boys.

Far from being bereft of support Tony found staunch allies in Peter Lawrence, Giles St Aubyn and James McConnell. David Macindoe was an old Oxford friend, Peter Pilkington was a trusted confidant as were John Anderson and Ray Parry. Others appreciated his kindness, advice and support. What resistance there was centred around a tight-knit circle of mainly Old Etonian housemasters who, traditional by instinct, could be vocal in their opposition. There was a grudging acceptance from this group of the need to make some concessions to the changing times, but to their dismay the new consensus on discipline never took root since the Head Master in league with the majority of their colleagues continued to drift irresolutely with the liberal tide without standing up to be counted. Tony's failure to offer a consistent educational philosophy bred uncertainty and division when precisely the opposite was needed. His later admission on Radio Scotland that he would never have made a successful king among medieval barons rings very true.

Aside from his vacillation Tony's relationship with disillusioned housemasters was further soured by his reluctance to observe the proprieties of the Head Master of Eton. It had long been the custom there that the responsibility for handling boys and their parents fell very much to the housemaster with the Head Master a mere adjutant, intervening only to deal with serious breaches of discipline. This arrangement had quite suited Birley who had thanked his housemasters in his farewell speech for shielding him from the parents. Not so Tony. He tried to recreate Bradfield ways at Eton in his attempts to see both parents and boys independently. Often at these meetings decisions would be taken at random without as much as a word to the housemaster concerned. When news leaked out of these trysts their hackles would be raised because their territory had been impinged upon. 'He seems to have made a hit with the Head Master', one housemaster commented acidly on one of his star pupil's report. Some weren't above expressing their dissatisfaction with the Head Master to senior boys in their house. When they looked to him for support as the alpha and omega of all disciplinary authority Tony again could be found wanting. Too often difficult pupils were treated with greater indulgence than it appeared they merited. Peter Pilkington, then Master-in-College and later Headmaster of King's, Canterbury, and High Master of St Paul's, recalls how a serious case of theft in his house was detected and the perpetrator sent to the Head Master. Instead of expelling him, Tony merely beat him, leaving it to the housemaster to brief his parents about the incident.

Embroiled for much of his time in the claustrophobic world of high politics Tony tried to escape whenever possible by taking refuge in the company of the pupils. Formal dinners where the Head Master would dine with senior boys was one outlet he normally enjoyed and he wasn't above accepting the occasional invitation to tea by the Library — the house prefectorial body in a boarding house.

Like Birley, Tony taught some dozen periods a week in his own classroom tagged to Upper School above the entrance to School Yard. His lessons in Latin, Greek and Divinity would invariably be well received as would his strawberries-and-cream tea-parties when, in relaxed form, he would organise party games. He also ran the Essay Society in his study once enticing Cassandra of the *Daily Mirror* to give them a scintillating talk.

When Etonians leave the school the tradition is that they take their personal leave of the Head Master whereupon he presents them with a copy of Thomas Gray's poems, the standard leaving book. Besides writing their name inside Tony would add some endearingly appropriate comment. He would, as a token of his gratitude, habitually reward leading office-holders by giving them a pair of inscribed cufflinks, a practice he followed in his other schools although one President of Pop, promised his cufflinks in the post, never did receive them.

In addition to those pupils Tony taught, consulted and disciplined, he set out to help a number in trouble but despite his efforts he remained, because of time and custom, a distant figure to the overwhelming majority, including even a number of his Captains of the School (the Etonian equivalent of Head of School). According to his daughter Jo, it used to upset him deeply that when leavers appeared in his study he was often bidding farewell to unknown faces. This, of course, was the predicament of presiding over such a vast establishment and most Etonian Head Masters over the years rested content with the way things were.

'Do you know all the boys?' a visitor once asked Dr Hornby the 19th-century Head Master. 'No,' he replied grimly, 'but they all know me.'

The boys weren't unduly disturbed either They were used to a distant figure of Olympian grandeur who commanded their respect rather than their affection; and in this guise Birley had certainly fitted the bill to perfection. It was unfortunate then for Tony that he lacked the presence of his imposing, charismatic predecessor. He used to recount the story of how striding down the Eton High Street during his first year he stopped a junior boy for some minor misdemeanour and asked him if he knew who he was talking to. 'No,' responded the boy. 'What do they think of the new Head Master?' continued Tony. 'Not a lot from what they tell me,' came the nonchalant reply.

The breezy, jocular approach which Tony had used to good effect elsewhere found fewer takers among Etonians. Their sophistication and patrician hauteur made them wary of friendly advances which they found unbecoming in their Head Master, particularly when Chummy — their nickname for him — mistook their identity for someone else. His outward bonhomie they felt to be something of a pose since promises made in public to gain popularity weren't always carried out in practice.

There were other problems. Eton at this time contained a sizeable component which, weaned on a life of leisure, found little incentive in taking their education seriously. Such boys considered the emphasis on participation and competition in school activities to be rather beneath them, thereby setting them sorely at odds with a Head Master whose own experiences had been exactly the opposite. Entranced by the magnificent facilities of the school, Tony was astonished and disillusioned that so many Etonians shunned the opportunities provided, preferring instead to frequent the betting shops of Windsor. His public comments to this effect in the *Chronicle* of November 1965 won him few friends amongst the professional window gazers who heaped scorn on his homespun values.

Bad manners were another bone of contention. Tony found the arrogance of some Etonians quite insufferable and would often fulminate in private about it. Michael Meredith recalls how, on visiting Eton in 1965 for an interview, he was unceremoniously pushed into the gutter by three advancing members of Pop proudly brandishing their canes. When Tony heard this he immediately summoned the President of Pop and demanded to know who the offenders were. These airs and graces weren't confined only to the elect. They were as much the preserve of the recalcitrant as Tony discovered when he had reason to caution them over certain breaches of school rules. There was precious little meeting of minds here and the antipathy between Head Master and the raffish element only deteriorated further after a series of notorious incidents in the mid-1960s involving these types led to a number of premature departures. When reliving his time at Eton at the end of his life Tony looked back with mixed feelings. 'The best boys at Eton were superb, moral and intellectual greyhounds of the first order,' he told *The Scotsman* in June 1979, 'and the worst were simply intolerable.'

'Be a reformer', the great Dr Warre once said of his own years as Head Master of Eton, 'but don't be found out.' It wasn't easy for Tony to adhere to this advice because it was as a reformer that he had been appointed to Eton with a brief to get things moving. Once there, Tony generally sided with the forces of progress but to depict him as a compulsive root-and-branch firebrand armed with an uncompromising charter for change would be to miss the point. His deepseated attachment to institutions and his political support for the Conservative party weren't mere coincidence. Schools such as Eton with their proud history were to him houses built on rock for they provided the adolescent with the skills and security to make a success of his life. Change, therefore, had to be justified in order to see the light of day.

It so happened, of course, that the Eton Tony inherited badly needed a good spring-clean and he was the new broom on hand to carry it out, but whenever the reforms appeared they were just as likely to emanate from masters or senior boys as they were from Tony himself. Such breadth of origin gave the reforms greater authenticity; on the other hand, without the Head Master's firm guidance from conception, their implementation was rarely a straightforward business as Tony found himself in the crossfire between the various rival factions.

He was only a month into his new posting when the first hint of controversy arose. An article in the *Chronicle,* calling for the abolition of boxing, by two senior boys, David Jessel and William Waldegrave, later a Cabinet minister in the 1990s, gained national prominence when the *Daily Express* ran the story on its front page of 17th February 1964. Caught off guard by all the media interest Tony seemed uncertain how to proceed, resorting to the tried and tested expedient of an internal inquiry into boxing. Judged by his comments a month earlier and his recent experiences at Bradfield, his own instincts veered towards abolition but facing vociferous opposition from the boxing lobby, he relented, leaving it to his successor finally to wield the axe on a sport which had outlived its usefulness in schools.

Other early initiatives included approving schemes to instigate social service at Eton and to broaden the concept of religious worship. The former sprang from a conversation between two young masters, Roger Thompson and Peter Pilkington, in December 1963; and when apprised of their plans on taking up office Tony gave them every encouragement, weighing in with some helpful suggestions of his own. Within a year 100 Etonians, including a number of the school's more roguish element, were participating in a whole variety of community projects in the surrounding area, be it visiting the elderly, teaching immigrant children or helping in hospices. Howard Moseley, who became master-in-charge of social services in 1966, remembers Tony being very supportive, especially when some boys were caught in a pub. Contrary to the misgivings of some housemasters he saw that the odd irritant along the way shouldn't deflect from the overall value of the project, which benefited school and neighbourhood alike. By the time he left, 120 were engaged in community work.

Overseas, things were stirring too. In 1964 Peter Lawrence, a senior housemaster, with Tony's wholehearted approval, had sent two of his boys to Tibet to teach in an independent Tibetan refugee settlement at Rewalsar, a remote village high in the Himalayan foothills. Tony also backed a fund-raising campaign the following year to support a self-sufficient community of Tibetans. Out of this small initiative and some other larger ones sprang Eton Action.

For a number of years the old Eton Mission at Hackney Wick, in east London, which served the neighbouring poor there, had appeared increasingly remote and irrelevant to Etonians in a world in which newer and more appealing causes cried out for support. An open meeting on 12th May 1968 marked the setting up of Eton Action as the new main channel for Eton's charitable activities. According to the *Chronicle,* Tony closed the meeting with a speculative peep into the future. He envisaged a rolling charity that would finance a variety of different projects rather than being tied to one particular project like Eton Mission. More than ever it would be up to the boys themselves to decide which charities to support.

Thanks to the work of Howard Moseley, Eton Action's first secretary, and others, Tony's challenge to the school's social conscience didn't go unanswered. Over the years Eton Action has organised numerous fund-raising projects, pride of place going to the popular annual fair which has enabled it to sponsor the school's social services as well as a host of other worthy causes.

Another priority concerned Chapel. Since almost all of the public schools were religious foundations, it wasn't surprising that communal worship should feature so strongly in their lives. Familiarity also often bred contempt and although the outward forms of worship were duly observed the arid presentation of much of the content left many pupils spiritually unmoved. In a more secular age iconoclastic forces began to single out compulsory chapel as an object for attack. Such critics at Eton didn't lack support. The clergy favoured a voluntary system of worship believing that congregations would become more receptive; and Tim Card records how Birley at one of his final masters' meetings let slip the revelation that he would have liked to have introduced voluntary chapel at Eton as he had previously done at Charterhouse.

Despite this clamour for change Tony was never tempted down the same road as Birley for three reasons. First, the temptations to be absent were too great. Second, the opportunity to listen to high thoughts and be at peace in school for ten minutes every day was educative in the best sense. Third, voluntary chapel sowed unseemly discord between attenders and non-attenders. But although retaining the compulsory principle Tony did reduce the number of Sunday services which Etonians were obliged to attend from two to one per day as well as providing an element of choice as to the type of service they attended. Weekday services also were enriched with a greater variety in content. Whether these changes were enough to keep the flicker of faith alive in those who might otherwise have lapsed into agnosticism remains a matter for speculation. They did meet with general approval, however, with the result that they form the basis of the college's approach to religious worship to this day.

Partially bound up with the debate over Eton's spiritual development was the future of the Eton Choir School, a prep school of twenty-eight boys who participated in all the main college services in addition to holding their own special church services on four afternoons each week. Early in 1965 the Fellows were alerted to the fact that all wasn't well with the Choir School since its numbers were down from twenty-eight to twenty-one. Moreover, its home in the Brewhouse was growing increasingly dilapidated and its continuing value was under critical scrutiny not least from the clergy, who, with Tony's support, felt that the choir with its institutional formality stood as a bar to further religious experiment in chapel.

A number of options to resuscitate the Choir School were outlined by Julian Lambart, the acting Provost, for the Fellows to consider. Tony favoured the more far reaching one of developing a fee-paying prep school like the one which supplied the choristers for St George's Chapel in Windsor, hoping amongst other things that through the teaching of Latin — a mandatory requirement for entrance to Eton up to 1968 — it would be one more way of slightly widening the college's intake. The cost, however, of this proposal rendered it impractical and the

Fellows fell back on the more modest one of constructing a temporary building to teach the choristers and awarding more bursaries to promote a growth in numbers. These changes brought some progress in the short term but, with the cost of a new building soaring beyond expectation, it simply wasn't enough. In March 1968 the Fellows, no longer able to enjoy the luxury of a temporary building, bowed to the inevitable and decided to close the Choir School in July 1969.

The end of the Choir School a year earlier than earmarked and with it a slice of Eton's heritage infuriated traditionalists but the majority of the staff tempered their regret with resignation. They appreciated not only the problem of cold financial logic in continuing with the *status quo* but also detected the new possibilities for music at Eton now that substantial funds, formerly allotted to the Choir School, could be channelled into musical scholarships. Once the surviving members of the Choir School had been taken care of these new scholarships duly came to pass, and these combined with a new voluntary choir of ninety to sing at congregational services ensured that the school's proud musical tradition continued to flourish.

If there was one area above all where Eton needed to modernise it was academically, since the school's curriculum seemed caught in a timewarp. The question was whether reform could be carried through without upsetting the fundamental Etonian way of life. Essentially its education had prided itself on its generalist approach so that ample opportunity was given to boys gaining a broad education untrammelled by the stultifying shackles of exam syllabuses. Specialisation and public exams had been delayed as long as possible whilst minimum time was given over to classes — an average of four and a quarter hours a day — so as to leave maximum opportunity for personal pursuits.

In deference to changing times Birley had introduced O- and A-levels to Eton in the early 1950s but as a staunch believer in a balanced education himself, he was in no hurry to alter the curriculum which had reigned supreme for the previous fifty years. Those wanting to gain entry to Oxbridge had been catered for by the Grand July, an exam which used to be held at Eton each July, set and marked by Oxbridge examiners. Those who entertained no such ambitions gently marked time, secure in the knowledge that their futures were safeguarded. The system was hardly a failure for the high achievers since eighty Etonians on average gained entry to Oxbridge each year but by the 1960s this cosy arrangement no longer sufficed. Confronted with a more open, mobile society, status and family connections ceased to be the automatic passport to better times. From now on two A-level passes were the minimum requirements for entry to Oxbridge colleges in addition to passing the entrance exam; and normally three A-levels were needed for the provincial universities. In this new climate Etonian parents, sensing the direction in which the current was flowing, began to push for a proper A-level curriculum in which a more serious academic ethos prevailed for the majority.

Their concerns were fully shared by Tony. 'The great question mark hanging over Eton is this,' he told Duff Hart-Davis in the *Sunday Telegraph* in January 1965. 'Our staff is without doubt the best qualified and hardest working in England; the boys have the inestimable advantage of single rooms; we've got the tutorial system. And yet, in spite of all this, the casualty rate — the number of boys doing not nearly as well as they should — is far too high. Why?'

Discussing the Hart-Davis article two weeks later, the *Chronicle* was unambiguous in its answer to the Head Master's question. 'We must face the fact,' it declared, 'that school work is still far from fashionable at Eton.' It went on to deride the absence of an English department and pointed to the shortcomings in the teaching of geography at a time when specialist teachers in either subject were still very much the exception not the rule.

It fell to Tony then, as had been made clear to him on his appointment, to cure Eton of this academic malaise. When he arrived he asked all heads of department to send him their views on the curriculum and suggest changes if need be. He then asked Christopher Gowan, head of modern languages and a known reformer, at the beginning of the Michaelmas half (the Christmas term) to chair a committee on how best to prepare boys more effectively for A-level and rationalise the curriculum in the Middle School. Once the committee discovered it was possible to allot the same teaching periods to each of the main faculties, opening up a rich array of subject choices, the inference to be drawn was that science and modern languages should have more time in the Middle School to prepare boys for specialist work at A-Level.

After six months of intense wrangling the committee came up with a new curriculum outlining arrangements for both A- and O-level study. Its main features were, first, a synchronisation of specialist hours to allow a whole series of new subject combinations that had not previously been on offer. Second, O-Levels were to be taken over two years which required eight extra periods and a new timetable. Third, English, geography and economics were to be elevated to full special subject status, and last, there should be a reduction of Classical hours further down the school and the teaching of English should increasingly be by specialist English masters instead of by the old Classical form-masters.

The implication of all these changes was profound, not least to the powerful Classical lobby who viewed them with extreme distaste. Most remained attached to the old curriculum with its strong Classical bias since not only were all boys in the Lower and Middle School placed in a Classical division (the Eton term for a class) under a Classical master but they were also assigned a Classical tutor who took a special interest in their academic progress, particularly in Latin and Greek, through a daily medium known as Pupil Room. As Classical masters also taught their pupils English-based subjects, Etonians profited from the close personal supervision they received from two separate sources, a privilege almost without parallel in any other school.

Under the new arrangements the time set aside for Pupil Room would fall victim to the extra periods now deemed necessary, while the teaching of English by specialist English masters, instead of by the Classical division masters, obviated the need for so many Classicists on the staff. This was a heavy blow for a department thirty strong, and comprising many senior Old Etonians of rare academic distinction. Outraged by recommendations which threatened to turn their world upside down, the Classicists sharpened their knives for the coming struggle. Their cause was initially aided by Tony's maladroit tactics. Instead of leaving it to the Curriculum committee to defend its own corner he summoned a masters' meeting and put the proposals forward himself with only Gowan besides him to explain where necessary. This inevitably drew all the fire to himself and Gowan, the chairman of the Curriculum committee, when it should have been made clear that the report had been drawn up unanimously by the whole committee including three Classicists and all the heads of department.

Shaken by this barrage of criticism Tony appeared now to have had second thoughts. Within a week he circulated a revised curriculum drawn up by a single Classical master which watered down many of the previous indications making it quite clear that he, Tony, thought it merited serious consideration. 'I can't let one man's view upset the whole staff,' Tony informed Gowan the next afternoon when out walking his dog, implying that the

Curriculum report was a solo effort although it had been signed by the whole committee with no minority dissent.

With hostilities suspended over the Easter holiday the Trenches went off to Greece on a Swan Hellenic cruise during which Tony regularly exchanged Classical asides with Harold Macmillan, the former Prime Minister and a fellow passenger. Elizabeth recalled how at Delos, Macmillan was reminiscing about Eton when suddenly he broke into a moving recitation from Prometheus in Greek which he had learnt there as a boy. It brought tears to his eyes. The holiday did much to renew Tony and he returned to Eton with new-found resolution.

Shortly after the beginning of the summer half Gowan and Fred Coleridge, the Lower Master, were requested to attend an informal meeting of the Provost and Fellows after dinner the following Friday to discuss curriculum reform. By the time they arrived at 9.15 pm the meeting had already begun and Tony much to their astonishment had put his weight behind Gowan's original committee report, informing the Provost and Fellows that it was official policy.

Caccia, chairing his inaugural meeting as Provost, spotted the implications of the Committee's proposals immediately since they necessitated another eight to ten extra masters to teach the new specialist subjects with all that that entailed for the salaries bill. Caccia asked Tony whether this was a permanent staff increase and Tony assured him it was not since Classical masters wouldn't be replaced when they retired. On this tacit understanding, never fully implemented by Tony, the Provost got his Fellows to authorise the proposals and put them into immediate effect.

It was a brave, historic decision which was soon to yield positive results. In the period 1965–1969 Eton won 100 university awards, twenty-two more than they had won in the previous five years. O- and A-level pass rates rose spectacularly and ap-plications to the new universities, which both Birley and Tony had encouraged, gained momentum. The new subjects, such as English and geography, given the opportunity to make their mark, responded with gusto as their numbers rapidly expanded. The stress on all-round academic standards which Tony pressed upon his staff filtered through to the pupils. The derisive term 'sap' once hurled at those with intellectual pretensions became less evident as Etonians began to grapple with futures they had previously taken for granted.

As the smoke cleared from the field of battle it was clear that the Classics department, as the reformers had intended, had suffered a major setback at a time when the popularity of their discipline was fast declining in schools and colleges throughout the country. By 1967 Classical subjects were no longer the major sixth-form subjects at Eton and from 1968 candidates were no longer compelled to offer Latin in either the scholarship entrance exam or in Common Entrance.* This was a break with the past because until then a place in College was awarded almost entirely on Classical prowess. From now on, although a brilliant Classicist could still get a scholarship, a scientist of similar ability could achieve this, too, providing he could still display some Classical acumen. The sum result was that the standards of pure scholarship were raised besides slightly broadening Eton's social intake since the easing of the requirements for Latin made a good prep school education less obligatory than before.

For all his procrastination over the curriculum Tony had at least made real progress in his efforts to make Eton a more meritocratic society. His attempts, however, to go further down this road proved much less successful.

The battle over school dress was part of a wider, if ill-defined, programme which, if implemented, would truly have

* In practice the overwhelming majority continued to take Latin at Common Entrance.

revolutionised Eton. Even before taking up the seals of office and again during his initial weeks Tony had rather given hostage to fortune with an uncompromising statement of his desire to widen the social intake of the college by offering greater oppor- tunities to intelligent pupils unable to afford the fees. These populist sentiments weren't mere window dressing. They repre- sented passionately held convictions based on personal experience whereby he and his three brothers, sons of a relatively impecunious father, had been the beneficiaries of generous scholarships which helped them receive a first-class education they would otherwise have been denied. The depressing spectacle of large numbers of Etonians wasting their opportunities would only have heightened these feelings.

During the Michaelmas half of 1965 the *Chronicle* ran a series of articles which cast aspersions on Eton's privileged ways. Patrick Wormald, the editor of the *Chronicle* and now Lecturer in History at Christ Church, Oxford, attributes the publication of a con- troversial article, condemning the exclusive entry system then in operation, directly to Tony's authority since not only had he agreed with its content but they had stayed up until 3 am to discuss it. Two weeks later in an interview with the *Chronicle* Tony linked his wish to make Eton more accessible to poorer pupils with an attack on that class 'which toiled not neither did they spin'. 'Naturally I have criticisms,' he remarked. 'Here, as elsewhere, there are some boys who are proud of the wrong things, who are professional spectators rather than performers, who are so "square" as to think that hard work is non-U.' He accepted that there was no obvious alternative to the entry system based then on individual House Lists which, in some houses, gave preferential treatment to the sons of Old Etonians but he concluded defiantly, 'I imagine no one would claim that entry at birth is necessarily the best system for parent, child or school.' His own preference was for an entry system based on a competitive

exam which in time would have transformed Eton into an establishment like St Paul's or Manchester Grammar School where
elitism was based on merit rather than birth.

It was against this background that the campaign to abolish
school dress took place. Patrick Wormald recalls Tony talking
about it incessantly, wondering if his designs would come to
fruition. 'I want brilliant young men from the east end of London
and how can I expect them to wear a tail coat?' he used to
remark. It so happened that over dress Tony found an ally in
the Provost who, besides having little patience for excessive
formality, felt that continuing with traditional dress sent the
wrong signals to a nation embracing the 'white heat of techno-
logical revolution'.

The debate became public knowledge and the tabloid car-
toonists made great play of Etonians strutting around College
decked out in gaudy garb from Carnaby Street, then the hotbed
of sartorial fashion. Unknown to the press the decision had been
as good as made. At a meeting of masters in December 1965,
Tony, much to his mortification, ran into a phalanx of opposition,
some of it stemming from unexpected quarters. There were those
who spoke in favour of the abolition of school dress but they
were in the minority and in any case they weren't united on
an obvious alternative. The case for retention seemed much more
coherent. Tail coats gave boys a sense of belonging, particularly
important in a large place like Eton. They were economic,
hardwearing and no more extravagant than any other form of
uniform. Tim Card recalls how Tony, sensing the drift of the
meeting flowing away from him, turned in despair to Dr Clerke,
an American master, on a year's exchange at Eton, and, unknown
to the Head Master, a stickler for wearing tails himself. 'You
must think our dress absurd,' said Tony.

'Oh no, I like my cutaway,' replied Dr Clerke.

On 29th January 1966, despite having previously assured the sixth form that the masters had voted to abolish all school uniform, Tony felt honour bound to inform the Provost and Fellows that the case for change wasn't a proven one. He affected an air of reason and insouciance when explaining the decision to the press but in private, the reverse, as his friend Peter Gladstone recalls, shattered him. It was the defining moment in his Head Mastership. Thereafter there was little further talk of changing the outward face of Eton. Instead Tony had to rest content with a couple of consolation prizes on these related issues. First, the Eton jacket, the preserve of the smallest pupils with its stigma for late developers, was abolished in 1967 so that everyone now wore tails. Second, and more important, there were to be more guaranteed places offered at the age of eleven to boys on the General List, an alternative method of entering Eton for those not admitted on the House Lists. This set in motion a trend which, under Tony's successor, led to many more boys entering the school through the General List, significantly reducing the Old Etonian element in the process.

One other reform, unrelated to the previous ones which bore Tony's imprint, was the ending of the fireworks on the Fourth of June, the school's principal festival commemorating the birthday of King George III, a well-known benefactor of the school. The highlight of the day for the large crowds of parents and old boys who flocked to Eton was the evening Procession of Boats at 9 pm followed by fireworks. As the years passed, this colourful spectacle had become increasingly subject to indecorous behaviour and in 1966 matters came to a head when Tony was hit by a beer bottle and boats were overturned by some Old Etonian frogmen, high on alcohol. Dismayed by these reckless antics Tony, with the support of the Provost, vowed that the time had come to clamp down on these nocturnal frivolities. From 1967 the Procession of Boats was brought forward to

6:30 pm and the fireworks abolished altogether, a decision which for all its rationale gained Tony few friends in Old Etonian circles.

If bringing Eton into the 20th century had consumed Tony in controversy then so did his individualist approach to discipline, which whether tough or tender in tone lacked nothing in unpredictability.

Discipline had for the most part been administered at house level by the senior boys with the Head Master on hand to deal with the more serious external cases brought to his attention by the housemasters. This led to considerable discrepancies within each house. In the majority the old authoritarianism remained but others were moving in a more liberal direction. These changes, already apparent during Birley's final years, broadly had Tony's support. Leadership, he felt, always imposed obligations as well as bestowing privileges. Hence his desire to reform Pop led him to persuade them to take over from masters the tiresome chore of checking boys into Lower Chapel and keeping order. Gross abuse of authority was something which repelled him. Jonathan Chenevix-Trench recalls how his father, shortly after arriving at Eton, went into the boys' entrance of one of the boarding houses and found himself standing behind a fagmaster who, unaware of the Head Master's presence, was in the process of berating a fag for being late for a boy call — a summons which all fags had to answer. The punishment meted out by the fagmaster was the relatively minor one of making the fag run up all the stairs in the House but Tony was so incensed by this that he promptly turned on the fagmaster and subjected him to the same treatment three times over.

These abuses were becoming rarer. In line with the more permissive climate sweeping the country, members of the Library and the Debate (Junior house prefects) came down from their pedestals to narrow the chasm which separated them from the rest of the house. House beating, House fines and personal fagging, already on the wane in some houses, became less popular in others so that by 1970 they were heading towards extinction. But if the new permissiveness was ushering in a more pleasant, temperate atmosphere it brought fresh headaches in its wake as the new post war generation weaned on a diet of rising affluence turned its back on their parents' values, opting instead for the new mass culture.

Such was the force of this new culture, which gave every opportunity for youthful self-expression, that no class or institution was left untouched by its populist gusts. Eton with its links with 'swinging London' was soon warmly embracing these new fads as houses reverberated to the music of David Bowie and the Rolling Stones, their strident lyrics a far cry from those of the *Eton Boating Song*. To some Etonians mouthing these lyrics was but a passing whim to which they paid only lip service. Others imbibed their intoxicating brew of idealism and protest more fully, setting them on a collision course with the school authorities as long hair, *outré* clothing, public protests and, in some cases, cannabis became the ruling passion.

Tony disliked the more militant forms of protest, particularly those which sought to criticise indiscriminately, and thought that those in authority should strongly caution against the modern Gadarene heresy which encouraged young people to run down steep places. Yet fond of quoting Dean Inge's maxim, 'There are two kinds of fools — those who say this is good because it is old and those who say this is good because it is new', he didn't completely turn his back on the new morality. Dress and appearance, to which Tony himself had always attached a low priority, were ripe in his mind for harmless innovation. With his tacit approval the steady drift towards long hair and Chelsea boots, discernible at Eton, as it was at most schools, went mainly unchallenged, so that Etonians increasingly cut a less than elegant sight in the High Street. The despairing pleas of many house-masters to get their Head Master to take firmer action on sartorial standards fell on deaf ears and even similar efforts by the Fellows in 1968 brought little detectable improvement so that the problem was passed on to Tony's successor.

Drugs were altogether more serious and knowing that the press were waiting like vultures to swoop on any scandal brewing Tony used to stalk the High Street looking for drug pushers. Tim Card recalls how steps were taken in 1966 to educate masters in the art of diagnosing drugs and boys were warned of their baleful consequences. Not all were persuaded and cannabis became fashionable in certain parts of the school. Some inevitable bad publicity did accrue when a number of well-known names left in unfortunate circumstances but, all things considered, it could have been worse. Unlike the majority of his colleagues in the Headmasters' Conference Tony adopted a more understanding approach to drugs, refusing automatically to expel a boy for such an offence. This prompted the observation in the *Chronicle*, in June 1979, that this tolerance induced more information from addicts, and that, compared to other schools, Eton suffered rela-tively little trouble in this area. The statement contains a grain of truth but a reading of *Eton Voices* and the reminiscences of those at the school in the late 1960s when the drugs culture was at its height, conversely suggest that such a verdict was a trifle wishful thinking.

Tony's mild stance on dress and drugs as well as his relaxation of leave rules, which enabled senior boys to visit London more often, caused consternation among a number of his housemasters, who already had their doubts about his whole approach to dis-cipline. To them, the Head Master was there to make judgements not to seek explanations when offenders were sent to him on the Bill, an official punishment by the Head Master with witnesses. Tony was rarely prepared to play it by the book, demonstrating

particular clemency towards amiable rogues by trying to appeal
to their better instincts. In February 1965, when confronted with
a spate of abscondings, Tony's attempts to get to the bottom of
the affair drew condemnation from traditionalists who felt his
policy to be soft.

In a letter to her mother, Elizabeth sprang to his defence. 'He
has always minded and always will mind about boys that fail or
run away. After having seen humanity reduced to its barest bones
in the war he cares deeply for his flock. Some of the older
masters here have become cynical, unimaginative and rigid and
implying to Tony that he cannot be so personal in a big school
— but how else can you really influence the boys' attitude to
work, morals and manners except to show them that there is
someone at the top who really cares. I'm sure Tony's policy is
right even if it is awfully hard work and I'm sure he will win
in the end.'

Her optimism proved rather misplaced. The upsurge of
permissiveness saw to that. In any case the more ruthless traded
on his kindness and continued on their merry path of delinquency.
However, if Eton became slacker under his leadership it became
at the same time a more caring, integrated community in which
individuals felt more at ease with their surroundings.

If the general thrust of Tony's disciplinary policy had been
towards tolerance and leniency there remained the curious paradox
over his taste for corporal punishment which caused a bigger stir
at Eton than at either of his two previous schools.

There had been dark mutterings about Tony's extravagant use
of the cane at both Shrewsbury and Bradfield but what reservations
there had been had barely materialised at official level. At Bradfield
the Council were well aware that their headmaster administered
sound beatings when the situation demanded it but as Sir Eric
Faulkner recalled, 'we were never worried by his use of corporal
punishment.' Consequently, it had barely been an issue when

Tony was being vetted for Eton. Tim Card relates how at a
dinner in the summer of 1963, Lord Cohen, one of the Fellows,
remarked that he and his colleagues had chosen the smallest Head
Master since Dr Keate whose penchant for beating pupils had
known no bounds.. 'I hope he does not resemble Dr Keate in
other ways', he said. 'Oh, but he does,' he was told.

When Tony arrived at Eton he found there traditions of
corporal punishment that had been perfected over five centuries.
It is true that grizzly rituals such as Pop tanning, a beating by
the President of Pop, was now out of favour. It is also true that
beating by senior boys in Houses was less fashionable than hitherto
as was Eight-tanning, a beating administered by the Captain of
Boats for offences committed on the river. Birching, the Eton
term for flogging, by the Head Master had survived, however,
and although it was rarely used by Birley it could be a lurid,
painful business for those summoned to the flogging block. The
unsavoury trappings of such a degrading spectacle in a more
enlightened era helped turn an increasing number of Etonians
against beating in general. Any new Head Master determined to
persevere with this archaic practice would in all likelihood have
encountered resistance. It was Tony's uncompromising stance
over not only flogging but beating in general which turned the
likelihood into a near certainty.

The opposition centred not only on the number of boys
chastised but on Tony's habit of beating in private, flouting the
Eton tradition of beatings being witnessed and recorded. In June
1965 the President of Pop, William Waldegrave, an implacable
opponent of corporal punishment, urged a debate on this subject.
Tony tried to stop both the debate taking place and a report of
it appearing in the *Chronicle* but Patrick Wormald, the secretary
of debates and editor of the *Chronicle*, insisted that the debate
should go ahead. In the event, after an outstanding speech from

Waldegrave, the honorary proposer, the motion to abolish corporal punishment was narrowly rejected by 78–72.

Behind the scenes the battle continued. Wormald, the following
November, was reported to the Head Master for staying up half
the night editing the *Chronicle*. Tony gave notice of his intention
to beat him to which Wormald retorted, 'I shall leave at once
and won't be chary of publicising your threat.' Tony backed
down but the problem didn't disappear.

In the Lent half, 1966, Tony found himself drawn into conflict
with his Captain of the School, James Mackay, a good friend of
the Head Master. Mackay recalls advising Tony in the strongest
possible terms against beating two senior sixth formers who had
returned late to school on the grounds that it was an inappropriate
punishment for a minor crime, and, more important, would undermine the Head Master's authority within the school once the incident became known. When Mackay aired his reservations Tony
didn't dissent from them but in a highly emotional state went ahead
all the same, causing great resentment to one of his victims, Nick
Fraser, who, ironically as the new editor of the *Chronicle,* had
written a series of hostile editorials attacking corporal punishment.

A few weeks later Mackay and his housemaster decided that
the best way of dealing with a compulsive rule-breaker in their
house was for him to be put on the Bill as a last resort before
expulsion. Tony expressed his agreement but then proceeded to
disregard this collective advice, and beat the boy in his rooms
without informing them. 'I seriously considered,' recalls Mackay,
'whether I had a duty to report my concerns immediately and
directly to the Provost and Fellows but I took the easy way out
and instead relayed them to masters who could monitor the
situation after I had left the school.' He did, however, convey
his unhappiness to his father, Lord lnchcape, who in turn informed
Caccia, a close friend. Similar tales of disapproval about Tony's
excesses with the cane emanating from parents and some house-

masters forced the Provost into taking action. He secured an undertaking from Tony that he would no longer beat boys in private, an undertaking he was subsequently unable to honour, further undermining his credibility.

And then there was the physical strain. Overseeing as large an establishment as Eton would have taxed the resources of any Head Master, particularly during the troubled 1960s. Part of the secret of Birley's success had been his phenomenal energy. After finishing meetings with housemasters at 10.30 pm he would then take himself off to College Library and bury himself in research until the small hours ready for Early School the next morning. Prior to Eton, Tony had been blessed with similar stamina but now the pace of life began to tell on him quite dramatically so that within a year of their arrival, Elizabeth under pressure herself continued to question the wisdom of their leaving Bradfield. 'This is the job we have taken on', she ruefully reflected to her mother, 'and we must endure and hope God will make it easier. I hardly have an ordinary conversation with Tony now and today he was so tired that he could hardly eat any lunch. Can you wonder that I worry and am not very happy?'

Crucial to the effective stewardship of Eton lies the art of delegation. Sadly, it was something Tony never properly mastered. Routine matters involving the staff tended to be dealt with through long personal letters, normally handwritten, copies of which would sometimes end up in the wrong files. In addition to the daily diet of teaching, committees and official entertainment there were all the pastoral duties which Tony willingly shouldered. Standard disciplinary rebukes were often prolonged into something more akin to sessions of personal counselling as he tried to flesh out the causes behind the pupil's offence and come up with possible solutions which often entailed regular return visits to the Head Master to monitor progress. It was admirable but in some ways self defeating because not only was he trespassing on someone else's domain, he was also needlessly adding to his toils, which in any case were to proliferate through a series of tragic deaths which blighted the community during Tony's time at Eton. One boy was drowned on the river in a boating accident. Another boy hanged himself and a master committed suicide. As was his wont, Tony proved wonderfully compassionate to the bereaved in these circumstances, but to a man as emotionally brittle as he was, the effects on him, as his family recall, were devastating.

It wasn't only the present conspiring against him since the dark shadow of war and its chilling legacy loomed ominously in the background. It is difficult to ascertain in those precounselling days how dire an effect this was to have on Tony as he, like so many of his colleagues in Siam, preferred not to relive his experiences. The evidence, though, does suggest that the physical and psychological defence mechanisms which Tony had erected to cope with his suffering began to break down shortly before he left Bradfield. Thereafter the ferocious pace of life with its attendant tribulations simply made matters worse. Now under supervision for his war-damaged liver he was also the victim of a bloodshot eye, failing sight and renewed malaria attacks all of which aged him quite conspicuously. Worst of all Tony suffered a recurrence of earlier nightmares, reliving the brutality of the concentration camps which might well explain his tendency to be physically sick before he went to bed.

There were other pressures, too, most notably Tony's non-Etonian background. This might not have mattered had he somehow looked the part but in a close-knit society where precedence and formality were all important the sight of a diminutive, dishevelled character with slightly outlandish features, out of place in the traditional black cassock, did him no favours.* Forever in

---

* Tony actually gave up wearing the cassock, setting a trend for his successors to follow.

the company of esteemed Etonian personalities, Tony always felt something of an outsider, a stranger within his kingdom. A Scottish headmaster attending a conference at Eton during these years recalls observing at a social gathering afterwards the Provost lording it in the middle and an insignificant figure sitting by himself in the corner having his tea alone. On further investigation he discovered it was the Head Master.

Tony had many friends within the community but rarely close enough or senior enough for him to be able to take them into his confidence. Consultation in any case wasn't something he excelled at. David Macindoe, his old Oxford friend, felt rather aggrieved that Tony never once sought his advice during his time as Head Master of Eton. When he did give vent to his feelings it tended to be either to junior members of staff or to outsiders, most notably Brother Peter, a Franciscan friar from Italy, whose benign influence, according to Jonathan Chenevix-Trench, fleetingly induced in his father a contemplative dalliance with Holy Orders. Michael Hoban, Tony's successor at Bradfield, recalls speaking to him on the phone during his first year and asking him how things were going.

'Hellish job this one,' Tony replied. 'Carry me back to Old Virginia.' Increasingly bereft of confidence, Tony found presiding over public occasions even more daunting. Chambers, the daily briefing to all masters by the Head Master, was a particular ordeal as were fractious committee meetings. Above all there was the strain of preaching in Chapel, an obligation which reduced him to taking tranquilizers. On one notorious occasion the school reacted to a verbose sermon by stamping the floor with their feet, drowning out the rest of his remarks.

Aware that his star was waning and disillusioned by the constant back-biting Tony sought solace in drink. Tales soon abounded of his inebriated state on formal occasions such as Chambers or in Chapel. The veracity of these tales was seemingly given added strength by Tony's habit of slurring his words, which owed as much to extreme fatigue as it did to alcohol. To what extent the drink compromised his headmagisterial duties is open to conjecture since for every person who found his personal dealings with him exacerbated by the problem there was another who claimed to have rarely or never seen him the worse for wear. Whatever the precise truth and the extenuating circumstances which gave rise to it there is no denying the fact that Tony's alcoholic excesses provided his critics with one more convenient stick to beat him with as they moved in for the kill. Their chance to wound mortally came over the Neal Affair which showed up Tony in a poor light.

Michael Neal was an affable colleague, a competent teacher and a conscientious housemaster with a genuine interest in his charges. Unfortunately, the extensive trust which he placed on them wasn't properly reciprocated and consequently discipline had began to break down in his house. Things came to a head during the summer of 1968 when three of Neal's boys were expelled and others demoted following various goings on after a midnight party. The incident attained a certain notoriety within the school and many assumed that the Head Master would take this opportunity of relieving Neal of his housemastership. Instead, Tony as the man ultimately responsible for discipline, offered up his own head on a platter to the Provost, an offer Caccia brushed aside.

That might have been the end of the affair had the Provost not gone to stay with the parents of a boy in Neal's house during the summer holidays. There Caccia was regaled with further unpleasant evidence of unruly behaviour. From this there arose the clear implication that the housemaster wasn't in control and the Fellows, already perplexed as to why Tony hadn't previously dismissed Neal, kept up the pressure for a change of housemaster as parental complaints continued to mount. Up

against such powerful forces Tony felt he had little choice but
to comply with their wishes. A month into the following half
and amidst great public agonising he used a much less serious
disturbance in Neal's house as a pretext for unceremoniously
ditching the housemaster, adding salt to the wound with his
edict that Neal should vacate his house within forty-eight hours,
a sentence later rescinded to the end of that half. The news of
Neal's fate was greeted with uproar by the boys in his house.
In a public show of solidarity they pasted walls and noticeboards
with vast slogans of 'Support Neal, Ban Trench'. Something
similar in weedkiller was planned for the cricket fields but was
never actually carried out. There was consternation, too, among
the masters, particularly the more liberally minded ones. According to Bobby Bourne, a senior housemaster at the time, many
of his colleagues accepted that Neal had failed to get a grip of
his house and deserved to go but the manner of his departure
grated. During the final weeks of Neal's housemastership when
feelings were running high the illusion that he had been victimised
made rapid headway. A gathering of housemasters called to
discuss the crisis felt compelled to support the Head Master but
even a number of Tony's previously loyal supporters aired strong
reservations over his handling of the affair. For others, less
committed to him, this was the point of no return. Their
confidence in him had been irretrievably shattered.

News of the Neal controversy percolated through to London
clubs and smart dinner-tables in the West End where Old Etonians
congregated in force. For some time they had sensed that all was
not well in the school. More alarmingly. they had heard the
rumours circulating about the Head Master's personal foibles. 'I
daren't go to London these days,' Caccia would confide to close
friends, 'because everyone immediately asks me, "Whatever is
happening at Eton?"'

With a modest decline in numbers adding to the sense of uncertainty, the future of the Head Master now became a leading issue in itself. Sir Michael Cary, successor to Lord John Hope, now Lord Glendevon, as the Masters' Representative, was instructed to carry out a straw poll of housemasters to sound their opinions. Doubts had soon arisen amidst a number of the Eton establishment that the wrong choice of Head Master had been made and at least one senior Fellow felt that Tony should have gone by 1966. For a while the loyalty of his Lower Masters, Fred Coleridge, later to be Vice-Provost, and Martin Forrest had taken the sting out of some of the damaging criticism but there were limits as to how far they could camouflage reality.

An isolated attempt to rally support for Tony was strangled at birth amidst a general consensus that with the Head Master's authority at a dangerously low ebb he should depart after a respectable time span. These findings were relayed back to the Provost and Fellows who were left to make the final judgement on the man they had so assiduously courted six years earlier. There were those Fellows like Lord Redcliffe-Maud who attributed many of Tony's problems to the disloyalty of 'bloody-minded housemasters (the rebel barons)', who resented his direct contacts with boys in their houses. But even he was forced to concede that Tony's indecision did the housemasters no favours and that their confidence had been irredeemably breached.

It was left to the Provost to transmit the decision of his governing body to Tony. Well aware that this fate might come his way, he accepted his dismissal philosophically and graciously. With tact and sensitivity all round a letter was dispatched to all parents at the beginning of the summer holidays in July 1969 to inform them of the Head Master's 'retirement' as from August 1970. 'The stress and strain on a Head Master,' Tony explained, 'have clearly increased.' The announcement evoked surprise intermingled with some relief.

'Thank you for you letter,' wrote Charles Willink, one of Tony's housemasters, 'I am sure that your decision is right and wise on every count.' Many parents and friends wrote in commiseration. Few were under any illusion concerning the demands of the job. The press for their part had little of substance to report although a measured article by Kenneth Rose in the *Sunday Telegraph* went some way towards explaining Tony's predicament:

> The incessant burden of dealing with boys, masters, parents, the governing body and the outside world has all too often exhausted him. These pressures have on occasion left him reluctant to immerse himself in detailed administration to the satisfaction of all his colleagues or to deliver unpopular but necessary judgements with authority.

Once term was over and the desks had been cleared Tony and Elizabeth took refuge in Norway where they informed the children en route that they would be leaving Eton. Later that December, once the dust had settled, Tony in a letter — earmarked confidential — to his brother Christopher put a more personal gloss on the reasons for his impending departure:

> My dear Christopher,
> I hope you will forgive my not having answered your letter before. It is difficult to put in words why I'm leaving Eton in July after just one term under seven years, without disloyalty to my Governors and without damaging Eton which I have come greatly to love. I think it is true that I am not sufficiently ruthless, and that I dislike power and the pomposities that accompany it. I haven't succeeded in getting 'the Old Guard' housemasters behind me to a real extent. In some ways indeed I am too small a man in too big a job. I've done some good and all the boys would agree.

And things can never be the same as they were, thank goodness. For one thing, boys do some work now, and the variety of intellectual and manual activities they can follow has very greatly increased. Nor have we had any 'Student Power' trouble (despite encouragement by the press!). But I do think it right for me to go. Things will be easier for my successor for some who have made things hard for me are now rather ashamed and even a little frightened! Eton will certainly benefit. One other point in this most confidential letter. My Provost and I have very different ideas. His ethics, you may say, are utilitarian — mine Kantian! We've no idea yet what we shall do — it may not be so easy to find something, but I shall have to, and pretty quickly!

Love to you both, Tony

Tony's final year brought its usual round of challenges and controversies but despite feeling the ravages of the past few years, the burden of office sat easier upon him as he began to get demob happy. Tim Young, Tony's penultimate President of Pop, recalls attending an excellent party given by the Trenches in April 1970 during which Tony threw eggs out of the drawing room window on the confident assumption that they wouldn't break on hitting the ground below. The festive mood continued through the balmy summer with the return of the Conservatives to power helping to still fears about the school's future, and a rare double over Winchester and Harrow on the cricket field.

If Tony's send-off lacked the grandeur of Birley it wasn't without its moments. The Provost and Fellows showed their appreciation by playing host to him at Brooks as well as providing him with a generous financial settlement. At a formal dinner the assistant masters presented him with silver candlesticks and the boys gave him a fine water colour of Eton by Edward Duncan, a younger contemporary of Turner, while at a separate reception for Elizabeth she was given a diamond brooch by the wives and dames. Finally the *Chronicle* paid their departing Head Master a gracious valediction:

> There can be little doubt that during his reign the Etonian has become more tolerant, more kindly, more considerate of others, more seriously disposed towards his work, more conscious of the outside world and of the need to train himself to take his place as a citizen.
> We are left with the picture of a gentle and considerate schoolmaster . . . always prepared to find some good in even the basest delinquent, always trying to help those who were down to pick themselves up and start again, always successfully recognising successful endeavour with a word of praise. We owe him much; we wish him well.

And with that clarion call ringing in his ears Tony, his future still unclear, departed leaving historians to argue over his legacy and whether it merited its place in the Etonian pantheon. It was a debate still raging passionately a quarter of a century later when Tim Card's history of the school since 1860 appeared.

Judged by his self professed desire to eliminate caste from Eton Tony fell a long way short of expectation. His idea that the school should be open to many more working-class pupils, a worthy aim in itself, nevertheless typified the 1960s thinking in its vagueness. If, however, his grand design remained something of a pipedream, Tony could rest content that Eton under his leadership had seen the curriculum transformed, new subjects introduced, the work ethic promoted and horizons broadened. In addition to the great leap forward in academic standards, the arts were encouraged, the facilities improved, Chapel reformed, the social services begun, discipline relaxed and relationships broadened. 'This is the modern Eton,' enthused the *Chronicle* in June 1970. 'A school which utilises its facilities to encourage self-expression while by no means neglecting its duties as a trainer of the mind and preparer for national exams.'

The fact that many of these reforms drew their impetus as much from outside the school as inside and that Tony's record rests mainly on the endeavours of his subordinates only qualifies his achievement, not negates it. For Eton, unlike a number of its principal rivals, at least had the innate sense to look the future in the face. The advent of league tables in the 1990s, in which Eton has ridden triumphantly high, show how this gulf to some extent remains. As to who promoted reform there is no denying the contention that Tony was rarely the instigator of it but his wholehearted unselfish support of others was crucial not only to their implementation but also to their depth. According to Peter Pilkington, 'Tony viewed schools in a romantic 19th-century way and, though a brilliant Classicist, was not deeply interested in either the politics of education or the curriculum. In a way this was providential for Eton as he allowed others to take over, and both in chapel and in the curriculum radical reforms were made which might not have happened had the Head Master been of a conservative disposition and deeply interested in these matters.' The process of change was by no means complete by 1970 and much remained to be accomplished by Tony's two eminent successors but to assert, as the *Sunday Times* did on 4th September 1994, that Eton's academic renaissance was entirely post-Chenevix-Trench is to overlook the good seed planted in the 1960s.

For all the college's seven years of plenty during his time there Tony was never able to dispel the impression that he looked out of sorts at Eton, his parvenu status and oblique methods being major handicaps to understanding the school or mastering the way it worked. Inadequate planning, consultation and consistency of purpose on his part bred undue confusion and resentment among his staff as they locked horns with each other over policy. Housemasters in particular felt the full force of his prevarication as they were exposed to the stormy blasts of the teenage revolution. Once personal factors came into play the steady erosion of their trust made a change of Head Master both desirable and inevitable. That the transition was effected so smoothly is a credit to all sides.

It is a matter of some conjecture as to whether Tony ever rued the day he donned the mantle of Eton. Within his family Tony sent out contradictory signals on the few occasions he deigned to reflect on his time there but to the independent observer the evidence points overwhelmingly to the affirmative. For Eton not only seriously undermined his health, it shattered the cult status which had accompanied him throughout his life and which had formed a vital ingredient of the Trench aura. Now bloodied and bruised in battle Tony was forced to drink from the bitter cup of failure sapping his confidence in the process. As afternoon gave way to evening and the lights began to fade it remained to be seen whether he could restore his battered pride by finding newer worlds to conquer.

CHAPTER 7

FETTES – NORTHERN SUNSET

'WHERE HAVE YOU BROUGHT US TO?', exclaimed Elizabeth in horror as the Gothic spires of Fettes College bore down upon the Chenevix-Trenches from their giddy heights, presenting a sombre salutation to a family on the move and somewhat adrift from their moorings. For migrating north to the windswept steppes of Edinburgh wasn't a natural step for a tribe which was deeply wedded to the public school culture of the south. Certainly as news of his Eton dismissal sank in a period of doubt gripped Tony as he pondered the years of uncertainty ahead of him. Eventually, in December 1969, he contacted his old mentor J.C. Masterman to seek his advice. Masterman's reply, dated 4th January 1970, makes interesting reading:

> Thank you very much for your letter. I am glad that you wrote and indeed I am pleased that you should write to me about your predicament. No, I didn't know that leaving wasn't your choice. I read the statement which you sent round and thought there was a curious ring about it, but I didn't understand the reason for this . . . You know how much I regret the whole affair. My instinctive feeling is that if Edward Bridges had lived and been ten years younger it wouldn't have happened but that's only a private thought and regret.
>
> The past is the past, we have to think about the future. You are in a very awkward position, for the Head Mastership of Eton is the top job in the profession and may seem to

debar you from most other posts, and the world will think that you did not succeed at Eton. Furthermore it will be difficult to explain to new employers or governing bodies what the real position at Eton was. But you must get another teaching job and for pension reasons if for no others.

I certainly think that a Teacher Training College would be glad to take you up, but opportunities of this kind are rare and often do not crop up at the right time. I agree that if you 'went state' your action would be misunderstood and might cause a good deal of difficulty and embarrassment. But I do not agree that you cannot go to another public school as headmaster. In my opinion that is your métier and I believe that you are the best headmaster in this country for a school of, say, 500 or 600 boys (or girls?). Why should this field of work be debarred? It should not be.

If you go in for another headmastership (and I hope you will) some difficulties will arise, for the governing board of the school concerned will have to be told the truth (in confidence of course) about the Eton business. You will also need some backing and it may be difficult to choose sponsors. If I may offer advice, I should ask Kim Cobbold for a letter if and when one is needed. He was long enough a Fellow to know about your work. He thinks that you did much for Eton; he would be anxious to help you, he was not concerned in your departure for he had by then retired. A present Fellow would no doubt do his best to help, but would be in a difficult position.

I'll take off my coat and do the best I can, though I am now rather fading out. Meanwhile I want you to give me leave to show your letter at my discretion, to say, a chairman of governors of a school – should the occasion arise. It is not right to allow your very handsome behaviour to sink you when the correction could be made by a knowledge

of the facts. So please give me this discretionary leave.
No more now but we'll have a talk later on if the situation
develops in the sort of way which I hope It will.

Yours,   JCM

PS The best brigadier is not necessarily successful when he
becomes a general of a division, but that doesn't debar him
from taking another job as brigadier and making a flaming
success of it.

Masterman's letter was a real fillip to Tony, confirming his own
predilection to remain in schoolmastering. In April 1970 he was
shortlisted for the headmastership of St John's College,
Johannesburg only for him to have second thoughts. The next
month his eye was taken by an advertisement in the *Times
Educational Supplement* inviting applications for the headmastership
of Fettes College, which would become vacant in August 1971.
Apart from holidays with the Gladstones at Fasque, Tony's Scottish
affiliations extended to little more than his great uncle having
been Professor of Greek at Edinburgh University. Given his
current plight, however, the idea of breaking new ground north
of the border had its attractions, especially since Fettes, a school
of 400 which Tony had briefly visited in 1958, would be perfect
for his style of leadership.

    With the Fettes job attracting a weak field, the name of the
Head Master of Eton among the fifteen contenders shone out
like a lighthouse. There were, of course, the difficulties with
Eton that Masterman had anticipated but if the Etonian version
of his dismissal was fully available to the Fettes board, as Eton
have claimed it was, then Fettes chose to ignore it. 'We did
examine his application to see if anything would invalidate his
application,' Francis Jamieson, chairman of the finance committee

told *The Scotsman* the day his appointment to Fettes became public knowledge, 'but of course there was nothing.'

The news in any case was by no means all dire. Before the short list was interviewed, one of the Fettesian governors had spoken to Eton's representative in the Governing Bodies Association and received a favourable report which supplemented Masterman's flattering testimonial. In addition, the then headmaster, Dr I. D. McIntosh, had been to Eton on 'a fact-finding mission' and met Tony. No such enquiries were made on behalf of the other candidates. When the short list of three presented themselves at Fettes in July 1970, Tony, up against the relatively unknown headmasters of Christ College, Brecon and Eltham College, London, was overwhelmingly the front runner. At his interview he told the governing body that there was nothing in headmastering that he hadn't encountered. His audience appeared convinced. Francis Jamieson, soon to become chairman, informed his colleagues that they were wasting their time considering any of the other candidates. Once Tony had fully satisfied the requirements of the medical examination he was, much to Eton's surprise, back in the saddle of a well-known educational establishment.

During the interregnum Tony spent much of his sabbatical in his Sussex cottage restoring his strength and devoting time to his family who often had taken second place to school commitments. Long walks with them in the neighbouring countryside, full of history he brought zealously to life, and competitive games of chess and bridge were particularly favourite pastimes.

Leaving Elizabeth to administer the discipline Tony had few expectations of or imposed few restrictions on his children. Initiatives on their part which brought them acclaim or happiness were warmly endorsed but in general their education was a matter of some indifference to him. Even promises to attend some important function were often broken when his presence was demanded closer to home.

The one exception to this rule occurred in rather unusual circumstances. During his sabbatical, the boys' prep school, Swancote, lost a master at short notice and Tony stepped into the breach to teach English, an arrangement that brought a smile to all sides. Richard Chenevix-Trench recalls his father one day sedulously smuggling packets of sweets into the car and directing his brother to the illegal treasure trove in the back.

Once his duties were over, Tony renewed a previous practice of lecturing on a Swan-Hellenic tour of Greece, Here his erudite, succinct talks mixed with his old world courtesy made him an ideal courier to the well-heeled clientele.

As time drew nigh for Tony's descent on Fettes, opinions differed as to his coming. The illustrious war record and the Eton pedigree, undoubted attractions for many, were offset by those who knew of his *Private Eye* notoriety. Tony himself, although deeply grateful to Fettes for resuscitating his career, approached the new challenge with apprehension. Elizabeth, for her part, still suffering from withdrawal symptoms over Eton, was reluctant about moving to a part of the world which, for all her ancestral connections, was foreign soil to her. Their initial months in temporary accommodation, whilst the Headmaster's Lodge was renovated, only added to her despondency. The pressure on Tony to supply quickly the Midas touch was thus considerable.

Founded in October 1870 from the substantial trust funds of a former Lord Provost of Edinburgh, Fettes had made its name predominantly on its renown at Rugby football, turning out fifty-nine internationals and seventy-one Blues. When Queen Elizabeth the Queen Mother had attended the school's centenary celebrations in 1970, Fettes could look back with pride over its first 100 years but for all the recent strides in academic accomplishment storm clouds were gathering elsewhere. Not only were the numbers and the finances in disarray, the community was in turmoil as the school's traditional values were increasingly being questioned by a new disaffected generation.

Entering this furnace of combustible youth was just the challenge Tony needed. If his personality had been out of step with the Eton of the mid-1960s, it was now perfectly in tune for the Fettes of the 1970s. From the moment he entered its precincts in September 1971 the place relaxed and began to rediscover its soul. 'I want you to remember,' Tony informed the school at his first Assembly, 'that my study door is always open to those who want to see me. I don't mind if you come and stare at me to see if my nose looks like Concorde.' True to form Tony was soon roaming his parish, his walking-sticks, pipe and white Scottish terriers as familiar a sight on the playing-fields of Fettes as once they had been at Bradfield. One afternoon with the light fading, Tony's failure to evoke any response from his dogs as he whistled to them was soon explained when closer inspection revealed they were two white rugby balls. 'We are a useful pair,' said Ian Sutcliffe, the semi-deaf PE master, 'I can't hear anything and you can't see a damn thing.' 'You old bastard!', cried a delighted Tony as he stumped off laughing.

Aside from his active support for the sporting fraternity Tony made it his business to attend as many school functions as possible and entertain vast hordes once he and his family were safely installed in the newly decorated Lodge. Here in these elegant confines with stately views overlooking the city of Edinburgh and the Pentland hills, Tony and Elizabeth would host a lunch party every week that brought together many sections of the Fettes community along with various Edinburgh dignitaries.

Courtly hospitality aside, Elizabeth retrod familiar steps by setting up the Monday Club, a monthly gathering for wives and matrons, and providing a nursery school for staff children. The moment any addition to the Fettesian family arrived, she would be around with a present to greet the newborn and to check that everything was in good shape.

Again, it wasn't only the teaching staff that were singled out. Secretaries, matrons and domestic staff likewise were warmly embraced inside the Chenevix-Trench mansion. Each Christmas the Common Room were prevailed upon to come to a party laid on for the wider Fettesian community and enter into the spirit of the occasion. Whilst the differing worlds of brawn and brain looked on apprehensively from their respective corners, Tony totally unabashed led the way dancing with the stoutest of the cooks before turning to his repertoire of party tricks. As with Bradfield the magic of the Trenches soon cast its spell upon Fettes. Ronnie Selby Wright, then an honorary chaplain, remembers visiting the school weeks after Tony's arrival and sensing a new mood afoot. 'What's happened?', he asked Tom Goldie-Scot, a senior member of staff. He replied, 'Tony'.

Beneath the glittering exterior there was work to be done and fast. A confidential note from the chairman of the finance committee, passed to Tony on his arrival, painted a bleak picture of the balance sheet. The cost of the various Centenary Appeal projects had amounted to £40,000 more than proceeds, and in addition to a deficit of £30,000 on capital account, the income and expenditure account had incurred losses of over £100,000, making a total deficit of £130,000. With current bank overdrafts then running at £57,000 the general fund of the Fettes Trust (excluding property owned and occupied by the school) was down to £37,000.

The unwelcome curse of inflation had become an unfamiliar terror for schools to accost. Fettes wasn't alone in finding its spending plans falling short of their necessary target and was already into a second appeal to modernise the college when Tony arrived. Clearly the shortfall in cash could only be resolved either by greatly supplementing numbers — then standing at 392 boys

and 3 girls — or selling off further sections of the Fettes estate.
Not surprisingly the first option was much the more preferable
even if it meant tinkering with standards of academic entry; a
move that Tony fully supported as he felt slow developers often
contributed more to school life.

Tony was no financier and indeed rarely bothered about the
workings of the Estates committee. Renovating the many struc-
tural deficiencies of Fettes left him unmoved. When Robert
Philp, one of his housemasters, complained about the dilapidated
state of his house, he was fobbed off by his fellow Classicist with
a quotation from Thucydides, 'It is people who make up a
community'. External impressions aside, however, Tony was
canny enough to appreciate the importance of good public
relations, particularly with the prep schools, as a means of attracting
recruits to Fettes. Alan Waddell, chairman of the finance committee, recalls Tony even wanting one of the royals to come to
the school, reckoning it would do much for the marketing. In
his first report to the governors, on 5th October 1971, he noted
that Fettes seemed to have acquired a reputation, particularly in
the south, for being a 'very tough school'. This was an image
he set out to redress partly by taking his message to the Scottish
prep schools but above all by reviving the spirit of Bradfield in
his welcome to prospective parents whatever the nature of their
visit. For all his administrative lapses, Tony unfailingly ensured
that any request for a prospectus was answered immediately and
appointments promptly arranged.

When interviewing, Tony preferred to conduct these sessions
in the more informal surroundings of the Lodge where he always
had something of interest to attract the child's attention such as
a tray of polished stones. During these meetings there would be
no question of blatantly selling the school to the parent. Instead
he would direct his questions to the boy always seeking to find
the hidden passion that would ignite a spark and draw out his

personality to the full. After a while they would be joined by a housemaster who, receiving a paean of praise from his headmaster, left with their visitors on an inspirational high, so that they had little trouble sounding the right positive notes.

Feted by such cordiality from one of the top names in British education, many parents were enticed into choosing Fettes at a time when its spartan facilities presented a rather bleak product to sell. Of course the smooth publicity machine didn't always run like clockwork. Gracie Gavine, Tony's long-suffering secretary, recalls the occasion when some parents were kept waiting while she scoured the school in vain for the absentee headmaster. Suddenly, just as she despaired of ever finding him, Tony, in an old coat, flung open the front door swirling his stick, casually remarking, 'Oh, my dear Gracie, what a beautiful day!' When she explained the predicament, Tony took it all in his stride, deflating any possible embarrassment by couching his apology in the most melodious of tones.

To help boost numbers, Tony was given discretion by the governors in February 1972 to reduce fees for certain categories of pupils. By January 1974 there were 435 boys enrolled, nearing the capacity of 450. Surprisingly, in view of repeated assertions from Tony that the extra numbers were causing strains (again shades of Bradfield), the self-imposed ceiling was ignored so that by January 1978 the figure had mushroomed to 491 boys with 41 girls, a record for the school and a relief to the bursar if not to the overstretched housemasters, whose houses were already splitting at the seams.

Tied to the strategy of enlisting more pupils was Tony's eager endorsement of a suggestion first mooted by Ian McIntosh that the old sanatorium, Malcolm House, could help open a new chapter in the school's history by housing a junior school of up to eighty boys for the 11–13 age bracket, serving schools other than Fettes. Apart from apportioning out a few boarders with masters' families the institution would be exclusively a day school, thereby causing little competition to the hard-pressed Scottish prep schools.

Tony's vision was first outlined at a governors meeting on 16th November 1971, and the following October the governors set the seal of approval on this venture — scheduled to begin in the following September — leaving the headmaster in control of the advertising. One of Tony's earliest decisions was to appoint John Arkell, then head of English, to be the new junior school's first headmaster, having struggled to convince him that such a daring concept could succeed. 'Oh, never mind, my dear. You'll have a lovely house to live in whatever,' was Tony's cursory rejoinder, alive to the fact that all new enterprises have a risk element attached to them. As it was, he need not have worried. His choice of Arkell, now headmaster of Gresham's School, Holt, was probably one of the best appointments he ever made. Together with his personable wife, Jean, they cut such a dash as lords in their own manor that soon the very best in Edinburgh were turning up to enrol. By the time Arkell attended his initial governors meeting in January 1975, he could tell his employers that burgeoning numbers had enabled them already to reach their target of eighty.

For the rest of the 1970s the junior school continued to prosper with a significantly higher proportion graduating to the senior school. This in itself was to have future ramifications not originally foreseen in these formative stages. In May 1974 the governors rejected the idea of a junior school boy moving up to the senior school with dayboy status because to do so would mean a complete reversal of policy. Eight months later, they appeared to have had second thoughts since they accepted a highly selective entry of about twenty junior school day boys to the senior school and in March 1976 they agreed that Fettes should start planning for 'a considerable expansion in day boy numbers.' What clearly influenced their volte-face was the fear that, in an era of falling birth rates, rampant inflation, then running at 25 per cent, would drain away the savings of the professional classes, placing the future of boarding schools in jeopardy. Because the immediate fall off in boarding that was expected never materialised, the senior day house that Tony anticipated never surfaced but the steady increase in day pupils continued, pointing a finger to the future. Indeed, the dilemma of how far boarding schools like Fettes should go to meet the demands of the profitable day market without losing their essential boarding character is still being addressed in the mid-1990s.

Hand in hand with the junior school and day pupils there arose the seeds of co-education with all its momentous consequences for the future. Like so many major changes, the scheme began almost by accident and proceeded far beyond the limits of its early preconceptions. When Tony arrived there were three girls in the sixth form and gradually this number expanded so that by the end of his time it had reached thirty-four. Had the facilities been available this figure would have been comfortably exceeded such was the demand for places. As it was the girls, all of them day, had to be siphoned off to the boys' houses rather in the role of a supporting cast devoid of their own identity. This mattered less to the more extrovert ones who particularly relished their proximity to the opposite sex but for others it made their minority status all the harder to bear. To Tony, the experience of presiding over girls was a complete novelty and one that left him rather uncertain as to how to handle them. In principle his policy was the laudable one of integration, leaving others to discover how this could best be carried out in practice. Because a limited entry system encouraged a discriminatory admissions policy in favour of high achievers, it wasn't long before tangible benefits of co-education could be cited by its supporters. In June 1976, looking back on his first five years at Fettes, Tony paid public tribute to the girls. 'They bring gaiety, grace and a great deal of brains to our society, and are never any trouble. What never? Well — hardly ever!'

Already the recipients of favoured status on such fundamental issues as games, prep and dress, those in more serious breach of school rules would often be sympathetically treated when the question of sanctions arose. Certainly, those required to report to Tony rarely went in fear of their lives, although the feminist in one offender, gated for anti-social behaviour, demanded a beating, a request Tony politely refused. Any leniency on his part towards the fairer sex caused some offence to the boys who felt that the girls were treated as a privileged caste within the state. From a female perspective, however, the chauvinism of many boys and staff grated, particularly in regard to sport where they were often left to fend for themselves. Eventually, changes began to filter through, such as the first female housemistress in 1975, the first girl school prefect in 1976, by wish of the other prefects, and the formation of the girls' hockey team which won a tumultuous reception from the boys on returning from their first match.

Girls who felt adrift in this alien world always had Elizabeth's shoulder to cry on as they sat eating scones in her kitchen. It was as much due to her efforts as to Tony's that Fettes survived the teething stages of this daring innovation. In his valedictory interview with *The Scotsman,* days before his death, Tony extolled the girls for their civilised influence yet cautioned against major further advances. 'In principle, I would love to hear of Fettes as co-educational but I'm not sure that thirteen and fourteen-year-old girls in a boarding school really mix with the boys.' Had he lived, he might well have had reason to reassess his judgement for within less than a decade the principle had become reality: a revolution with few tears.

Away from the pressures of filling the school Tony turned his attention to equally pressing internal matters. His determination to resume at Fettes the kind of pastoral headmastership he had practised at Bradfield accorded well with a Common Room that had been held in thrall by a series of domineering headmasters whose word was law. The invitation to address their new headmaster by his Christian name — unprecedented in Fettesian history — was simply the outward show of a more fertile relationship that sprang up between the staff and Tony. They, like others elsewhere, came to appreciate the infinite time he would spend with them in private and the support he would offer them in adversity. Similarly, his appearances around the school — be it in congregational practice, which he never missed, or on the sports fields — served to raise morale, his presence often enlivening a fairly mundane occasion. Ian Winstanley, the master-in-charge of debating, recalls an incident at the Vawdrey Reading Prize when a boy was reciting from Mallory and Irvine on Everest. Tony, who had slipped in unnoticed, heard out the extract before announcing, quite misleadingly, that he had been privileged to know Mallory well, and 'if he was here this evening,' he continued, 'do you know what he would have said? Max, go and climb that mountain!'

Released from the circumspections of a more cautious regime, individual members of staff were trusted to go about their work in the way they thought best, with a special seal of approval to those breaching the orthodox or stalking the unknown.

John Arkell, in charge of the transport of the Cadet Force, which amongst its other objectives taught boys how to drive, remembers a chance encounter with Tony when mistaken reports reached them that one of his group had been involved in an accident. 'Tony,' exclaimed Arkell, 'perhaps we shouldn't do this.' 'Oh no, my dear,' Tony assured him, 'a crash is no reason to stop boys learning under your instruction.'

With a word in their ear or a note in their locker the staff were motivated enough to intensify their already high work-rate extending the range of cultural and recreational activities on offer. It was only when less appealing responsibilities attracted few takers that a touch of headmagisterial initiative was called for. Unsuspecting candidates would be summoned to the study and softened up by a charm offensive as to why they were just the person to supervise the junior film society. Such flattery normally worked to perfection but when two overstretched masters resisted alluring entreaties to join the naval section of the Cadet Force, the reservations of the third man were firmly brushed aside.

For all his relaxed demeanour Tony could be singleminded about getting his way. John Arkell's excuses for not producing the school play were cut to pieces, much to Arkell's subsequent delight; and Tom Goldie-Scot, a former Second Master, found himself unable to resist Tony's vigorous approaches to become head of modern languages, at the age of sixty-five. Appointments, too, were very much at his personal whim. David Kennedy, head of physics, and Peter Coshan, head of biology, remember their joint venture with Tony to appoint a new science teacher. Having met Douglas Barnes-Graham, their second candidate on a short list of six, they registered their approval with the headmaster the next time they saw him. 'Yes, I thought he was good, too,' replied Tony 'I've appointed him.'

Continuing the policy he began at Eton, Tony readily enlisted grammar school or state educated teachers, as well as making his first female appointments. Some of these new outsiders found adapting to more privileged surroundings a difficult bridge to cross but most were helped on their way by the unpretentious nature of Tony's regime. In keeping with this style, official meetings were kept to a minimum and intimations on the headmaster's noticeboard were as much a source of general entertainment as a call to further endeavour. One minor classic he unearthed ran as follows:

THE FETTESIAN'S EASY GUIDE
TO POLITICAL SYSTEMS SACRED COWS

SOCIALISM: You have two cows, and you give one to your neighbour.

COMMUNISM: You have two cows; the government takes both of them and gives you milk.

FASCISM: You have two cows; the government takes both cows and sells you milk.

NAZISM: You have two cows; the government takes both of them and shoots you.

BUREAUCRACY: You have two cows; the government takes both of them, shoots one, milks the other and pours the milk down the drain.

CAPITALISM: You have two cows; you sell one of them and buy a bull.

As was his wont Tony left day-to-day administration in the capable hands of his deputy, Dick Cole-Hamilton, giving him the cue to pay lip-service to rules and regulations. On the rare occasions on which housemasters' meetings were held (often at irregular hours) Tony's reluctance to discuss contentious issues could often frustrate his housemasters. When Robert Philp, unhappy about a lead from the centre on some controversy, reminded him that they, the housemasters, were at the sharp end, Tony clutched his arm, grinned and retorted, 'And am I delighted that you are.' As ever he was happy enough to let his housemasters get on with ruling their own roosts, interfering only if prevailed upon to do so. This meant that when he wished to eradicate something as sensitive as personal fagging he didn't impose his will by edict but merely communicated his wishes and left each housemaster to act as each saw fit.

In general, relatively few issues frayed relations between Tony and his Common Room at Fettes but the vexed question of pay was one that did rear its ugly head. For some time there had been rumblings of discontent about the failure of the Fettesian salary scale to keep pace with the inflation of the early 1970s. Thus when the Houghton Report was published in January 1975, recommending rises of 30%, backdated to May 1974, for those teaching in the state sector, matters were brought to a head. Knowing the financial implications of Houghton to cash-strapped Fettes, Tony circulated a confidential note to all staff outlining the dilemma and beseeching them to forego backdating which would add £18,000 to the school's overdraft. He continued:

> Every independent school is now fighting for survival. At the moment, touch wood, our prospects are healthier than they once appeared to be and healthier than most of our rivals. I think we have to think very carefully before jeopardising these prospects for otherwise we could all be out of this job!

In addition to the financial reasons, Tony cited more general ones in support of his policy of restraint:

> Compared to state schoolmasters, Fettes masters do get a few 'extra perks': free house (or living-out allowance), very cheap education for sons and in the sixth-form for daughters, free lunches, local telephone calls. Bachelors pay nothing like a realistic rate for board and lodging. I do not mention intangibles such as size of classes, type of pupil, surroundings, shorter terms and a school still small enough to be a family, and the right to refuse to take or to remove impossible boys.

Placing his final card on the table Tony let it be known that he had already asked for his own salary not to be raised. The circular met with a mixed response and when one of the sceptics expressed his doubts in writing to the headmaster, Tony's reaction was to lay bare his soul rather melodramatically in response:

Thank you so much for your reply to my circular about Houghton. Believe me, I wish to put no pressures on anyone! I too have no home but the Lodge, and my capital is about £3,500. I am on the government schoolmaster insurance/pension scheme. You may think it odd that an ex-Head Master of Eton should not be better 'lined'. But expenses there were very heavy – royals to dine etc. and I could save only £3,500. Here, my salary is £2,000 less than a minor school and much less than a state school headmaster.
Agreed this has been my choice. Also I get half fees for my sons (my salary is £4,750). They cost me £13,000. I lunch off bread and cheese and eat meat once a week on Sunday when we usually have masters and children in. We have no daily help. But we are cushioned against inflation in that the college pays for our food. The bursar will, I think, confirm that we are very cheap! We live in a super home but it is not our own and we have no other. We do get heat free and also light. And I get car expenses on college duties. So I am not on the 'bread line'! All the same, I am near retiring age; then what? But I love the place and am understandably happy.

What you say about the governors' 'administration' of the Fettes Trust is true. But this is now ancient history. Our present finance committee meets four times a term to budget termly. It has also been entirely reconstituted; a major task for me. Sandy Hodge (the director of finance) has no illusions. When I came, we met briefly twice a year.

From a sinking school of 392 boys when I came we have risen to 459 and 20 girls. Cash flow has therefore improved, but at present, the legacy of the past leaves us with some £14,000 overdraft 'down the drain'. It has been for me a long, long claw to windward — not a pleasant one. But vis-à-vis Loretto, Glenalmond, Sedbergh, we are to windward. As for Merchiston all very well for now!. But I would lay longish odds against their survival in three years time . . .

So far the count is about 3 to 1 for 'c' (acceptance of his recommendation). But there are many from whom I have yet to hear. I must emphasise that my letter is not 'propaganda' but a real attempt to find out what you all feel and I am very grateful for yours, which is constructive. I think we ought to have a meeting of interested parties fairly soon.

When the meeting duly took place the discontent still simmered beneath the surface and it needed a passionate speech from Tony extolling the vocational ideal in education and their universal commitment to Fettes to bring a number of doubters into line.

For all his reluctance to tackle administrative and material matters, Tony couldn't dispose of them as easily as he might have wished. It remained the bane of his relationship with his colleagues since his age-old desire to placate gave rise to promises he couldn't deliver. Inevitably in such circumstances the flak began to fly and Tony had to withstand some bitterness from disillusioned Young Turks denied their share of the spoils. 'I was shocked and saddened to receive your letter this morning,' wrote Tony to one. 'I have indeed told you that I saw you as a housemaster, and I do. But never to my knowledge have I ever promised you a particular house or the next one.'

John Arkell, another victim of broken promises, recalls giving
Tony a piece of his mind only to be stopped short by a pained
riposte of, 'My dear John, one day you'll be a headmaster and
I hope nobody ever speaks to you just like you've talked to me.'

Similarly, with staff accommodation: it is rare for any boarding
school to abound in quality housing to the satisfaction of all its
employees, and the necessity of establishing a pecking order is
an invidious one for any headmaster. Now that more married
staff were being appointed, the shortages became acute and Tony
found it a monumental task to keep all his troops happy. Again,
a tentative promise of preferential treatment let slip in casual
conversation could return to haunt him when demand began to
outstrip supply. In response to conflicting parties staking out their
rival claims, Tony's replies would often take the form of a lengthy
confessional in which he would make play of the competing
pressures he had to contend with. 'I fear it would take Solomon
if not the Archangel Gabriel to satisfy all,' he lamented. 'At least
one is going to be disappointed, for not even I could predict
the explosion of matrimony in the past six months.'

Tony's ability to extricate himself from the tightest of corners
although no longer quite so ingrained as in the past, was still
sufficient to ensure that most chill winds of discontent blew over
fairly quickly. 'May I add that your letter in no way lessens the
affection and respect in which I hold you to avoid further misunderstanding,' was a typical soothing rejoinder after one of his
more bruising encounters when he was left reeling on the ropes.
The deep well of affection that he generated with his staff in
spite of the breaches of trust was because of his deep affinity to
them and their families. Those who departed for fresher pastures
weren't being unduly nostalgic when they looked back to the
camaraderie of the Chenevix-Trench era at Fettes as something
of a lost Elysium.

If Tony opened doors to his staff, the same could be said of his relationship with the pupils. A strong constituency from both England and overseas gave the school a cosmopolitan flavour but the overriding ethos was a stolid Presbyterian reserve that might well have dismissed the new headmaster with his cultivated voice and eccentric mannerisms as an effete southerner. Such suspicions weren't entirely erased by the sight of Tony, arm sloped around individual pupils, addressing his charges as 'My dears' or starting the school steeplechases with a 12-bore shotgun in a manner reminiscent of the madcap Prendergast in Evelyn Waugh's *Decline and Fall*.

As the years progressed, the oddities became more distinct so that to some he did become a caricature. Yet, however much individuals might smirk at the foibles within his personality they rarely lost their respect for him. Although Tony had long since disliked addressing mass gatherings he could still leave a mark when he felt the need. In those days the summer term finished with the traditional end-of-year service in the chapel after which everyone dispersed. Such proximity to the holidays was an open invitation for all the refuseniks to gather in the gallery and cock a snook at authority by carrying on with their own entertainment oblivious to the solemnity around them. Ross Leckie, then a boy in the school, recalls how one year the sheer power of Tony's reading from the book of Ecclesiastes, 'Remember thy maker in the days of thy youth', stilled the ranks of the opposition as one by one they were mesmerised by the performance of their headmaster whose figure they could barely discern above the lectern.

When it came to combating antisocial behaviour Tony would assemble the school and instead of raising the roof he would invariably talk through the problem trying to make them see reason in the process. Just occasionally threats would be used, but even these might take an unusual form. When some lockers at Loretto had been vandalised by a Fettesian rugby team, Tony, playing on his undoubted popularity, declared that if such behaviour should recur then the school could find itself a new headmaster. Ronnie Selby Wright remembers another occasion in the dining-hall when having given the school a scolding he ended by saying, 'I'm so sorry to be cross with you, my dears, but don't let it ever happen again.'

As a teacher Tony had probably lost some of his earlier brilliance, but his passion for his subject remained undimmed and those privileged to sit in on his classes in the top fourth form Latin or the Classical upper sixth were richer for their experience. Ross Leckie, a Classical scholar both at Fettes and at Oxford, rated Tony as the best teacher he ever came up against subscribing to the earlier contention that had more people taught the Classics in the Trench manner its demise neither would have been quite so sudden nor complete.

Besides his wisdom and sparkle the secret of Tony's rapport with Fettesians lay in his age-old openness. Within weeks of his arrival names began tumbling off his lips as he met them around the grounds or in a more formal setting. Knowing the lie of the land enabled him to build up a profile of each personality — albeit a mistaken one in some cases — and gave him something of substance to relate to during his frequent encounters with them. Gracie Gavine, the headmaster's secretary, recalls earning herself a rebuke from Tony when turning away a boy who called in to see him. 'Gracie, never ever refuse to let a boy see me. I'm free to see a boy any time. Always say 'yes', and I'll put myself out.' Tom Goldie-Scot, too, has recollections of Tony interrupting a leaving party in the Lodge for school prefects in order to advise a boy. 'If I hadn't seen him now,' explained Tony on return, 'I wouldn't have been able to see him.'

An open-door policy was particularly refreshing to the outcasts of Fettesian society. Cameron Cochrane, Tony's successor, remembers being down in his cellar past midnight one Saturday evening during his first term, when he was aroused by a knock on the window. Heading gingerly for the front door, Cochrane was astonished to find a Fettesian late back from up-town leave in an inebriated state, ready with the following words, 'Mr Trench said if I was ever in trouble to ring his door, and I'm in trouble, Sir.'

With a return to the open-door policy and his close rapport with Fettesians, Tony rediscovered his flair for report-writing. Chris Carruthers, housemaster of School House, and no slouch with his charges, reckoned to learn something new about 10 per cent of his boys when copies of the headmaster's reports were sent to him. Parents, too, liked what they read. It was as always a highly useful selling point. Tony's accent as always was on the positive. Phrases such as 'dear boy', 'alpha person' and 'excellent fellow' — natural stamps of approval — frequently recur in his comments. When idleness threatened to still the roar of his young lions Tony resorted to personal evangelism to arouse the fainthearted: 'Come on, Fergus;' 'Buck up, Tom;' 'Don't let me down, Neil;' 'He is a nice fellow but learning is a two-way business not a one-way street.' Ever willing to save the sinner from damnation, Tony could even turn on the boy's teacher in a public show of professional disloyalty. 'Toby and he don't, I fancy, get on all that well nor do I think the fault is all on one side.' It was only a motley collection of the graceless, ill-mannered and insufferably conceited that bore the full force of his unforgiving obloquy. 'Creature of moods is all very well,' he wrote on one, 'but we're getting a bit tired of them. He needs to brace up — fast!'

Of course, an open-door policy, however ideal in concept, wasn't without its flaws. As Tony had discovered at Eton, a headmaster who is all things to all men runs the risk of over familiarity, and Fettesian housemasters discovered that

threatening the unruly with a visit to the headmaster carried
scant conviction as rogues positively enjoyed seeking out Tony's
company. More reprehensible was the habit of Fettesians abusing
their access to the headmaster by manipulating the system to
their advantage. Ian Winstanley remembers taking his opposite
number from Gordonstoun to a pre-arranged drink in the Lodge
after a tennis match and being confronted with the unseemly
sight of a boy bitterly denouncing a number of his teachers to
an apologetically defensive headmaster. The spontaneous concessions to individuals which had always been Tony's stock in trade
mounted as advancing years made him even more favourably
disposed towards the young and their whims. Such favours were
often extended to parents too. 'We are here to do your duty,'
Tony reassured the parents each Founder's Day and the more
demanding took him at his word, peppering him with requests
to which he would normally readily accede.

George Preston recalls how one of the boys in his house,
about to depart with the Cadet Force for a Field Day was
suddenly, without a word to anyone, given permission to miss
it so he could be with his mother on her birthday. Fettesian
housemasters, like their Etonian counterparts, found it difficult
to hold a consistent line on discipline in face of Tony's accommodating gestures made on the spur of the moment to individuals
without any prior or subsequent consultation.

As has become clear during this study, Tony's bent for personal
relationships amongst his pupils wasn't simply the means to an
end, it was the end in itself. School regulations were merely the
outward apparel of something deeper. To enrich a community
you had to change attitudes. This was the responsibility of those
in authority.

When there is a changing of the guard it is usual for those
entering office to criticise their predecessors for leaving unwelcome skeletons lurking in some hidden cupboard to dispose of.

Tony was no exception although he appreciated this was the way of the world. Many facets of Fettesian life under his predecessor, such as its academic and sporting prowess, stood comparison with the best but the harsh repressive ways of the old order left much to be desired.

Despite the enlightened disposition of a new breed of housemaster the responsibility for day-to-day house discipline was still in the hands of the prefects and their acolytes. In common with their counterparts in other Scottish schools, where the Dark Ages still reigned, few were willing to forego their powers. Presiding over a draconian regime, where manliness and house spirit were all the rage, those who were young, weak, artistic and nonconformist were often given a harrowing time. The sight of a petrified third former shaking with fear outside the prefects' room before being exposed to some lurid initiation ritual wasn't unknown. Victimisation of the vulnerable — the bane of the boarding school over the years — be it through excessive punishment or being shunned by the peer group, was still alive and kicking.

In a world where trusted values were creaking it was only a matter of time before the upheavals that had disrupted life south of the border would hit Scotland. Indeed the advance guard with its slogans had already arrived, forcing the resignation of Malcolm Muggeridge as Rector of Edinburgh University in 1968, because of his opposition to contraceptive machines in the students' union. Tony Blair, a pupil at Fettes between 1966–71, and now leader of the Labour Party, was amongst those who dared challenge hallowed Fettesian shibboleths, receiving short shrift from the austere, upright Dr McIntosh whose final years resembled a fragile autocracy at odds with the spirit of the age.

The minute of a meeting of the governors on 3rd March 1969 notes that McIntosh had reported various acts of indiscipline, some of them without particular significance, some of them, however, symptomatic of this new found restlessness endemic in schools and universities. During this period of disquiet the beleaguered headmaster was constantly on the phone to his chairman of governors seeking moral support as his tottering edifice lay under siege from outside. Had the old order remained another year, then a host of teenage Dantons and Robespierres might have engaged in embarrassing shows of public protest. With the recently released film, *If*, for all its grotesque fantasies of revolution in a public school, causing uneasy tremors in a number of Common Rooms, this was no time for official inertia. Action was needed and fast.

Tony at his first governors meeting had already set out to alter the image of Fettes as a 'very tough school'. In addition to his at-home style, Tony wanted to break down the walls of mistrust by encouraging individuality. Fettes's position on the edge of a great city had to be exploited, he said, and older boys had to be trusted to use the educational opportunities afforded by the city. Intelligent use of leisure had to be learnt by pupils and the older ones should also be encouraged to study on their own without invigilation. Words were soon translated into deeds. Fettesians were granted greater access to venture into the city on half-holidays. Sixth formers were permitted entry to pubs on a Saturday evening and to have study periods back in house, as opposed to compulsory invigilation in the library.

Dress was another area ripe for reform. The teenage craze for long hair, flared trousers, and boots was hardly at one with the school's sartorial code. Undeterred by mutterings at Eton when acting in a similar manner Tony took the sting out of the issue by relaxing the edicts, fondly hoping that once rid of official restraints members of the school would respond positively by taking a pride in their appearance. Old photographs of the 1970s emphasise only too clearly the general shabbiness that crept in but efforts to revive the old guidelines largely fell on deaf ears.

Robert Philp recalls how Tony would roll his eyes to the heavens
in boredom if someone deigned to raise the matter at a housemasters meeting. To Tony there were simply more important
questions to discuss. 'Of course it matters that the young should
be clean. It matters more that they should be considerate,' he
told the assembled ranks on Founder's Day in June 1972. Nine
months earlier, in his inaugural speech to the school, Tony had
voiced a similar message. 'The only thing I can't stand is bad
manners, for they are the oil that makes society work smoothly.'
Of exemplary bearing himself, it wasn't surprising he afforded it
such a high priority. Those who transgressed on this score were
rarely shown much mercy.

David Brydon recalls how some unruly behaviour by Fettesian
supporters at a 1st XV match against Stewart's Melville on their
ground at Inverleith led to an extended school detention on a
half-day with a string of unusual questions that he set and marked
himself. In 1977 he felt the matter of courtesy sufficiently important to warrant inclusion in his Founder's Day address as an
area to improve on. 'Manners are the happy way of doing things:
some of you may say that they are superficial but so are the
dew drops that give such depth and beauty to the morning
meadow. I really do feel that when we live in a civilisation that
is breeding from the bottom and dying from the top we might
give this point a serious thought.'

Such strictures weren't simply applied to basic courtesies; they
were concerned with fundamental human relationships. Few
might have appreciated it at the time, but he was, in essence,
appealing for a revolution in attitudes particularly from those in
authority towards the younger, more vulnerable types. This meant
not simply refraining from excess punishment or fagging; it meant
positively seeking them out and befriending them. 'A community
thrives on love,' reflected Tony on Founder's Day in 1977, 'and
cannot long endure without it. As Chesterton says, "In her best

days, men did not love Rome because she was great: she was
great because men loved her"'

Given his mistrust in legislation as a means of changing attitudes
Tony knew the onus was on him as headmaster to communicate
his gospel to the prefects so they in turn could put it into practice.
Groups of them would be invited in for sherry to discuss issues,
for Tony felt the secret of conversion was to ask questions not
formulate judgements. That isn't to say his ways won complete
and immediate backing — far from it. When he encouraged his
prefects to ape the *aristoi* of Athens by shouldering responsibilities
as well as enjoying rights, he was laughed out of town by hard
core traditionalists. They bitterly resented any attack on their
fiefdoms and stubbornly resisted such attempts, but they were
clearly bucking national trends. The majority sympathetic to these
more permissive modes of behaviour proved more receptive. A
major bridge was built between the year groups helped by headmaster and prefects working in harness towards the same end.

From the moment Tony, true to form, was stuffing chocolate
biscuits into their pockets at the new boys' tea, he was doing
his bit to ease their transition into this strange new universe.
Ross Leckie, the product of an austere Scottish prep school,
remembers being flabbergasted as a fourth former when Tony
hailed him in the street. Headmasters didn't do this kind of thing
but soon such informality became second nature.

A number of junior boys availed themselves of the opportunity
to visit him. In House, their low estate was still readily apparent
but as the rigidities of the hierarchy began to wither their lives
were made more tolerable. Fagging became less arduous, restrictions less petty and punishments more apposite. Of equal importance was the closer integration with their peers so that house
spirit became less a narrow edict from on high and more a
genuine expression of collectivist will and endeavour.

In this more relaxed atmosphere the school began to shed some of its inhibitions and increasingly became a community at one with itself based on a confluence of the old and the new. Fettesians would still turn out in force to cheer on the Rugby XV against Merchiston while at the same time enjoying the novelty of listening to *Jesus Christ Superstar* in chapel or performing *Zigger Zagger* on stage. More free time meant more time up town yet paradoxically the pupil input into school societies was as prolific as it ever had been and greater than in subsequent years. In line with Tony's other schools, a better balance between sport and culture was achieved whilst the opportunities for serving the local community multiplied.

Throughout his career the challenge of dealing with the recidivist element was the one that fascinated Tony. Adhering to John Buchan's dictum, 'That the task of leadership is not to put greatness into humanity but to draw it out, for the greatness is there already', no effort was spared with any troublemaker. Reprobates who had parted company with their previous schools could always expect a sympathetic hearing if they applied to Fettes. 'Don't let the housemaster see that file,' was Tony's instruction to his secretary when he agreed to take on a boy from down south with a highly dubious past. Knowing the reluctance with which any housemaster would view these newcomers he would resort to type explaining why only that person had the qualities to cope with such problem pupils. When Alan Waddell, a Fettes governor, quizzed him about taking a boy expelled from elsewhere in Scotland Tony's forceful rejoinder was, 'How would you like to be given one chance in life?'

Once they were admitted, Tony would play his part in ministering to the needs of these boys along with the other rebels. Ross Leckie, with a chequered history behind him, remembers as a senior boy being summoned to the headmaster's study.

Fearing the worst, Leckie was astonished to hear the verdict, 'I'm not going to expel you. I'm going to make you a school prefect but you will contribute.' In order to drive his point home he made Leckie sit down and read aloud in Greek the Funeral Oration of Pericles from Thucydides *History of The Peloponnesian War* — a piece familiar to him in class — extolling the Athenian values of good citizenship. Such personal faith in one so previously temperamental proved totally inspired. Leckie, finally seeing the light, changed tack and gave his all to the school. His transformation was but one of the most spectacular that Tony helped to bring about in others. Simon Scott, a friend of Leckie, remembers being weaned away from a life on the fringes by the painstaking approach of the headmaster who spent hours with him making him see the point of sensible rules.

As was the case at Eton, Tony's reasoning made less headway on more raucous types, often to the despair of the housemasters who longed to rid themselves of first-rank troublemakers. One pupil, the perennial scourge of the Common Room, repeatedly seemed doomed for an early departure but Tony, determined not to be beaten, dreamt up all kinds of mitigating factors in the boy's defence. After one of the boy's more outrageous episodes, Tony, drawing on friends at Alnwick Friary, sent him there for a fortnight in the hope that a spell on retreat in the cloisters would teach him the true meaning of communal behaviour.

In general, Tony saw expulsion as an admission of failure by the school towards one of its individuals and would thus go to inordinate lenghts to avoid this if he could. One of his favourite ruses with those condemned on Death Row was supposedly to play the prosecuting counsel himself and to invoke the name of their housemaster who had successfully intervened on their behalf. In that way they could be given another chance without losing face.

Some seized their remission gratefully; others, ignoring the olive branch on offer, proved they were beyond redemption. In the case of Alnwick Friary this remedial approach proved no more than a palliative compared to other more traditional methods, and Tony eventually had to concede defeat. 'I have tried', read the rather poignant postscript to the note announcing that the boy had left Fettes.

As with almost everything in Tony's career there were no logical criteria by which expulsion would occur. He used to say, 'I expel for what they are and not for what they've done.' David Rhodes recalls reporting a drugs-related case in his house to the headmaster and Tony asking him whether he wanted the boy to stay or not. Rhodes said he wished him to stay because the boy was young and had been misled. Bill Kennedy, head boy of Fettes in 1973, remembers being awoken one evening by his housemaster and informed that the headmaster would like to see him. On arrival and over a drink, he heard Tony expound on a serious incident of a boy who contributed nothing to the life of the school, being caught running a gambling and marijuana racket from his study. 'Mr Chenevix-Trench then said to me, "I believe I must expel him. Can you think of any other way in which he can be punished short of expulsion?" I couldn't and enquired as to whether or not the situation would be reported to the police. The answer was no. The boy left the next day.'

Even when expulsion was the necessary verdict, Tony would go to great lengths to cushion the blow by helping the victim to rebuild his shattered life. So quick was the hand of forgiveness that one boy, even as he waited in the Headmaster's Lodge for his final departure, was prevailed upon by Tony to keep one of the precious first editions he happened to be reading. A sixth former's propensity for drug-taking earned him an all too brief sojourn at Fettes but he still remained on excellent terms with Tony after his expulsion.

With the evidence rather intangible it is extremely difficult to quantify precisely the effect on Fettes of Tony's system of self-discipline. Everybody is agreed that the change when it came in 1971 was sorely needed and that a more relaxed style was one that accorded with the aspirations of the vast majority. In this new climate the cultural heresies of the 1960s became the ortho-doxies of the 1970s so that the Fettesians of this vintage evolved into a happier, more fulfilled generation under the gaze of a benevolent authority capable of grasping the nettle when the need was felt. Drugs, for instance, a running sore in the inde-pendent sector during these years, were adequately contained if not totally eliminated.

But for all the virtues of Tony's system it wasn't, as he fully admitted, without its imperfections. In his more cynical moments, he used to remark that 'if you trust pupils they let you down and if you don't they do you down.' Placing his faith very much in the former Tony hoped that his appeal to reason would ultimately persuade the majority to reciprocate trust with respon-sibility. His hopes were by no means completely misplaced. Old Fettesians recall the onus it had placed on them to think twice about cutting corners particularly since there was little kudos in outwitting a popular headmaster, but, inevitably, to a dissolute minority the temptations became irresistible. As the 1970s pro-gressed and even before Tony's grip began to slacken, a corrosion of standards crept in, not helped by the lower calibre of some of the pupils then in residence. Reports of Fettesians breaking bounds and abusing rules on alcohol became increasingly common as they were frequently spotted imbibing in Edinburgh hostelries often at unholy hours. Soon tongues began to wag, giving op-ponents of the school a soft target to aim at.

For all the desire to still the current of damaging rumours and innuendoes the search for solutions proved more problem-atical. Margaret Buchanan-Smith, the wife of the housemaster of

Glencorse, recalls the occasion late one Saturday evening when, as she was collecting her daughter from a disco, she recognised a number of familiar faces out on the town. Having persuaded the resident tutor to conduct a bed check on her return she, in the immediate absence of her husband, then rang Tony to tell him about the incident. The next day, much to her dismay, Tony beat the head of house but exonerated the others, accepting their word that they had just gone out for a walk.

Unwilling to grapple with absenteeism Tony left his housemasters with a lonely furrow to plough. Consequently, his successor was presented with an unwelcome legacy so tragically brought home during his first term when a Fettesian, breaking bounds, was killed, asphyxiated by a falling window as he clambered back into his quarters past midnight.

In the laxer years of the late 1970s it wasn't only the housemasters who harboured fears about wilting discipline. A couple of senior boys took the liberty of writing to their headmaster to express their own reservations. One pinpointed the mood of informality between Common Room and senior pupils which he felt compromised the professional integrity of the staff and their standing in the eyes of the school. The other referred more generally to declining standards and the need to alleviate the situation quickly. 'Fettes, which was the Eton of Scotland, isn't any more,' he concluded ominously. Tony was grateful indeed for such frankness but was less accommodating to the Old Fettesian who complained that the headmaster was too liberal and the school too slack. 'A lobster shell,' his critic wrote, 'may be hard on the outside and yet underneath it is very soft.' 'Crabs to you,' was Tony's dismissive reply upon reading it.

Although Tony's increasingly lenient approach to discipline appeared to fit the temper of the times, his continued belief in corporal punishment stood out as a quirkish paradox. Even in the most Dickensian of institutions the cane by the late 1970s was rarely the trusted companion of old to those exercising authority. The advent of co-education in the independent sector served only to further highlight its obsolescence, and for many schools this change seemed the moment to part company, but for Tony it remained an effective deterrent against teenage delinquency. The increasing reliance upon suspension as an alternative for serious breaches of school rules was one that found little favour with him, first, because it removed the person from the scene of his crime, second, it disrupted his education and, third, it dragged out the penitential process. Consequently, beatings continued as before. The majority accepted it with little resentment but some, buffeted by their experience, took umbrage. The matter wasn't allowed to drop.

Following a series of heated parental complaints about the ferocity of the beatings handed out to their sons, two housemasters, after consulting their senior colleagues, decided to confront Tony about the allegations. Unhappy with his explanation, they took their case to the governors who reviewed the whole affair at their meeting on 4th December 1978. After an extensive debate they decided to retain corporal punishment, providing that there was a uniform policy in all houses, the punishment was administered only by the headmaster and housemasters, that the punishment was administered without fuss or ceremony, infrequently, and as the last resort and that a 'factual record' of beatings should, in future, be kept. It was a face-saving compromise offering some respite for the headmaster yet addressing a number of the issues raised. Little more was needed at this stage. Within months, the Chenevix-Trench era was history and so, more or less, was beating. When Cameron Cochrane, his successor, officially abolished it the decision was but a formality.

If reputation from the court of history was the sole judge of men's actions then surely it is a cause for regret that Tony's tenure at Fettes didn't end, say, in 1977. He had achieved much but now he was a mere shadow of his former self and his system, essentially built on personal trust, began to disintegrate. Back in the 1950s he might well have got away with it when the constraints of conformity still held much deviance in check. But twenty years on with the devil permissiveness on the rampage no such effective safety valve existed. Thus the priorities for the future would be the restoration of authority at the centre and the closing of the various loopholes in the system without losing sight of the essential humanity that Tony had brought to Fettes. It was a tall order for any successor and one that took a number of years to accomplish.

'Tony is in great form,' reported Elizabeth to Ronnie Selby Wright after a month at Fettes, 'and so pleased to be back in the saddle in a small school with such a good staff and friendly boys.' Responding to the challenge in this new environment did much to raise his spirits and keep them intact when he could concentrate exclusively on school affairs. On his final Founder's Day he went as far as to claim that he had loved Fettes more than any of his former three schools. Superficially, this statement might have contained some validity, but in truth, it was only half the story.

The Tony Trench of Fettes was but a shadow of the carefree dynamo who had galvanised Bradfield twenty years earlier. The flesh was still willing but the spirit ever increasingly weak. Richard Chenevix-Trench recalls how his father used to emerge from his study pale and pregnant with thought after a draining session of report writing, obsessed by the nagging doubt as to whether he was giving the parents an accurate picture of their child. Even during the holidays the pace of life rarely slackened and the family, rather to their resentment, came second to everyone else.

When the opportunity to wind down did present itself, Tony increasingly opted for the more gentle medium of television compared to the more intellectually demanding schedule of reading and writing book reviews.

Weighed down by fatigue it was not unknown for Tony to fall asleep in front of guests in the Lodge, or his colleagues at a meeting. On one famous occasion playing host at a concert at Fettes, he raised a few eyebrows by dozing off on the shoulder of his guest, the headmistress of a prestigious Edinburgh girls' school. Public platforms again took their toll and major pronouncements were avoided whenever possible. Founder's Day was even cancelled one year on the spurious grounds of cost. Invitations to social gatherings were shunned wherever possible, Elizabeth sometimes going to parties unescorted. When friends or acquaintances passed Tony in the street there would be no guarantee that their identity would be detected. Even more, personal conversations could find him less alert and more preoccupied than ever before.

There were other worries too. The deaths of his father in 1964, Christopher in 1971 and Richard in 1977, besides being the cause of much grief, meant more work for the surviving brothers on behalf of their ailing mother. Financially, the omens weren't favourable. Elizabeth's own dowry had suffered at the hands of the stockbrokers in 1974 and Tony, with retirement looming, had little in reserve for the expenses of private life that school life had cushioned them from. Above all there was the stigma of failure that time couldn't remove.

After leaving Eton, Tony rarely mentioned it by name, alluding instead to it as 'life in a previous existence' but to a proud, sensitive soul the regrets were etched too deep to avoid open wounds. In particular, he felt remorse for undermining Elizabeth's self-esteem by the manner of their departure. Her disillusionment at these turns of events lingered, serving only to fuel Tony's own sense of inadequacy. For all the loving support of his daughter Jo, who unlike her brothers and sister was often in residence, and of friends such as Ronnie Selby Wright, the burden rarely lifted from his shoulders, particularly as his health continued to deteriorate. Cameron Miller, a part-time teacher and friend, recalls Tony twice putting up notices which read, 'I shall be away for the next forty-eight hours', only to inform him personally that 'I can't stand the pain'. Once the bursar had to show parents round the school because Tony wasn't fit to see them.

In this despairing state it is perhaps not surprising that he again resorted to drink. The effects could become glaringly obvious. Those ringing Tony in the evening could wait an eternity before the phone was answered whilst those boys bidden to his study might be subjected to erratic treatment. Tales of the wrong boys being beaten weren't simply the stuff of ill-informed gossip; and housemasters increasingly resorted to spurious excuses as to why their boys weren't available if Tony issued a peremptory summons down the telephone. On one occasion, with a prefects meeting pending, Tony was discovered in an inebriated state by George Buchanan-Smith, the chaplain. Shocked by his condition, Buchanan-Smith remonstrated with his headmaster that he wasn't fit to preside and that to do so would damage the reputation of the school. Such candour found little favour with Tony who became very obstreperous. He eventually relented and the next day he sent his chaplain a penitential letter poignantly declaring, 'You're the only person who will stand up to me.'

As Tony's behaviour became more unpredictable, concern began to mount. The pupils, including the majority of those discriminated against, proved remarkably tolerant but in the Common Room the senior masters were at a loss as to how to proceed. Eventually Dick Cole-Hamilton, the Second Master, decided to take their anxieties to Elizabeth, who replied, 'This is my cross and I have to bear it.' She raided her husband's study and found hordes of empty bottles. Cole-Hamilton also contacted Lord Grieve, then a senior member of the governing board. They agreed to keep the matter to themselves.

On 2nd February 1978 Tony was taken seriously ill with a severe internal haemorrhage in his intestine resulting from his wartime experiences and was rushed to the local Western General Hospital. Jonathan Chenevix-Trench recalls flying up from Eton to be at his father's bedside. He justified his presence with soothing words but his explanation left Tony unconvinced. He knew he was seriously ill. He rallied sufficiently in the short term to enable the governing body a month later to minute that 'his health was reported as greatly improved'. They did take the precaution, however, of asking Dick Cole-Hamilton, who had interrupted his short-lived retirement, to deputise as acting headmaster, to continue to the beginning of the next term. They also persuaded Tony, very much against his will, to announce his retirement as from August 1979, as soon as possible.

A sub-committee was set up to oversee the appointment of a new headmaster. Accepting the governors' stipulation that his successor should be a disciplinarian, Tony overtly supported Christopher Turner, headmaster of Dean Close School, Cheltenham, pointedly placing him in the seat of honour in chapel on the morning of the interview. The governors, however, decided otherwise, choosing Cameron Cochrane, headmaster of Arnold School, Blackpool.

As Tony prepared for his final year he seemingly appeared light years away from his ills of a few months before. July saw the happy marriage of his daughter Jo to John Homfray in the Fettes chapel while August marked Tony and Elizabeth's silver wedding anniversary. Tony treated his wife to a ten-day holiday in Ireland before the whole family congregated in Norfolk on the appropriate day for a picnic. The celebrations continued when weeks later Tony was elected to the Royal Society of Edinburgh and the Order of St. John, savouring the thrill once again that recognition brings. His final term proved one long recessional as school magazines, BBC Scotland and *The Scotsman* queued up to be party to Tony's last professional will and testament. As he looked back on his thirty-two years of teaching from his St Helenean vista, he poured scorn on the modernist tendency to theorise: 'I hate talking about education because there has been too much gas about education altogether. It is a thoroughly empirical business.'

These same undeviating principles were again elaborated on when he bade his farewells to the Fettesian faithful on Founder's Day, 2nd June 1979. As the school and its guests waited at the appointed hour for the formal entry of the dignitaries there was no sign of Tony.

'Where is he?' the Second Master asked Elizabeth.

'I haven't the faintest idea,' she replied.

Suddenly Tony appeared, and hared down the platform before composing himself to give a brief but heartfelt *Apologia Vita Mea*. Acknowledging that the sophisticated clubland parents of Eton had regarded him as a naive fool because of his propensity to believe boys, whatever the evidence, he reiterated his age-long commitment to the individual, 'for it is he that matters'. Having profusely thanked the Fettes community for their friendliness and support he ended with this humble peroration: 'I rather think I am a fool, but I've been a happy one rewarded beyond my deserts. For my memory I should be well content with the words of the Saxon thane, Eldred, in G.K.Chesterson's *Ballad of the White Horse* before his great death fighting for Alfred against the Danes at Ethandune.'

> The Kings go up and the kings go down
> And who knows who shall rule
> But men and birds and dogs may weep

At the burial of a fool.
O lodgers in my cellars,
Boys in my apple trees,
The world grows stern and strange and new
And wiser men shall govern you,
Yet some fools weep for me.'

Having taken his curtain call and listened to the official tributes
to him, Tony then heard the head of school pay his own farewell
in the *Vive-La*, the annual Founder's Day review of the Fettesian
year set to verse and music.

We honour today our retiring headmaster
A kindly adviser, a scholar and pastor
And something that one is inclined to forget is
His promotion, from Bradfield, through Eton, to
    Fettes

A headmaster comes when a headmaster goes
But although *tempus fugit, plus c'est la même chose.*
How weak is our Latin! How rotten our French is!
But *Salvete* the Cochranes! Adieu to the Trenches.

By the end the formalities had exhausted him. The head
groundsman on his evening rounds detected what he imagined
to be a tramp curled up on a seat by the cricket pavilion. On
investigating further, he found it was Tony and helped him back
to the Lodge.

After half-term the valedictions continued. Dinners in Tony's
honour were held by the Scottish Headmasters' Conference and
the Fettes governors when he and Elizabeth were presented with
a substantial cheque from Old Fettesians. Both occasions found
him in vintage form. At the former, Sir Roger Young, then
headmaster of George Watson's College, Edinburgh, recalls

Tony's gracious speech. 'I have an unusual request,' he concluded, 'I want all the men here to rise to their wives because it is to them we owe everything for what we are.'

On Tuesday 19th June, Tony entertained his successor to lunch at the Roxburghe Hotel in Edinburgh, holding Cameron Cochrane spellbound with a résumé of his love and future hopes for Fettes. After they had parted company Tony returned home and announced to Elizabeth, 'I've handed my life's work over to Cameron and I'm happy.' Cochrane, much inspired by Tony's optimism and faith in people, was also well pleased with their meeting. When he rang Tony two evenings later to express his appreciation it was Elizabeth to whom he spoke.

'Can I have a word with Tony?' began Cochrane.

'I'm sorry, Cameron,' replied Elizabeth, 'You can't. He has just died.'

Tony had realised the gravity of his illness the previous year and although able to reassure a wellwisher in June 1978 that 'he was now fully recovered', the omens were far from propitious. His secretary recalls him looking a pale shadow of his former self and Cameron Miller has recollections of a conversation with Tony that suggested he was living on borrowed time. 'The doctor says I should give up whisky,' he declared. 'I've taken a considered view. The quality of life is more important that the quantity'.

On 7th April 1979, perhaps with premonition, Elizabeth wrote to Ronnie Selby Wright. 'Ronnie, before next term's bustle and farewells take over I did just want to say that if anything were to happen to Tony, I would like you to talk about him at any memorial service Fettes and even Eton might hold for him . . . I am not anticipating anything but it is always wise to be prepared.'

A month later, Tony, during his interview with Radio Scotland likewise appeared a trifle fatalistic when peering into the future: 'Whether God will give me a chance after I retire to do a little teaching in some way or another I don't know.'

Retirement wasn't something he viewed with equanimity. Bowing to Elizabeth's wishes, they had spent his savings on a house at Watlington, near Kings Lynn, in Norfolk. The choice of location seemed strange and self-defeating. Apart from being close to Tony's mother and brother it had little to commend it. Not only did the house lack character, it was remote from their friends and their memories. In public, Tony made all the right noises but in private the prospect left him cold. When he gazed into the crystal ball and contemplated an obscure retirement separated from his 'glorious young', whose glittering futures were his pride and joy, he saw his life's purpose drifting painfully away.

On Wednesday 20th June 1979, Elizabeth went into the Lodge at lunchtime and found Tony unwell in bed. It was a recurrence of his previous intestinal trouble. He had to have an emergency operation the next day and died without recovering consciousness. He was barely sixty. The impact on the school was a shattering one as the news of his death filtered out. Jean Weekes, wife of the Church of England chaplain, remembers consoling a tranquil Elizabeth in the hall of the Lodge, when, suddenly, the door was flung open and a young boy charged in quite hysterical. 'Where is he'? he screamed. 'It can't be true'. They managed to quieten him down but his outburst was only a more dramatic expression of the general mood that soon ensued.

The school was officially informed at house prayers that evening when Robert Philp in Carrington House closed with Tony's favourite prayer of Newman. The reaction ranged from stunned silence to outward grief. David Rhodes remembers boys in his house rushing out of prayers to the phone to break the news to their parents, many of them in tears. Most signed letters of condolence to Elizabeth. This was one of them:

Dear Mrs Chenevix-Trench,
The members of Arniston House would like to express our
deepest sympathies and offer you and your family our con-
dolences on the loss of your husband who was a great man
and friend to us all.
Our thoughts are with you.

On the morrow, as the country basked in warm sunshine, it
wasn't only at Fettes that the flag hung limply at half-mast and
black ties were the order of the day. At Bradfield and Eton,
similar marks of respect were observed. Eton's Head Master,
Michael McCrum, paid an emotional tribute to Tony in Chambers. The following Sunday a special Requiem Communion was
held for him in the College Chapel and the next day the Head
Master led the Eton contingent to the funeral in Edinburgh. In
the Warriston Crematorium the pall-bearers, with the coffin in
tow, struggled to cut a swathe through a sea of mourners, young
and old, Fettesian and non-Fettesian alike, who had assembled
to pay their respects to a man whose personality had touched
so many lives, rescuing many from the crooked turnings. Inside,
the congregation heard the head boy of Fettes evoke the spirit
of Christian pilgrimage by reciting Bunyan's famous words about
Mr Valiant-for-Truth, 'So he passed over, and all the trumpets
sounded for him on the other side.'

After the formalities of the funeral, Fettes held their own
special service of Thanksgiving. Elizabeth had wanted this to be
in the College Chapel, but Dick Cole-Hamilton, once again
acting headmaster, mindful of the confines of space, advised on
St Luke's, Comely Bank, as a more suitable alternative. There,
on the following Sunday, the whole Fettes community gathered
en masse to hear Cameron Cochrane read from Rudyard Kipling's
The Dead King and Ronnie Selby Wright in his address pay
tribute to Tony's scholarship, courage, kindness and humility,

reminding the pupils how much they meant to him. The words seemed to strike a chord. Dick Cole-Hamilton, with forty years behind him at Fettes, reckoned he had never heard the school in such rousing voice. 'They sang their hearts out. They seemed to be paying their tribute to their headmaster, in the only way they could do it.'

In the midst of all the grief, life had to go on although the dying embers of the term were devoid of that sense of expectation normally associated with the onset of the summer holidays. Elizabeth, so often a steadfast rock amidst the storms raging around her, kept her head high during those difficult days cocooned within a wall of protective love. Her final act of public service to Fettes was a dignified presentation of the cups at the junior school prizegiving, followed by a fond farewell to the Common Room once the term had ended. With Dick Cole-Hamilton's arm around her she stood on the bank over the Headmaster's Garden, thanking everybody at Fettes for restoring Tony's confidence after the Eton experience. Then it was down to the exacting business of packing up and moving off to an uncertain future in Norfolk, bereft of her husband whose ashes were consigned to the fields of Fettes by his daughter Laura and Mike McIntosh Reid, a good friend of the family.

In the College chapel a plaque was erected in his memory, the only headmaster to be accorded such an honour since Dr Potts, the school's first headmaster and, ironically, like Tony, a distinguished Salopian Classicist. It bears the inscription:

In loving memory of Anthony Chenevix-Trench, a great scholar, a dedicated teacher whose door was always open for he loved his fellow men.

It was an appropriate epitaph and one of which Tony would doubtless have approved.

TONY CHENEVIX-TRENCH

'I 'VE NEVER BEEN A POLITICIAN nor, that ghastly word, an educationalist. I'm a teacher and to be a teacher you have to know your children,' so Tony publicly asserted on Radio Scotland weeks before his death. It was an uncompromising, accurate self-assessment of a headmaster who, throughout his years in high office, had never deviated from the ideals which he had formulated at an early age. Uncomfortable with committees or with the trappings of power Tony continued as headmaster to make the needs of his pupils paramount, teaching and tutoring the young whenever possible. His approach, unorthodox by the standards of his time, was more akin to the practices adopted by headmasters of Victorian public schools, their elevated gospel of duty and enlightenment making a willing convert of someone who found his basic security in this closeted milieu.

But for all his roots in the past Tony wasn't chained to it. His prescience alerted him to the danger of blind reaction in a perennially fluctuating world. Consequently, he charted his own personal odyssey between continuity and change, particularly appropriate during the turbulent years of the 1960s and 1970s, when headmasters suddenly found their authority under siege as they battled with alien forces. It wasn't a time for fainthearts to be in charge.

Tony Chenevix-Trench was something of a rarity in that three well-known schools were entrusted to his keeping at critical points in their history. Whether it was by fate or design each of them was in need of renewal when he answered the call to be their leader. It was fortunate for Bradfield, Eton and Fettes that they found in Tony a headmaster whose personality met many of their priorities, breathing fresh life into creaking limbs without undermining the fabric of the body politic. His passion for human enlightenment which had survived the horrors of Siam was now given a free rein as he broke down the fetters of the narrow education then on offer and went in search of that elusive spark which enabled each individual to find his special worth. Hundreds flocked to his standard with only a hapless few of the many who came under his influence being consigned to outer darkness, their talents left untapped; for human waste was the enduring legacy from war which Tony couldn't abide.

His work, however, was by no means complete. In each of his schools Tony never lasted longer than eight and a half years. This was no mere coincidence. His inspirational aura shone brightest during the hours before noon when the adrenalin was in full flow. Thereafter repetition dulled his enthusiasm and because he lacked the practical nous to give substance to his ideas a number of them were left hanging precariously in limbo. Consequently his successors needed to be consolidators to tie up the numerous loose ends and make a virtue out of routine.

Tony's lack of administrative dexterity called into question the long term viability of his brand of headmastering. Oversensitivity also severely compromised his effectiveness. When asked by one of his housemasters at Fettes to adjudicate between two contenders for a position of high authority, Tony suggested the one who could best say 'No'. It was advice he himself honoured more in the breach than in the observance. A lifelong desire to please left him often serving more than one master. The lack of clear-cut consistency that this threw up not only led to a number of bruised egos, it also created a vacuum at the centre which the overbearing eagerly exploited — a formula for confusion and bitterness. This was particularly apparent at Eton since its size and status proved less accommodating to the allure of the Trench magnetism, Tony's constant talisman hith-erto. His refusal to change tack and depart from the habits of a lifetime only compounded his problem. It paradoxically drew attention (as Tony later acknowledged) to the drawback of an idyllic childhood as an adequate preparation for the more sullied adult world where dreams were often trampled upon.

Inevitably Tony's enforced departure from Eton cast a shadow over a life which until then had been crowned with a myriad laurels. Unconditioned to failure, he naturally found it all the harder to stomach once its curse assailed him. It was a personal tragedy that this crushing blow to his self-respect should come shortly after the ghastly legacy of the war years had returned to haunt him with a cruel vengeance. The infirmities it unleashed not only blighted his final years; they overshadowed the richer memories of earlier decades.

It goes without saying that Tony's leadership skills, long on inspiration and short on resolve, were found wanting in the supreme challenge of his career, a bubble waiting to burst in the eyes of his detractors. Conversely, it is undeniably the case that for all the travails of his tenure at Eton, Tony's legacy there was by no means negligible. An élite based on birth gradually trans-formed itself into an élite based on merit so that whatever charges were levelled at the college thereafter, mediocrity was not one of them.

Academic scholarship, however, for all its importance to Tony, paled into insignificance compared to the overriding need of boarding schools like his to create leaders of men. Much time was spent expounding the virtues of good citizenship and his exertions were by no means wasted. No sooner had seeds been sown than green buds began rapidly to appear. Those buds now flower to good effect in the world, in addition to the environments that Tony once graced with his presence. For, today, a number

of our leading headmasters in the independent sector were reared
in the Chenevix-Trench stable and have remained faithful to his
memory. Their allegiance wasn't born of blind devotion, because
Tony's shortcomings were too readily obvious. Yet overshadow-
ing the flaws stands his passionate concern for the individual, a
vital quality for any leader to possess but, sadly, one too often
subsumed by cold statistics and personal ambition. And that is
not all. We live in an increasingly consumer-orientated age where
machines abound in the name of progress. Of course they have
their place and schools must adapt accordingly to feed on their
pickings. But for all its merits, high technology can never replace
the basic moral absolutes governing human behaviour that mark
the surest route to true happiness and progress.

It would be idle to pretend that as we hover on the brink of
a new millennium the pressure for commercial acumen will ease.
Teachers will need to develop further their professional skills and
most would say Amen to that — but in their quest for greater
efficiency they would do well to avoid the human pitfall that
awaits those with limited vision. A brief glance around any
modern industrial society reveals its deserts of human waste which
tell their own bleak tale of how the left-out millions can, through
extreme anti-social behaviour, extract their bitter revenge. With
this unedifying spectre to guard against, not to mention the scores
of divided families now in vogue, the following words uttered
by Tony Chenevix-Trench over forty years ago should strike a
resonance in the ears of those responsible for moulding the leaders
of tomorrow. Not only do they capture the essence of the man,
they point to a timeless truth about a vocation to which he
devoted the bulk of his working life and in whose service he
reaped a rich reward.

'What is a boy? He is a person who is going to carry on
what you have started, to sit where you are sitting and,

when you are gone, attend to those things you think are so important. You can adopt all the policies you please, but how they will be carried on depends on him. Even if you make leagues and treaties, he will have to manage them. He will assume control of your cities and nations. He is going to move on and take over your prisons, churches, schools, universities and corporations.

All your work is going to be judged by him. Your reputation and the future are in his hands. All your work is for him, and the fate of nations and humanity is also in his hands.

So it might be well to pay him some attention now'.

Index